SOCIAL AND LABOUR RIGHTS IN A GLOBAL CONTEXT
International and Comparative Perspectives

The active pursuit of social and labour rights is seen as a crucial response to globalisation. This book brings together leading scholars from the United Kingdom, Ireland, France, Germany, Italy, Japan and the United States, who question the effectiveness of the new rhetoric of rights such as those to decent work and security, equality of opportunity, adequate food and housing, and healthcare. The authors examine emerging new approaches in several European countries, Japan and the United States and in codes of practice of multinational companies. Recent attempts by the International Labour Organisation to promote core rights and decent work, and new techniques of enforcement at regional level by the European Union and the North American Free Trade Association receive special attention. The authors help us to understand how far the law can act to restrain public and private power for the benefit of at least some of the people for some of the time. This book will interest students and teachers of law, human rights, politics and corporate governance, as well as policy-makers in government, the European Union and international bodies, corporate management, trade unions and non-governmental organisations.

BOB HEPPLE QC is Master of Clare College and Emeritus Professor of Law in the University of Cambridge.

SOCIAL AND LABOUR RIGHTS IN A GLOBAL CONTEXT

International and Comparative Perspectives

Edited by

BOB HEPPLE

CAMBRIDGE UNIVERSITY PRESS

CAMBRIDGE UNIVERSITY PRESS
Cambridge, New York, Melbourne, Madrid, Cape Town, Singapore, São Paulo

Cambridge University Press
The Edinburgh Building, Cambridge CB2 8RU, UK

Published in the United States of America by Cambridge University Press, New York

www.cambridge.org
Information on this title: www.cambridge.org/9780521818810

© Cambridge University Press 2002

First published 2002
Third printing 2005
This digitally printed version 2007

A catalogue record for this publication is available from the British Library

ISBN 978-0-521-81881-0 hardback
ISBN 978-0-521-04732-6 paperback

CONTENTS

CONTRIBUTORS

Takashi Araki is Professor of Law in the University of Tokyo.

Catherine Barnard is a Fellow of Trinity College and University Senior Lecturer in Law in the University of Cambridge.

Simon Deakin is a Fellow of Peterhouse and Robert Monks Professor of Corporate Governance in the Judge Institute of Management Studies, University of Cambridge.

Cynthia L. Estlund is Professor of Law at Columbia University, New York.

Ivan Hare is a Fellow of Trinity College and University Lecturer in Law in the University of Cambridge.

Bob Hepple QC is Master of Clare College and Emeritus Professor of Law in the University of Cambridge, and Honorary Professor of Law in the University of Capetown.

Antoine Lyon-Caen is Professor of Law in the University of Paris-X (School of Law) and Professor at the Law School of Social Sciences (EHESS).

Paul O'Higgins is Honorary Professor of Law, Trinity College Dublin, Emeritus Regius Professor of Law, Trinity College Dublin and Emeritus Professor, of Law King's College London, and former Reader in Labour Law, University of Cambridge.

Silvana Sciarra is Professor of Law in the European University Institute and in the University of Florence.

Lord Wedderburn of Charlton QC FBA is Emeritus Cassel Professor of Commercial Law at the London School of Economics. He taught in the Cambridge Faculty of Law from 1953 to 1964 and founded the course on 'Industrial Law' (later called Labour Law) in 1961.

Manfred Weiss is Professor of Labour Law at the J. W. Goethe University in Frankfurt, and is President of the International Industrial Relations Association.

ACKNOWLEDGEMENTS

Drafts of the papers in this book were discussed at a conference held on 21 July 2001 to mark the fortieth anniversary of the establishment of a course on Labour Law (at first called 'Industrial Law') in the Cambridge Law Tripos. We are grateful to the Cambridge Centre for European Legal Studies, the Centre for Public Law, and the Economic and Social Research Council Centre for Business Research for hosting the conference. We also wish to thank all those who contributed to the discussion, and whose comments were helpful to the authors in revising their work for publication. In particular, we were fortunate to have as lead discussants or chairs a number of those who undertook doctoral research at Cambridge in the 1970s and 1980s, namely Professor Brian Bercusson, the Hon. Mr Justice (Patrick) Elias, Professor Keith Ewing, Dr Sonia Mackay, Professor Gillian S. Morris, and Professor Brian Napier, as well as two other colleagues with whom we have long collaborated, Professor Paul L. Davies (LSE), Professor Sandra Fredman (Oxford) and Andrew Duff MEP. Diane Abraham organised the conference and helped edit the contributions with enormous efficiency, care and tact.

ABBREVIATIONS

AC	*Law Reports, Appeal Cases*
ACAS	Advisory, Conciliation and Arbitration Service
BJIR	*British Journal of Industrial Relations*
Brit. Jo. Soc.	*British Journal of Law and Society*
BYIL	*British Yearbook of International Law*
CA	Court of Appeal
CAC	Central Arbitration Committee
CBI	Confederation of British Industry
CE	Committee of Experts on the Application of Conventions and Recommendations (ILO)
CEEP	Centre Européen des Enterprises Publiques
CFA	Committee on Freedom of Association (ILO)
CFI	(European) court of first instance
CIME	Committee for International Investment and Multinational Enterprises
CIPD	Chartered Institute of Personnel and Development
CLJ	*Cambridge Law Journal*
CMLR	Common Market Law Reports
CRE	Commission for Racial Equality
DfEE	Department for Education and Employment
DRC	Disability Rights Commission
DTI	Department of Trade and Industry
EAT	Employment Appeal Tribunal
EC Treaty	Treaty establishing the European Community (as consolidated by the Treaty of Amsterdam)
ECB	European Central Bank
ECHR	European Convention for the Protection of Human Rights and Fundamental Freedoms

ECtHR	European Court of Human Rights
ECJ	European Court of Justice
ECR	*European Court Reports*
ECSC	European Coal and Steel Community
EHRLR	*European Human Rights Law Reports*
EHRR	*European Human Rights Reports*
EIRR	*European Industrial Relations Review and Report*
ELA	Employment Lawyers' Association
ELJ	*European Law Journal*
EMU	European monetary union
EOC	Equal Opportunities Commission
ERA	Employment Rights Act 1996
ESC	European Social Charter
ESRC	Economic and Social Research Council
ETUC	European Trades Union Congress
EU	European Union
HL	House of Lords
HMSO	Her Majesty's Stationery Office
HRLJ	*Human Rights Law Journal*
HRQ	*Human Rights Quarterly*
ICCPR	International Covenant on Civil and Political Rights
ICESCR	International Covenant on Economic, Social and Cultural Rights
ICR	*Industrial Cases Reports*
IER	Institute of Employment Rights
IIRA	International Industrial Relations Association
IJCLLIR	*International Journal of Comparative Labour Law and Industrial Relations*
ILJ	*Industrial Law Journal*
ILO	International Labour Organisation
IMF	International Monetary Fund
IRLR	*Industrial Relations Law Reports*
ITWF	International Transport Workers' Federation
JSPTL	*Journal of the Society of Public Teachers of Law*
LQR	*Law Quarterly Review*
MAI	Multilateral Agreement on Investment
MLR	*Modern Law Review*

MNC	multinational corporation
MNE	multinational enterprise
NACAB	National Association of Citizens' Advice Bureaux
NAFTA	North American Free Trade Agreement
NGO	non-governmental organisation
NLRA	National Labor Relations Act
NLRB	National Labor Relations Board
OECD	Organisation for Economic Cooperation and Development
OJ	*Official Journal of the European Community*
OMC	open method of coordination
SI	statutory instrument
TEC	*see* EC Treaty
TEU	Treaty on European Union (as consolidated by the Treaty of Amsterdam)
TNC	transnational corporation
TULRCA	Trade Union and Labour Relations (Consolidation) Act 1992
TUPE	Transfer of Undertakings (Protection of Employment) Regulations 1981
UNICE	Union des Confédérations de l'Industrie et des Employeurs d'Europe
WLR	*Weekly Law Reports*

TABLE OF CASES

Introduction

BOB HEPPLE

I. Why rethink social and labour rights?

Social rights, such as the rights to work, to education, to adequate food and housing, to healthcare and to social security, are claims on society which are recognised as having special importance and universality. They are usually asserted by those without power against governments. Labour or employment rights, such as the rights to decent conditions of work, fair pay and job security, and the right to participate in trade unions and to engage in collective bargaining, are usually asserted against private holders of power, in particular employers. Both social and labour rights are referred to as 'fundamental' when they are 'put beyond the reach and revision of ordinary legislation and shifting democratic majorities'.[1]

The essays collected in this book rethink the nature of and justifications for social and labour rights, their constitutionalisation and legal enforcement. The perspectives are those of international, European and national human rights and labour laws. The authors have based their contributions on the varied experiences of several countries, in particular the United Kingdom, France, Germany, Italy, the United States, Japan and post-apartheid South Africa. Drafts of the papers were presented and discussed at a conference held in Cambridge on 21 July 2001 to mark the fortieth anniversary of the foundation of a course on Labour Law (at first called 'Industrial Law') in the Cambridge Law Tripos.

The rethinking of social and labour rights is necessary because the social, economic and political environments in which they were first conceived (e.g. in the Mexican Constitution of 1917, the Russian Constitution of 1918 and the German Weimar Constitution of 1919) have

---

[1] See Estlund, below, Ch. 8.

been fundamentally affected by modern globalisation and the expansion of the network society. These developments have diminished the power of nation states and national laws to control the flow of capital, finance, technology, information and migrants across their borders. The political legitimacy of modern globalisation is supported by the rhetoric of neoliberalism, a belief that market forces should rule and that the state should have a minimal role. Social rights at international, regional and national levels are increasingly seen as beacons of resistance against the disempowerment of local communities, trade unions and other social organisations which globalisation and neoliberalism entail. In their own different ways each of the contributors deals with this question: does the new rhetoric of social rights – as embodied in instruments such as the ILO Declaration of Fundamental Rights and Principles at Work (1998) and the EU Charter of Fundamental Rights (2000) – match the reality of the new world of market regulation and growing global inequality?

II. The weakness of current responses to globalisation

The scene is set by Professor Lord Wedderburn in the opening chapter. In 1961, when he initiated the Cambridge Industrial Law course, it was a distinctive feature of the law of the United Kingdom – unlike several other countries[2] – that there were no legally entrenched social rights. There was no right not to be unfairly dismissed, no rights against unfair discrimination, and (with limited exceptions) no universal rights to minimum pay or maximum working time. These matters were subject only to the contract of employment which masks the inequality of power and bargaining position in the relationship of employer and employee. Collective bargaining was seen as the principal means of offsetting this inequality. So confident were the unions of their industrial power that before 1970 they 'wanted nothing more of the law than it should leave them alone'.[3] Fundamental social 'rights' were seen as political values and not legal rights. The 'rights' to associate, to engage in collective

---

[2] In 1944, a committee appointed by the American Law Institute to draft an international bill of rights noted that the 'current constitutions' of many countries recognised social rights, e.g. forty in the case of the right to education; nine the right to work; eleven the right to adequate housing; and twenty-seven the right to social security.

[3] K. W. Wedderburn, *The Worker and the Law* (Harmondsworth, 1965), p. 9; 2nd edn (1971), p. 3; 3rd edn (1986), p. 1.

bargaining and to take industrial action depended on fragile negative immunities granted by Parliament against common law liabilities. Reflecting this reality, the syllabus devised by Wedderburn took students through the analysis of the complex common law, but it also went behind this to probe the social policies and ideology of the law.

In Chapter 1, Wedderburn examines where we have travelled in the United Kingdom since the days when labour rights were dependent upon what Kahn-Freund characterised as collective laissez-faire. Wedderburn argues that it was wrong to vulgarise the idea of 'abstention of the law' into some kind of shorthand for an 'absence' of law or an impotence of the law to change the relations between labour and capital. But the very structure of British collective labour law, built on a 'fabric of liberties and "immunities" from common law illegalities and an incomplete excape from master and servant law, was at the end of the twentieth century unlikely to provide an easy modern basis for such fundamental labour rights as could be found in France, Italy or Germany or in the ILO Conventions'.

In seeking an 'alternative labour law', Wedderburn is critical of the contemporary focus on 'regulation', which – even when it leads to the conclusion that some fundamental labour rights are necessary – 'cannot in itself determine the value judgements in assessing any "proper" balance between freedom and subordination'. The school of thought which concentrates on regulation for the purposes of competitiveness puts at centre stage the individual employment relation and seeks a rationale for labour market regulation in 'market failures' and the limited correction of 'unacceptable' distributive outcomes. This frame of reference, Wedderburn argues, 'ignores the reality of modern power, especially in an age of global capital'. He examines the post-1997 labour law measures introduced by New Labour in the United Kingdom and finds in them a continuation of the 'fundamental defect of our labour law', namely 'extravagant individualism'. Paradoxically, 'the English common law notion of individualism, based more on ideas of property than of citizens' formal equality, has not given us any parallel protection for the dignity or privacy of the individual worker'. In this the United Kingdom compares unfavourably with countries such as Italy and Germany, where a combination of fundamental rights and collective bargaining or (in Germany) the works council's powers of codetermination have provided individuals with greater protection.

Globalisation, according to Wedderburn, is the reason why 'the active pursuit of human rights and labour standards is so crucial'. 'Given the conflicting aims of multinationals and weakened states, all means must be considered whereby fundamental labour standards and principles can be created, upheld and – somehow – enforced in the global market.' In this, 'few things are as important as discovering new ways of fostering "countervailing workers' power"'. He finds little comfort in EU law, which is dominated by competition law, despite well-intentioned attempts to generate new social and labour rights. However, he urges a continuation of the search 'for new mechanisms for the enforcement and improvement of international and national labour standards'.

At the centre of any such consideration stands the International Labour Organisation (ILO). During the interwar years and in the first decades after the Second World War, the ILO adopted international minimum standards on a wide range of matters which might be described as social rights, including freedom of association and the right to organise trade unions, the elimination of child labour and forced labour, and freedom from discrimination. Professor Paul O'Higgins, who led the Cambridge Labour Law course from 1964 to 1984, ensured that students were made aware of the activities of the ILO, the OECD and the Council of Europe. He also broadened the students' approach by arranging lectures on industrial relations, as well as the traditional law lectures.

In Chapter 2, O'Higgins explains the motivations for ILO standards, in particular the fears of social revolution and of 'social dumping'. He examines critically the relationship of ILO standards with social rights established under later regional institutions, in particular the Council of Europe's European Convention for the Protection of Human Rights and Fundamental Freedoms (ECHR), its 'large footnote' the European Social Charter of 1961 (ESC) (revised 1996), the Treaty on European Union (TEU) and the Treaty establishing the European Community (EC Treaty). There is a disturbing lack of ratification of ILO conventions, and even states which have ratified them, including the United Kingdom, fall a long way short of meeting their obligations. The relevance of many of the standards may be queried because of the failure to adopt instruments directly addressed to the multinational corporations. O'Higgins's conclusion is that there is considerable confusion between the different standards-setting bodies. In his view the primacy of standards set by the ILO should be ensured by some overall supervisory authority, preferably a court, where authoritative interpretations could be given.

III. The potential of fundamental social rights in the EU

The most recent attempt at a regional level to develop fundamental social rights has occurred in the EU, with the adoption at Nice in December 2000 of a Charter of Fundamental Rights, including many social rights in addition to civil and political rights. In Chapter 3, Professor Manfred Weiss examines the political and legal background and possible implications of this Charter. Fundamental Community rights have been an issue since the early days of the EC. The EC Treaty accorded primacy to the four freedoms of movement: of capital, goods, services and labour. Accordingly, there was a danger of deconstruction of fundamental rights at national level. This led to a celebrated controversy between the European Court of Justice (ECJ) and the German Federal Constitutional Court. Only when it was established that the ECJ's interpretations in Luxembourg would not conflict with those of the European Court of Human Rights in Strasbourg did the German court accept the supremacy of EC law. This respect for the Council of Europe's instruments is now confirmed in the TEU. In view of this, why was a new Charter considered to be necessary?

Weiss suggests a number of reasons. One is the need for greater transparency, given the lack of clarity in the TEU and the EC Treaty as to the extent to which the European Social Charter (ESC) and Community Charter of Fundamental Social Rights of Workers (adopted in 1989) are to be observed. Another reason is that the integration of fundamental social rights into the TEU and EC Treaty 'was understood to be a tool to guarantee the social profile of the Community' – which has so far had a pragmatic and weak approach to social policy – 'and to make sure that the possibility of opting out in this area was no longer available'. Weiss defends the case for putting social rights on the same footing as the classical civil rights. However, he is critical of the chapter of the EU Charter on 'Solidarity', which contains some of the social rights, because it puts in one and the same chapter political goals and subjective (legally enforceable) rights. There is also a 'dramatic inconsistency' between the misleading Article 28 of the Charter, which obliges the Community to promote the right to negotiate and conclude collective agreements and to take collective action 'at appropriate levels', and Article 137(6) of the EC Treaty which denies the Community any legislative competence to do this. In some ways the Charter does not go as far as existing Community law (e.g. in respect of rights to information and consultation), and it includes some rights (e.g. on working time), which cannot be regarded as 'fundamental', while excluding or being ambiguous about others (e.g. the rights as workers of third-country nationals).

Weiss believes that the EU Charter is important in several ways: as a signal to the candidate EU states; as a guide to interpretation of the Treaties for the ECJ and national courts (between February and July 2001, it had already been relied upon in eight cases by Advocates-General, once by the Court of Justice and once by the Tribunal of First Instance, as well as by courts in Spain and Germany[4]); and as a source of inspiration for new Community measures. The only remaining question, in Weiss's view, is not whether, 'but rather when, how, and by what procedure' the Charter should be integrated into the Treaties.

The EU Charter has the potential, Weiss suggests, to provide a source of 'constitutional patriotism' (in Habermas's language) in the EU and, thereby, a safeguard against excessive nationalism. Above all, in his view, 'social policy can no longer be understood merely a marginal annex to EU policies'. But how then are social rights to reconciled with the economic freedoms which are at the heart of the EC? This is the crucial question to which Chapter 4 on 'Market freedom and fundamental social rights', by Professor Silvana Sciarra, and Chapter 5 on 'Corporate governance, European governance and social rights', by Catherine Barnard and Professor Simon Deakin, are devoted.

Sciarra, like Weiss, argues that labour law is central to European integration. While emphasising the need to re-establish social priorities in a 'market without a state', she also accentuates elements of compatibility of social rights with market principles. Her arguments are grouped under four heads: re-forming, re-balancing, re-establishing and re-thinking. First, the inclusion of labour law reforms in macro-economic policies, far from heralding the disappearance of this discipline, provides an opportunity to find new legal methods to ensure that efficiency is combined with the achievement of social goals. Secondly, labour law contributes

---

[4] Note from the Commission's Legal Service, July 2001.

to the re-balancing of economic and social forces which becomes necessary when there are drastic changes in government or in the equilibrium
between management and labour. In place of a sharp conflict between
market freedom and social rights, labour law offers a new dimension to
the market. Not only is it possible to make an economic case for social
rights, but it is also arguable that the different systems of social and
labour rights across the EU enhance the competitiveness of the EU as a
whole, provided core labour standards are maintained.

Sciarra pays particular attention to collective bargaining as 'the most
consolidated and powerful institution contributing to bringing some
equilibrium to unbalanced economic situations'. This leads, under her
third head, to a detailed analysis of the European Court of Justice's decision in the *Albany* case, in which competition law and labour law were
reconciled.[5] Fundamental social rights and collective bargaining, which
are long established in national legal systems, were 're-established' in the
European legal order. Finally, she argues that re-thinking is necessary
in order to transform the weak processes of European labour law into
permanent gains. Two examples are the involvement, under the Employment Title of the revised EC Treaty, of the social partners in national
and supranational employment policies, and the consultation of civil
society in the drafting of the EU Charter of Fundamental Rights. The
underlying issue in both cases is that of strengthening the legitimacy of
EU policies and law. This, in turn, rests on the 're-birth' of the discipline
of labour law 'which over the years has so notably expanded the breadth
of European legal culture'.

Barnard and Deakin continue this theme. They argue that social rights
are a means of controlling or channelling regulatory competition. They
take a procedural, as distinct from a substantive approach to social rights.
According to this approach, 'reflexive harmonisation' is needed in the
EU 'to preserve a space for local-level experimentation and adaptation,
contrary to the "levelling down" agenda of negative harmonisation,
but also in contrast to the idea that harmonisation in the form of a
"European labour code" must occupy the field at the expense of local
autonomy'. The essence of this approach is that regulatory interventions
are most likely to be successful 'when they seek to achieve their ends not

---

[5] Case C-67/96, *Albany International BV* v. *Stichtung Bedrijfspensioenfonds Textielindustrie*
[1999] ECR I-5751.

by direct prescription, but by inducing "second-order effects" on the part of the social actors'. 'Reflexive law' aims to encourage autonomous processes, in particular by supporting mechanisms for group representation and participation, rather than by imposing particular distributive outcomes.

Barnard and Deakin apply this approach first to the question of corporate governance in the EU – 'the system by which companies are directed and controlled' – in particular the role assigned to the various stakeholders and to workers' participation in the corporate enterprise. They examine the company law harmonisation programme and the diversity of company laws in the EU member states. A vital issue is whether the shareholder-orientated model which is associated with US and (to a degree) British practice, or the continental model involving some degree of worker participation, will become dominant. They link this issue with that of European governance, in particular the European Commission's strategy of involving new players, such as regional and local authorities, social partners, non-governmental organisations (NGOs) and third-sector associations. They examine the involvement of the social partners in the process of social legislation since the Maastricht Treaty in 1992, and find that more emphasis has been placed on these procedures than on the quality of the end result in terms of substantive social rights. They identify the risks of lack of representativity, and the alienation of individual citizens who are spectators in a discussion 'between elites for elites' which 'does not furnish them with detailed, legally enforceable rights'. For these reasons, they advocate a core of protection based on substantive rights alongside a framework for devolved law-making which recognises the role played by institutions of civil society.

IV. Constitutionalisation and enforcement of social rights: some comparisons

The remaining five chapters focus on the comparative experience of the constitutionalisation and legal enforcement of social rights. In Chapter 6 Ivan Hare considers whether social rights should be protected as constitutional rights, concentrating on four basic rights: to education, housing, health care and minimum income. His basic theme is that although many of the traditional objections to constitutional protection of social rights are either simplistic or overstated, there are substantial principled and pragmatic obstacles to granting to the judicial branch the ultimate decision-making power over the extent of such rights. Hare argues that there is judicial reluctance to impose positive obligations on the state in the fields of civil and political *and* social rights, because of the difficulty in quantifying and balancing substantial obligations on the state within the confines of the judicial process. A related but distinct point is that judges are thought to be particularly ill-suited to substitute their view for that of elected politicians and professional civil servants on how spending on social programmes and other areas of government expenditure should be balanced.

Hare examines recent decisions of the UK courts, the European Court of Human Rights and the South African Constitutional Court to see how far social rights are already enforced. He finds that the UK judicial review cases where some protection has been given are all explicable on traditional administrative law grounds and do not support the case for constitutional as opposed to statutory protection for social rights. The Strasbourg court has given an expanded meaning to 'civil rights' so as to include some social benefits, but this has purely procedural consequences and does not affect questions of distribution. Moreover, in recognising social rights as legitimate objectives of state policy which can limit the right to property, the Court of Human Rights has not upheld any positive social right. The post-apartheid South African Constitution explicitly recognises social rights. But an examination of two leading decisions of the Constitutional Court leads Hare to conclude that it has applied only the familiar standards of administrative law based on reasonableness, rather than an intense form of judicial scrutiny appropriate to the vindication of an inviolable right. For Hare, the case for the constitutionalisation of social rights is not proven.

Whether or not the new EU Charter of Fundamental Rights is part of a new constitutional framework for Europe, there are rich lessons to be drawn from the experience of European countries in respect of the legal efficacy and significance of fundamental social rights. In Chapter 7, Antoine Lyon-Caen draws some general hypotheses from this experience. His starting point is a critique of the traditional distinction between *droits-libertés* and *droits-créances*. The former are negative defences against the state, while the latter, usually identified with social rights, require positive intervention by the state. Lyon-Caen points out the necessary complementarity between freedoms and social rights: social rights enable people to make the choices protected by the freedoms. Moreover, social rights take effect in a variety of ways: as a means of orienting the interpretation of other legal rules, as a method of justifying rules, mechanisms and institutions, as a means of challenging the legality of rules laid down by public authorities which conflict with social rights (an impeding effect known in France as the jurisprudence of the *cliquet*), and as a way of securing access for individuals to public facilities and services. The legal significance of social rights in the European context is increasingly as a vehicle of change. One does not 'apply' social rights as if they have automatic effects. They have to be 'implemented', that is translated, interpreted and mobilised. They are principles of action, provoking not a top-down hierarchy of norms, but rather a complex exchange between a plurality of actors. This idea is closely linked to the current movement (referred to earlier by Barnard and Deakin) towards the proceduralisation of social rights. Lyon-Caen's reinterpretation aims to provide a framework for recreating a link between rights of positive status (*droits-créances*) and the rights of citizens to take an active part in defining the conditions of collective life.

In Chapter 8, Professor Cynthia Estlund presents an American perspective on fundamental labour rights. Just how fundamental are American labour rights and how did they get that way in a country where the market is ascendant and there is believed to be a receding role for state regulation? Federal constitutional rights play essentially no role in labour matters. Part of the explanation of this is the state action requirement – the rights secured by the federal constitution (apart from the 13th Amendment's ban on involuntary servitude) operate only against government. In private sector employment constitutional rights arise only when the government intervenes, and this it rarely does. Estlund recounts the pivotal history of 'the right of employers to be left alone' which still shapes American consciousness on the role of the law. She concludes that 'the net result has been a system of collective labour relations that has been almost entirely insulated from ordinary democratic politics, yet equally insulated from the potentially progressive influence of constitutional commitments to liberty and equality'. 'By leaving more to the domain of contract, the American labour market has gained flexibility, and perhaps job growth, while American workers experience greater economic insecurity and inequality than their employed European counterparts.'

Estlund identifies one area in which 'fundamental' rights have been established. This is under Title VII of the Civil Rights Act and other federal laws developing the equal employment opportunity principle. To this there are two significant caveats: the steps taken by the current Supreme Court to limit congressional power as against the states, such as the limits on the liability of the states to suits for damages; and the privatisation of employment discrimination claims by the increasing use of mandatory arbitration. Finally, Estlund notes that state constitutional provisions have played their greatest role in the proliferation of individual employment rights, such as privacy and protection against dismissal. She points to the paradox that the lack of 'fundamentality' and universality – leaving these developments to lower and more local sources of legal authority – 'sometimes yields rather ambitious and durable employment rights'. She contrasts the vibrancy of the area left almost entirely to the states and the virtual stagnation of the law of collective labour rights that is exclusively federal and largely insulated from majoritarian control. In principle the solution may be to create federation-wide minimum standards – the most fundamental rights – while allowing local variations above that minimum.

The enforcement of social rights is heavily dependent upon the cultural context in which constitutions and social and labour legislation are enacted. This is shown in Chapter 9, where Professor Takashi Araki reviews the impact of fundamental social rights on Japanese law. The Japanese constitution contains a number of such rights, including the right to a minimum standard of living, the right to education, the right to work and to decent working conditions, and the right to organise and bargain collectively. These rights have been a source of inspiration for legislation on subjects such as employment security, labour standards, trade unions and collective bargaining. Fundamental social rights have also affected the judiciary, but the courts have generally been reluctant to go against the wishes of the democratic legislature. In judging the legality of actions in the private sphere the courts have been able to translate fundamental social values into principles of public policy, but Araki demonstrates that in practice the courts have generally upheld existing employment practices, such as the life-time employment system, even where this infringes fundamental rights, such as the right against age discrimination. However, the public policy concept has been actively utilised – even in the absence of specific legislation – against sex discrimination and also to restrict arbitrary dismissals. Araki uses the development of equal opportunity law to illustrate another feature of Japanese social policy, namely a soft-law approach using administrative guidance, which is thought to be more effective than direct legal intervention in Japanese culture.

The lack of effective procedures and sanctions for the enforcement of social rights is a recurring theme in this book. In Chapter 10, I discuss three tendencies which make it difficult to realise the potential of social and labour rights.

The first of these is the growth of soft law, that is non-binding recommendations, codes of practice and guidelines. In public international law, ILO recommendations are the best-known example, but I argue that the distinction between these and non-ratified ILO conventions is more a matter of theory than practice, particularly given the declining rate of ratification of ILO conventions. The 1998 Declaration on Fundamental Principles and Rights at Work was an attempt to strengthen compliance with non-ratified core conventions, but the follow-up procedures are 'strictly promotional', with the possibility of trade sanctions for breach of the fundamental rights being explicitly excluded. Other examples of soft international law are the disappointing ILO Tripartite Declaration of Principles Concerning Multinational Enterprises and Social Policy, and the rapid proliferation of voluntary corporate codes of conduct issued by transnational corporations. There has also been an increasing use of soft law in respect of EC social policy, and in the United Kingdom.

I argue that some soft law may help effective enforcement, where it recommends voluntary action and 'best practice' which goes beyond minimum legal standards. But soft law is unacceptable where it is treated as an exclusive alternative to binding instruments. International and national experience shows that voluntary codes never work on their own. While they may influence some organisations, regulators need to be able to rely on progressively more deterrent sanctions in order to secure cooperation and compliance.

The second tendency is the privatisation of enforcement, as illustrated by the expansion of mandatory arbitration in the United States, discussed by Estlund in Chapter 8, and the new 'arbitration alternative' in individual employment disputes in the United Kingdom. The latter is criticised by me for its failure to address the inequality of resources of employer and employee in a system of individual rights, and for the substitution of the unfettered discretion of an arbitrator for the rule of law in the workplace. These are worrying national counterparts to the privatisation of public enforcement that has already occurred through transnational corporate codes of conduct at the expense of improved mechanisms of national and international public law.

The third tendency is the growth of restrictions on transnational collective solidarity at a time when 'strikes' by international capital – moving enterprises and plants freely between countries – are increasingly commonplace. The ILO's expert committees and the OECD have been equivocal in their interpretation of international standards, while the EU has no legislative competence in this area. National legislation either prohibits such industrial action or imposes severe conditions. I propose that sympathy action should be allowed where the workers involved genuinely believe that the action relates directly or indirectly to their social and economic interests.

Effective legal procedures and sanctions are preferable to the use of industrial action, but I conclude that to have any chance of success these will have to transcend the narrow ambit of classical labour law and embrace all those who work in both the formal and informal sectors of the global economy: 'to become effective labour law must become social law'.

V. Rhetoric and reality

What conclusions, if any, do these rich and varied contributions enable us to make in answer to the question raised at the beginning: does the new rhetoric of social and labour rights match the reality of globalised market regulation and growing socio-economic inequality?

First, it is apparent that globalisation has changed the way in which we think about social and labour rights.[6] Throughout the world, governments now believe that trade, investment, jobs and development will come to those countries which have 'flexible' 'business-friendly' policies. One attempt to achieve this has been through economic and monetary

---

[6] See Harry Arthurs, 'Globalization of the Mind: Canadian Elites and the Restructuring of Legal Fields' (1998) 12 Canadian J.L.& Soc. 219; and 'Reinventing Labor Law for the Global Economy' (2001) 22 Berkeley Journal of Employment and Labor Law 271.

policies which reduce the capacity of organised labour and individual workers to resist the forces of the labour market. Another attempt has involved the degrading of social and labour rights, either by failing to update them or by rewriting them in ways hostile to workers' interests. Even where rights have been expanded these have been highly individualised and enacted against a background of diminishing or limited support for collective institutions.

Secondly, globalisation has exposed the weaknesses of both national and international methods for promoting social and labour rights. Although some philosophers have argued in favour of the constitutionalisation of social rights,[7] the evidence offered by lawyers in this book indicates that entrenchment has made little difference to their effectiveness in practice. In general, their enforcement has become increasingly problematic as a result of trends such as the growing reliance on soft law, the privatisation of enforcement and restrictions on traditional methods of collective solidarity. Notwithstanding the 1998 ILO Declaration, more than half the world's workers are still not covered by 'core' ILO conventions, and even states which have ratified them fall a long way short of meeting their obligations. The effectiveness of transnational standards has been undermined by the confusing disarray and conflict between international standards and (often weaker) regional ones. All of this reflects the way in which globalisation puts workers in different countries in competition with each other, fearful that assertion of their rights might lead to jobs being moved to other less rights-conscious jurisdictions. Not only are workers separated by inconsistent national and local legal regimes, but even within those regimes there are hierarchies of rights between traditional full-time employees and the expanding array of part-time, temporary and contingent workers of uncertain legal status. This undermines traditional solidarities.

Despite this gloomy picture, there are many indications of a rebirth of social and labour rights in the global economy. This can be seen in the attempts, so far unsuccessful, to make compliance with core human rights and labour standards (as embodied in the ILO 1998 Declaration) a condition of membership of the World Trade Organisation; in the 'labour side accord' of the North American Free Trade Agreement; and, most notably, in the EU Charter of Fundamental Rights, which, despite

---

[7] See esp. Cècile Fabre, *Social Rights under the Constitution* (Oxford, 2000).

its many defects of structure and drafting, is capable of being an inspiration and guide to Community social and labour standards.

This new dawn of social and labour rights has several features. First, social and labour rights are no longer seen as outside or in opposition to the market but are treated as integral to it. Social and labour rights are now presented as a necessary component of efficient and competitive markets. Secondly, the traditional analysis of social rights as being dependent upon positive interventions by the state is being questioned by a broader and more sophisticated approach. Social rights are increasingly relied on as a means of interpreting and justifying rules, mechanisms and institutions, or of challenging the legality of rules laid down by public authorities which conflict with social rights, and also as a way of securing access for individuals to public facilities and services. Social rights are becoming an important vehicle of change. They are not 'applied' in the orthodox legal way, but are mobilised as part of a dynamic interaction between the state, citizens, employers, consumers and workers. Social rights are demanded and realised not by courts and lawyers but by new social movements such as those of women, consumers, environmentalists, ethnic minorities, and development and human rights groups, often working with trade unions.

Thirdly, the role of law in the achievement of social and labour rights is being redefined. There is a movement away from substantive regulation to proceduralisation. The law is increasingly used as a means of supporting the participation of local unions and social groups as well as individuals. Paradoxically, strengthening local autonomy and participation is regarded as a more durable and realistic means of securing social rights in the face of globalisation than the imposition of top-down substantive redistribution. This approach could lead to greater inequality between undertakings and societies because of the unequal distribution of power. For this reason, its advocates stress the necessity for a core of minimum social and labour standards at international, regional and national level.

Fourthly, it is a feature of the emerging new structure of rights that, unlike classical labour law, it does not presuppose the existence of a contract of employment or an employment relationship. It is not limited to dependent or subordinated labour, on which labour rights have traditionally been focused. An objective of the ILO's 'decent work' programme, and of other movements, is to break down the inequalities between different categories of workers, between the employed and self-employed, and between those who work and those who are unemployed.[8] From this new perspective, labour rights and other social rights are interdependent.

Finally, one must acknowledge that our views about social and other human rights are shaped by our personal and intellectual histories. My own experience and study have neither led me to view social rights as absolute moral principles, nor to indulge in an ethical evaluation as to which rights are more worthy than others. The contributors to this volume share an instrumental approach, concerned with the kinds of interests which the law protects through rights which have 'teeth'. Rights in this sense imply that power can be wielded. The exercise of these rights, like war, is 'politics by other means'.[9] But rights are not simply the reflection of the existing distribution of power in society. Study of the process of creation and enforcement of social and labour rights helps us to understand how far the law can act relatively autonomously to restrain public and private power for the benefit of at least some of the people for some of the time. This is an integral part of processes of social and political change.

[8] See Amartya Sen, 'Work and rights' (2000) 139 Int. Labour Review, 119; B. Hepple, 'Equality and empowerment for work' (2001) 140 Int. Labour Review, 1.

[9] See R.Abel, *Politics by Other Means: Law in the Struggle Against Apartheid 1980–1994* (London, 1995), ch. 1.

I

Responses to globalisation

1

Common law, labour law, global law[1]

LORD WEDDERBURN

I. Introduction

Social rights cannot escape intimate association with labour standards. John Stuart Mill's belief that the nearest approach to social justice would be reached by associations of labourers working cooperatively with joint ownership of resources sprang from his perception of the conflicts inherent in the traditional relationship between the capitalist-as-chief and subordinated workpeople. English lawyers, by contrast, have habitually approached the subject through the eye of a common law based on a very different set of premises about the nature of employment relationships. The journey from common law to labour law is one in which legal and social analysis is inevitably joined by personal, ideological value judgements, and those who through hubris or repression are unable to recognise this human condition are unsafe guides. But today as lawyers we are also obliged, above all when offering ourselves as pretenders to the education of the young, to extend our imagination to the problems of a global economy and transnational power that pose new and dangerous social tensions.

When in 1960 I proposed that the Cambridge Law Faculty should introduce a 'Labour Law' option, I was taken aside and told that, interesting though this syllabus was as a presentation of the employment law of master and servant and law of economic torts, it was too 'political' a subject for the faculty to adopt. A year later, the same syllabus with the heading 'Industrial Law' was accepted. It included what we know as

---

[1] For the sake of brevity, footnotes below include references to argument and material in earlier publications which support propositions in the text, for example in *Labour Law and Freedom* (London, 1995; hereafter *LLAF*) and *Employment Rights in Britain and Europe* (London, 1991; hereafter *ERBE*).

individual and collective labour law, health and safety and mentions of social security law and company law on directors and of the ILO. After my departure, Paul O'Higgins admirably succeeded in having the 'Labour Law' title reinstated. Yet at the time the Faculty was in a sense right by its own lights in its first rejection of the subject before new members moved it on – even if those lights were, as was said of George III, 'few and dim'. Stallybrass's thesis that the 'objectivity' required of lawyers 'is difficult when you come to sociology' prevailed.[2]

Great teaching of the common law from Jack Hamson and others in Cambridge extended our imagination in various ways, but few of them could stomach inquiries into the social policies behind, say, *Rookes* v. *Barnard*[3] – in Laski's phrase the 'law behind the law'. Though new appointments soon afterwards began to turn the tide, it was not thought appropriate in 1960 to probe the social policies or ideology of the common law itself; nor was it commonly accepted in the Old Schools that labour law makes special demands on its apprentices, that whoever discussed labour law 'made apparent his attitudes', and that this was 'a place where law, politics and social assumptions meet in a man; and whoever believes that he is so "objective" or "impartial" as to be above the policies and prejudices is either arrogantly *naif* or dishonest with himself and others'.[4] It does no harm to repeat that in the light of modern developments.

It may not be a bad moment now in a new century to see where we have travelled since then. The relationship of the common law to our labour law is still of importance. The prospects of an 'alternative labour law' now seem to be weak in Britain, even in the light of European developments. The reality of transnational capital which can create and control the global market with the aid of the new information technology requires a reconsideration of labour law itself. These may be useful guideposts for a preliminary investigation into fundamental rights. It is a perilously extensive agenda for a brief survey, but we cannot paint an impression of such rights at work today on a canvas of any lesser width.

The need has certainly not passed to avoid lax statements of the common law which addle general analysis, such as the error that in England

---

[2] W. Stallybrass, 'Law in the Universities' (1948) 1 JSPTL 157, 164. Our generation owed a special debt to such teachers of Jurisprudence as Brian King and Mickey Dias for lifting our eyes to some wider horizons.

[3] [1964] AC 1129 HL.

[4] K. W. Wedderburn, *The Worker and the Law* (Harmondsworth, 1965) 339; in the somewhat sexist usage of the time, 'man' is used in the sense of the German *man*.

as in France collective agreements create inderogability in minimum employment conditions[5] or the opacity that for employment relationships the 'ordinary law of contract provides... rules against fraud and coercion during the bargaining process'.[6] We still need as jurists to emulate Sinzheimer, whose method was to 'work through the black-letter analysis of the law, in other words he neither went round it nor got stuck in it'.[7] If we ignore such a discipline we cease to be lawyers and become mish-mash, dare one say untrained, sociologists.

Before leaving the era of the 1960s, however, we may recall today, when labour law is the subject of research and teaching in so many of our universities, that in 1959 only four of the twenty British law faculties taught anything which we would now recognise as a 'Labour Law' course, as opposed to 'Master and Servant', 'Factory Law' or 'Trade Union Law'. Exceptionally, the labour law course at the London School of Economics traced its pedigree back long before Otto Kahn-Freund's arrival in 1933 to the lectures by Mr (later Lord) Wright in 1903, with Robson adding a course on European *comparative* labour law in 1934 – the first 'recommended books' being two publications of the ILO and subjects ranging from France, Germany, and the United States to the Soviet Union![8] In the 1950s the good fortune of having an

---

[5] See Advocate-General Jacobs's Opinion in *Albany International BV* v. *Stichting Bedrijfspensioenfonds Textielindustrie* [1999] ECR I-5751, paras. 178, 182. *Cf. LLAF* ch. 6. But it may be noted that 'contractual' collective clauses may have individual normative effects in some systems: see G. Riganò (2001) 1 Arg. di Dir. del Lav. 289, 294 on Cort. Cass. (It.) 11718/2000, ibid., 357–60. Normative terms impliedly derived from collective arrangements may benefit employers as much as employees: *Henry* v. *London General Transport Services* [2001] IRLR 132.

[6] H. Collins, 'Justifications and Techniques of Legal Regulation of the Employment Relation', in H. Collins, P. Davies and R. Rideout (eds.), *Legal Regulation of the Employment Relation* (London, 2000), 6. Economic coercion or 'duress' affords legal protection for the multinational enterprise at common law against industrial action, but not for the individual employee against the employer's power of 'command in the guise of agreement', at any rate where there is any welfare net for the unemployed: *Hennessy* v. *Craigmyle* [1986] ICR 461, 468 CA, and the *Dimskal* case [1992] ICR 37 HL. The common law has a habit of using protective legislation as an excuse not to develop its own protections: *Johnson* v. *Unisys* [2001] 2 WLR 1076 HL.

[7] O. Kahn-Freund, 'Hugo Sinzheimer 1875–1945', in *Labour Law and Politics in the Weimar Republic*, ed. R. Lewis and J. Clark (Oxford, 1981) 73, 77; see ibid., 108, for his ideological analysis of the case law in 'The Social Ideal of the *Reich* Labour Court'(1931), probably Kahn-Freund's greatest juridical work.

[8] See K. W. Wedderburn, *The Present State of Law Teaching and Research in Labour Law: Great Britain*, Theme III, National Report, 6th International Congress of Labour Law and Social Legislation 1966, and *Appendix* (Stockholm, 1966); and a later account of labour law research and teaching in Britain in S. Edlund (ed.), *Labour Law Research in Twelve Countries* (Stockholm, 1986) 193–211.

interest in labour history was compounded for some of us by the happy chance of coming across Kahn-Freund's rationalisation of the British labour law system in his remarks of 1954 (at the point when it was only just being released from war-time regulation) and – much more – in the seminal analysis of British *collective laissez-faire* of 1959,[9] after

> he fell in love with British industrial relations (in which) virtually every fault that he had seen in the industrial relations of the Weimar Republic could be matched by a virtue.[10]

He carefully analysed the long tradition of legislative regulation on which trade unions had struggled to erect the dominant pattern of collective bargaining but was quick, in retrospect perhaps too quick, to judge that the system might be qualitatively changed by the minor new regulation of 1963 and 1965 – 'something entirely new is happening in this field in Britain'.[11] At the time of what he called his 'Damascus' concerning the legal character of the British collective agreement, he introduced British lawyers to an analysis with roots in Weber and Marx.[12] Whatever the label put upon this approach emphasising the fact that British collective labour relations were remarkably dependent upon social rather than legal sanctions after trade unions had carved out a space in which collective bargaining could be relatively lawfully conducted and had beaten off attempts to juridify it and with it trade union status,[13] it is still a central element in understanding comparison with other systems, such as in France where it was, and is, a different orthodoxy to say of collective bargaining:

---

[9] 'Labour Law' in A. Flanders and H. Clegg, *The System of Industrial Relations in Great Britain* (Oxford, 1954), ch. 2; also 'Intergroup Conflicts and their Settlement' (1954) 5 *Brit. Jo. Soc.* 193, 'Collective Labour Relations' (1960) 3 *Rev. di Dir. Int. e Comp. del Lav.* 353; and his authoritative, insufficiently consulted chapter in M. Ginsberg (ed.), *Law and Opinion in England in the 20th Century* (London, 1959), 216.

[10] H. Clegg in Wedderburn, R. Lewis, J. Clark (eds.) *Labour Law and Industrial Relations* (Oxford, 1983) 6; see too Kahn-Freund's account for the German reader of the British system, ibid., ch. 1, written in 1978 (trs. J. Clark).

[11] O. Kahn-Freund, *Labour Law, Old Traditions and New Developments* (Toronto, 1968), 50–52.

[12] Especially in his Introduction and Notes to Karl Renner, *The Institutions of Private Law and Their Social Function* (London, 1949).

[13] See 'Collective Bargaining or Legal Enactment' in (2000) 29 ILJ 1, 26–28, especially on the place of S. and B. Webb.

Just as in the individual contract of employment, it is the lack of equality of the parties to the (collective) negotiation which explains the need for legislation.[14]

Unhappily Kahn-Freund also bequeathed the semantic confusions of the maxim 'abstention of the law', though he rarely used the phrase after 1954.[15] In a system where there had been 'not so much an abstention on the judges' part as an exclusion of them',[16] the concept of 'non-intervention' in autonomous collective bargaining became widely misunderstood. Subsequent work on Kahn-Freund on all our parts unmistakably exhibits, for those who wish to see, that 'primordial ambivalence of feeling towards the father. His sons hated him but they loved him too.'[17] 'Abstention' was vulgarised by some into shorthand for an 'absence' of law on labour relations, even at the time of the new literature on the subject; and even very eminent scholars ascribed a 'pure abstentionist position' to proposals for legislation to ban race discrimination in employment while opposing new rights for non-unionists.[18]

Moreover, among the extravagant claims, 'abstentionism' was blamed for its alleged mistaken belief in the impotence of law to change the relations between capital and labour.[19] We may have to be more cautious about confident ascriptions of state competence to change social patterns by edict when we re-examine below the context of global capital and the decline of collective workers' organisations essential to *collective laissez-faire*. Even in the domestic setting, enactment does not necessarily produce social effect, especially in the absence of adequate sanction. That is a special problem in the British legal context. Consider the number of pregnant workers unsupported by union help who suffer dismissal or discrimination when that is supposed to be an impossible fate under protections supposedly afforded to them but flouted

[14] Gérard Lyon-Caen, 'À propos d'une Négociation sur la Négociation' 2001 Droit Ouvrier 1, 5. Consider the extensive legislative framework surrounding French collective bargaining: G. Lyon-Caen, J. Pélissier, A. Supiot, *Droit du Travail*, 19th edn (Paris, 1988), 746–832.

[15] In many ways they were immediately more important in emerging comparative labour law; see G. Giugni, *Introduzione allo studio della autonomia collettiva* (Milan, 1960), 21–34, 93–139, 145–149.

[16] Wedderburn, *The Worker and the Law* (Harmondsworth, 1965), 20.

[17] S. Freud, *Civilization and its Discontents*, Penguin Freud Library (Harmondsworth, 1964 [1930]), XII, 325.

[18] P. Davies and M. Freedland, *Labour Legislation and Public Policy* (Oxford, 1993), 253.

[19] H. Collins, 'Against Abstentionism', in John Eekelaar and John Bell (eds.), *Oxford Essays in Jurisprudence*, 3rd ser. (Oxford, 1987), 79, 94.

by employers.[20] The power of the multinational enterprise is especially prominent in individuals' litigation.[21] There is an urgent need to re-assess here, as elsewhere in employment law, the procedures, sanctions and remedies (from compensation, reinstatement, burden of proof to interim relief) to make meaningful the commitment to equality and non-discrimination.[22] Rights, fundamental or otherwise, which lack adequate remedies are fantasies. The comparison has often been made with protective legislation in the field of health and safety at work, where virtually every means of enforcement is utilised from civil and criminal court sanctions in the web of statutory and common law duties, state inspection under a Commission and Executive, administrative orders, codes of encouragement and workers' representatives.[23] Despite the fact that some research has pointed in a new direction of 'smarter regulation' or even less regulation based on 'reflexive rationality', to confront stubbornly high workplace accident rates,[24] the next development in the United Kingdom may well with justification follow France in increasing the personal liability of directors and executives for unsafe conditions that still kill, infect and maim British workers.[25] The place and nature of 'regulation' are still an open question.

But the very structure of British collective labour law, derived from an early industrial revolution and from the character of the labour movement's struggle, and still built upon the fabric of liberties and

---

[20] R. Dunstan, 'Birth Rights' (NACAB Evidence Report, 2001); compare the NACAB Report on paid holidays under the Working Time Regulations 1998: *Wish you were here* (NACAB, 2000).

[21] See the libel case of *Steel and Morris* v. *McDonald's Corpn.*, 31.3.1999, CA (hearing took 313 days; judgment below was 762 pages; appellant defendants of Greenpeace allegedly 'attacked McDonald's Corporation's commercial image'; they were unrepresented for most of the hearing and in the CA). Cf. T. Royle *Working for McDonald's in Europe* (London, 2000), 17–18 ('the longest running ever civil court case in the UK'); cf. E. Schlosser *Fast Food Nation* (Harmondsworth, 2000); J. Vidal *McLibel* (London, 1997).

[22] B. Hepple, M. Coussey and T. Choudhury, *Equality: A New Framework*, Report of the Independent Review of Enforcement of UK Anti-Discrimination Legislation (Oxford, 2000), esp. ch. 4; cf. K. Purcell, 'Gendered Employment Insecurity?', ch. 6 in E. Heery and J. Salmon (eds.), *The Insecure Workforce* (London, 2000).

[23] See J. Hendy and M. Forde, *Redgrave, Fife & Machin: Health and Safety*, 3rd edn (London, 1995).

[24] See the discussions in Neil Gunningham and R. Johnstone, *Regulating Workplace Safety: System and Sanctions* (Oxford, 1999); T. Wilthagen 'Reflexive Rationality in Regulation of Occupational Health and Safety', in R. Rogowski and T. Wilthagen (eds.), *Reflexive Labour Law* (Deventer, 1994).

[25] See the proposals of the Health and Safety Commission and arguments of its Chairman B. Callaghan in (2001) 22 Company Lawyer 147.

'immunities' from common law illegalities and an incomplete escape from master and servant law, was at the end of the century unlikely to provide an easy modern basis for such fundamental labour rights as could be found in France, Italy or Germany or in the ILO Conventions.[26] Certainly a mere change of form from immunities into positive rights would not, even if achievable, necessarily guarantee new fundamental rights for working people.[27] We might examine below how far this aim was pursued in the 1999 legislation.

II. Theories and reality

Given the changes in economic and social relations since 1980, not to speak of technological advance in an information society, it is not surprising that interest has moved on. Globalisation is said to imply the need that 'labour lawyers, like lizards sitting in the sun, throw away their old skin and generate a new one, by taking fresh views at the subject.'[28] Among the new varieties we may note, on the one hand, that work on 'regulation' as a focus of interest in law generally, studying the need of regulators 'to balance the pursuit of efficiency against the social objectives that statutes, political parties and commentators designate as appropriate',[29] has been matched by research which sees an increase of regulation in labour law, far beyond the old-fashioned concept of a 'floor of rights', as beneficial to economic efficiency and necessary for social progress.[30] Regulation of discrimination is proven, it is claimed,

---

[26] 'Companies and Employees: Common Law or Social Dimension' (1992) 109 LQR 220, in *LLAF*, ch. 2; also (1980) 9 ILJ 65, in *ERBE*, ch. 3; cf. S. Deakin 'Legal Origins of Wage Labour', in L. Clarke, P. de Gijsel, J. Jansssen (eds.), *The Dynamics of Wage Relations in the New Europe* (Dordrecht, 2000), 32; and 'The Changing Concept of the Employer in British Labour Law' (2001) 30 ILJ 72–84; and for a current note, S. Deakin and F. Wilkinson, *The Employment Contract* Working Paper 171 (ESRC, 2000) in the light of M. Cully, S. Woodland, A. O'Reilly and G. Dix, *Britain at Work* (London, 1999) and N. Millward, A. Bryson and J. Forth, *All Change at Work?* (London, 2000).

[27] Contrast P. Elias and K. Ewing [1982] CLJ 32, 35–8, discussed in 'The New Politics of Labour Law' (1983), *ERBE*, ch. 4.

[28] S. Sciarra in T. Wilthagen (ed.) *Advancing Theory in Labour Law and Industrial Relations in a Global Context* (Amsterdam, 1998) X, 101–2.

[29] R. Baldwin and M. Cave, *Understanding Regulation: Theory, Strategy and Practice* (Oxford, 1999), 329.

[30] See S. Deakin and F. Wilkinson, 'Rights vs. Efficiency? The Economic Case for Transnational Labour Standards' (1994) 23 ILJ 289; and *Labour Standards – Essential to Economic and Social Progress* (1996 IER); now 'Labour Law and Economic Theory: A Reappraisal' in G. De Geest, J. Seegers, R. Van den Berg (eds.), *Law and Economics in the Labour Market* (Cheltenham, 1999).

to be necessary for efficiency and productivity.[31] This school of thought is led inevitably to advocate fundamental labour rights for workers,[32] and collective rights and procedures are indeed 'custodians' of individual rights and central to their application.[33] Substantive economic freedoms are sought, as 'institutionalised forms of capabilities', by extending fundamental social rights far beyond the limits imposed by minimalist, Hayekian doctrine.[34] The right of individual workers to programmes of education, for example, is best effected on a base of statutory rights affording facilities for union 'learning representatives'.[35] What is more its exponents take an interest in the rules and realities of corporate governance.[36] Regulatory labour standards are relevant not just to 'market failures' but 'form one of the conditions which *both permit and require* firms to pursue a high-wage, high-productivity strategy, based on continuous improvements in labour quality'.[37] The impact of the national minimum wage has not, it seems, caused discernible adverse effects on employment and has had other beneficial effects.[38] In general, normative regulation can affect the character of the 'incompleteness' of

[31] V. Pérotin and A. Robinson, 'Employee Participation and Equal Opportunities' (2000) 38 BJIR 557.

[32] For example, the extensive survey by U. Mückenberger and S. Deakin, 'From Deregulation to a European Floor of Rights' (1989) 3 Zeitschrift für auslandisches und internationales Arbeits- und Sozialrecht 157.

[33] W. Brown, S. Deakin, D. Nash and S. Oxenbridge in (2000) 38 BJIR 611.

[34] See the interesting paper by S. Deakin and F. Wilkinson, 'Capabilities, Spontaneous Order and Social Rights', ESRC Centre (Cambridge, 2000), now in (2000) II *Il diritto del mercato*, 317–44.

[35] *Learning at work* (Labour Research Dept, 2001) 13–15.

[36] Space forbids detail on this important aspect of labour law: for useful discussions see S. Deakin and A. Hughes (eds.) *Enterprise and Community: New Directions in Corporate Governance* (Oxford, 1997); S. Deakin, R. Hobbs, S. Konzelmann and F. Wilkinson, *Partnership Ownership and Control: The Impact of Corporate Governance on Employment Relations* (Cambridge, 2001); K. Hopt and G. Teubner (eds.), *Corporate Governance and Directors' Liabilities* (Berlin, 1984); S. Worthington (2000) 116 LQR 638 and (2001) 64 MLR 439. The current proposals in Britain are disappointing: see the *Final Report* by the Company Law Steering Group on *Modern Company Law* (DTI URN 01/492 and 493), below n. 78. On the French literature, G. Auzero, 'Le corporate governance et les salariés' (2001) Droit Ouvr. 150; and the *Vienot Report Part II* (Paris, 1999) and subsequent moves towards disclosure: *Financial Times*, 21 July 2000. In Italy, *Codice di Autodisciplina* (Comitato per la Corporate Governance, Milan, 1999). Cf. *Corporate Governance Codes* (Comparative European Corporate Governance Network, 1999, www.ecgn.ulb.ac.be/ecgn/codesreference. htm).

[37] S. Deakin, 'Labour Law as Market Regulation', in P. Davies, A. Lyon-Caen, S. Sciarra, S. Simitis (eds.), *European Community Labour Law: Principles and Perspectives Liber Amicorum Lord Wedderburn* (Oxford, 1996), 63, 86 (emphasis in original).

[38] *The National Minimum Wage: Third Report*, Low Pay Commission (London, 2000) I, Part 3; cf. A. Beattie, 'Monopsomy Revisited', *Financial Times*, 20 June 2001.

the employment contract, for example on the intensity of the work effort and precise content of the obligation to work, and supplement private ordering in pursuit of efficiency.

Yet the very depth of expropriation, poverty and powerlessness among the world's workers in today's global economy, and increasing relative poverty even in developed countries, and the widely acknowledged need for national and transnational core labour standards – the central issue for labour law tomorrow – illustrates the problem of applying such a thesis internationally and of supplying the protection which only collective organisation and struggle can make stick. Regulation cannot in itself determine the value judgements assessing any 'proper' balance between freedom and subordination. In the form of regulation *as* labour law aimed at efficiency and equity, it has achieved a new place in the subject, even if the new weakness of the state and the inherent deficiencies of the method itself limit its capability to explain or to solve such issues. And certainly the case for a British 'exception' to Simitis's iron law of *Juridification* in advanced industrial societies, a thesis 'best understood by looking at the origin and development of labour law', is now much weaker than it was before our regulatory interventions of recent decades.[39]

On the other side, there has arisen a different school which concentrates on 'regulation', or limits on it, for the purposes of 'competitiveness', putting into centre stage a priori the individual employment relation. In a sense this is an older approach, focusing on such pre-labour law, market-oriented questions as: *why regulate the employment relation?* This is an old, Anglo-Saxon question, one to which continental labour law authorities find a simple answer in the inequalities of the relationship. Subordination and inequality are acknowledged by this school as justifications for regulation, but treated by themselves as inadequate. Two lines of argument are admitted to justify special regulation of the employment relation – economic 'market failure' and distributive outcomes of an 'unacceptable' degree, though caution is urged on the latter intervention for worker-protection since the 'costs of protection of rights should be kept proportionate to their benefits' – 'benefits', we may reasonably infer, to the 'competitivity' of the employer, not to the welfare of the human being at work. The state today makes quick use of such theory to limit even access to enforcement procedures both to avoid costs for

---

[39] S. Simitis, 'Juridification of Labor Relations', in G. Teubner (ed.), *Juridification of the Social Spheres* (Berlin, 1987) 113; for the now doubtful British 'exception', J. Clark and Wedderburn, 'Juridification – A Universal Trend?', ibid., 163.

the employer and to protect its public funds, for example by institut-
ing charges on workers who use the tribunals.[40] The 'regulatory techniques' thought most suitable are those 'encouraging self-regulation and
self-monitoring of compliance'.[41] Moreover, the preferred 'flexible firm
undermines the conditions for worker organisation that had pertained
under mass production',[42] while on an individual level the primary aim
must be to mould the worker's 'employability' for the needs of capital.
The ideal is a cooperative, flexible employee who solves conflicts of interests by acting in the interests of the employer and on an uncertain
notion of 'partnership'. But, as has been pertinently observed by employers: 'Of course partnerships do not necessarily require trade unions.'[43]
Nor is there any great hint in British usage that an employer must be put
to proof that its mass dismissals should satisfy a test of *compétitivité*.[44]

The 'employability' programme is of course already at the centre of
current political ideology, together with an approach to the obligation
to work like a new Poor Law administered by Dr Ure,[45] and it has not
escaped commentators that overall this approach to workers, actual and
potential, means that:

> Human beings are thus reduced to the level of capital equipment, and
> learning ... is merely the fuel which makes them go.[46]

---

[40] See the remarkable proposals, later dropped, by the DTI to make charges on workers institut-
ing complaints in employment tribunals: *Routes to Resolution: Improving Dispute Resolution
in Britain* (DTI, July 2001) paras. 5.9–5.11 (On new restrictions on workers' access to employment tribunals in the Employment Bill 2002, Parts 2 and 3, see Parl. Deb. HL 26 Feb.,
13–26 Mar., 11 Apr. 2002.)

[41] See H. Collins, 'Justifications and Techniques of Legal Regulation of the Employment Re-
lation', in H. Collins, P. Davies and R. Rideout (eds.), *Legal Regulation of the Employment
Relation* (2000), above n. 6, esp. at 6, 12, 27. For a similar, though not identical, approach,
see the contributions in: R. Mitchell (ed.), *Redefining Labour Law* (Melbourne, 1995); cf.
S. Deery and R. Mitchell, *Employment Relations, Individualisation and Union Exclusion: An
International Study* (Sydney, 2000).

[42] H. Collins in Wilthagen (ed.), *Advancing Theory in Labour Law and Industrial Relations in a
Global Context*, n. 28 above, at 121.

[43] Digby Jones (CBI Director General) (2000), 910 *The House Magazine* (Parliamentary Communications London) 25 Sept. 2000, 18.

[44] Compare France, especially via the 'social plan': Code du Travail Art. L.321-1; Ass. Plén. 8
déc. 2000, see G. Lyon-Caen, *Semaine Sociale Lamy* (Paris) No. 1010, 8 Jan. 2001.

[45] See J. Fulbrook, 'New Labour's Welfare Reforms: Anything New?' (2001) 64 MLR 243, 249. In
June 2001 the government announced that it would require partners to attend for interview
along with unemployed workers to ensure that they too became employed.

[46] R. Harris, *Sunday Times*, 20 May 2001. Compare the analysis in *Productivity in the UK: The
Evidence and the Government's Approach* (London, 2000).

Accordingly, among the first steps of the new UK government in 2001 were a request to the Financial Services Authority to advise on how to 'embed an entrepreneurial culture' in schools, and proposals for selected fourteen-year-old children to end full-time schooling and work part-time as part of their training.[47]

Many of the economic market nostrums employed as rules in 'market failure' labour law remind one of Amartya Sen's comment on similar axioms such as 'revealed preference' (the prisoners' dilemma): 'the whole framework is steeped with implicit ideas about preference and psychology, not based on empirical verification'.[48]

It is even now suggested with panache that, setting aside Adam Smith and 'Marxian' notions of inequality in the employment relationship, from the 'perspective of game theory ... it is the *employee* just as much as the employer in whom economic power is vested'.[49] This frame of reference whereby individual employees and employers (the latter already in truth a concentration of capital or of state power, imbued by the law itself with personality and privileges of limited liability)[50] seemingly haggle about terms at the office door or factory gate ignores the reality of modern employment. But the issues of collective relations, corporate governance and fundamental rights in labour law are barely relevant to this new orthodoxy, one erected naturally as the superstructure of the new economic relationships. Such writers have long denied the maxim that 'Labour is not a commodity', and declared:

> Labour service is bought and sold daily ... All the considerations of interpreting the demand and supply analysis of price and output effects are applicable to labour services ... Underlying is the assumption that people are free agents and can quit or change jobs when they wish and that at least some will change jobs when knowledge of more attractive openings is available.[51]

---

[47] *The Times*, 19 June 2001.

[48] Amartya Sen, 'Behaviour and the Concept of Preference' (1973) XL 159 *Economica* (n.s.) 241–259, now in idem, *Choice, Welfare and Measurement* (Oxford, 1982), ch. 2.

[49] H. Collins in 'Justifications and Techniques of Legal Regulation of the Employment Relation', above n. 41, at 43 (emphasis in original) and see generally pp. 42–46 for such views.

[50] English judges maintain very close ideological control of any exceptions to these privileges: see *Trustor AB* v. *Smallbone* (No. 2) [2001] 1 WLR 1177, 1183-6 *per* Morritt V-C.

[51] A. Alchian and W. Allen, *University Economics*, 3rd edn (Belmont, CA, 1972), 407, 443; cf. M. Reynolds 'The Myth of Labour's Inequality of Bargaining Power' (1991) 12 Jo. Lab. Res. 167.

In fact, the market failure model of labour law acknowledges few justifications for intervention in the interests of workers 'who require regulatory intervention in their dealings with employers in order to secure different aspects of their *human freedom*'.[52]

It is that freedom of the individual which is at stake in the inequality of the employment relationship and to which fundamental rights must always be addressed. For those who, like the writer, regard the need for collective organisation by workers as essential to their freedom, or in Kahn-Freund's phrase that in reality 'on the labour side, all power is collective power', and that collective bargaining is a need and a right which springs from the nature of that relationship, such ideological closures on justifications for worker-protection are not likely to be attractive. It is notable that continental labour law theory takes the need for protection for granted. For the labour market is not just another market,[53] nor is the employment contract just another contract.[54] Nor is labour power just another commodity. It has, in Marx's phrase, 'no other container but human flesh and blood'. These choices go to the heart of the 'market failure' brand of labour law and its ideological base. The increased difficulty of attaining goals of human freedom in the global market is no good reason for submitting to new values, more convenient to those in power. As the ILO tradition insists, values can be defended even when markets demand change.[55] Although it was not nominally the essence of Thatcherite ideology, which purported to adopt formulae closer to the purer free market doctrines of Hayek albeit with strong state regulation,[56] this theoretical reversion to market dominance is acceptable to the ideologues of business and is today their preference in the business schools. Harvard studies of entrepreneurial strategies are found to spend little or no time on collective industrial relations.[57]

---

[52] B. Langille and G. Davidov, 'Beyond Employees and Independent Contractors' (1999) Comp. L. L. & Pol. Jo. 7, 44 (emphasis in original).

[53] See P. Weiler, *Governing the Workplace, The Future of Labor and Employment Law* (Cambridge, MA, 1990).

[54] C. Summers 'Similarity and Differences between Employment Contracts and Civil or Commercial Contracts' (2001) 17 Int. Jo. Comp. L. L. and Ind. Rels. 5.

[55] M. Hansenne, *Defending Values, Promoting Change*, Director-General's Report, ILO (Geneva, 1994).

[56] See 'Freedom of Association and the Philosophies of Labour Law' (1989) 18 ILJ 1, now *ERBE*, ch. 8.

[57] See for example R. McGrath and I. MacMillan, *The Entrepreneurial Mindset* (Boston, MA, 2000).

Common to the programmes favoured by it is the need to strip collective labour of its legal defences in order that the 'natural' economic processes should not be delayed by conflict. Law may be marginal to economic trends; but workers must still be shorn of effective advantages which it provides: 'family friendly' help perhaps, but not a collective voice in decisions or a right to pursue struggle for new freedoms. Steps towards 'enterprise confinement' in Britain by way of redefinition of a 'trade dispute', the end of protection from common law liability for secondary or sympathetic action, and the limitation of lawful picketing, matched by the regulation of union security, an expanding control over union rules and autonomy,[58] and the addition of extravagantly complicated rules governing ballots for lawful union industrial action, have all pursued this authoritarian aim.[59] The refusal in 1999 to reconsider the ban on all 'secondary' and sympathetic industrial action offended elementary labour standards and handed extensive legal powers to employers by maintaining the doctrine of 'enterprise confinement' whose boundaries are drawn by them. All jurisdictions have legal rules about the formation of trade unions and legal limits to their activities. In a decade Britain became, and remains, one of the most illiberal regimes on collective labour law, affronting fundamental principles.[60]

III. An alternative labour law in Britain?

All hope of speedy movement towards an 'alternative' labour law in Britain was lost in 1999. It is difficult to see how the Employment Relations Act 1999 went in a substantial degree 'some way to addressing the concerns' of the ILO on British labour standards since 1989.[61] Tania

---

[58] See (1988) 17 Bull. Comp. Lab. Relns. 107–131 (now *LLAF*, ch. 5).

[59] Although, as Bob Simpson points out, the effects of Millett LJ's judgment in *London Underground* v. *RMT* [1996] ICR 170, may lend new strength to a union's powers of action: (2001) 30 ILJ 194, 195.

[60] Such as the ILO Conventions 87 on Freedom of Association and 98 on the Right to Organise and Collective Bargaining: see especially K. Ewing, *Britain and the ILO*, 2nd edn (IER, 1994). On European jurisdictions and the right to strike, see Wedderburn in W. McCarthy (ed.), *Legal Interventions in Industrial Relations* (Oxford, 1992), 147–208, and *ERBE*, 276–353.

[61] K. Ewing, 'Freedom of Association and the Employment Act 1999' (1999) 28 ILJ 283, 298. On what follows see the argument in Wedderburn, 'Collective Bargaining or Legal Regulation: the 1999 Act and Recognition' (2000) 29 ILJ 1, 13–42; also P. Smith and G. Morton, 'New Labour's Reform of Britain's Employment Law' (2001) 39 BJIR119.

Novitz has persuasively argued, perhaps even understated, the oppo-site.[62] British law appears to offend ILO principles in respect of trade union elections, discipline of union members, strike ballots, and the aims, methods and effect (on employment contracts) of industrial ac-tion. In that context, the 1999 Act moved forward only a fumbling pace. Nothing in the Human Rights Act cures that defect. No change was made to the new structure of trade dispute immunities against common law liabilities in favour of positive rights. Minor if useful provisions, such as the right to be represented in grievance and disciplinary proceedings (s. 10), left the status of the trade union at common law unlawful.[63] The new Schedule on a modest duty to 'recognise' unions,[64] in theory a big step forward, creates an obligation of somewhat opaque content – imposing a 'method' in the form of a procedure, as the government de-scribed it, 'simply to meet and talk' (which appears to admit of 'take it or leave it' *Boulwarism*); applies an arbitrary test of 40 per cent ma-jority of the bargaining unit as a requirement; fails to ensure adequate access for unions to the workplace and to penalise anti-union behaviour by employers; attaches largely to pay, hours and holidays only; ex-cludes employers most resistant to recognition, those employing (along with associated employers – other than foreign employers) fewer than 21 workers – few large companies have so far been involved;[65] and offers some of its important protections only to 'employees'[66] (a not unimportant point in the context of the battle between labour law and competition law for hegemony over self-employed, atypical or

[62] 'International Promises and Domestic Pragmatism: To what extent will the Employment Relations Act 1999 Implement International Labour Standards Relating to Freedom of As-sociation?' (2000) 63 MLR 379; see too her 'Freedom of Association and Fairness at Work' (1998) 27 ILJ 169.

[63] *Boddington* v. *Lawton* [1994] ICR 478 (the common law principle cannot be changed). Union status is of course made lawful by the protection in s. 11 TULRCA 1992. But s.11(2) had to be added after the challenge by the judges in *Edwards* v. *SOGAT* [1971] Ch. 3654 CA.

[64] Itself not even compatible with ILO Convention 98 in the view of K. Ewing (2000) 29 ILJ 267.

[65] See the helpful TUC analyses: 'Statutory Recognition: Recent Developments' (March–April 2001), 'Meeting with CAC' (May 2001), [and 'Focus on Recognition' (Jan. 2002)].

[66] For an interesting attempt to extend an effective right to bargain to workers who are non-dependent, self-employed workers, see the Canadian Status of the Artist Act 1992; B. Langville and G. Davidov (1999) 21 Comp. L. L. & Pol. Jo. 7, 37. On collective agree-ments with labour-only contractors: F. Raday (1999) 20 Comp. Lab. Law & Policy Jo. 413, 436.

'third-type' work, in the light of changing work patterns and of EU legal developments[67] and of new classifications of 'public' and 'private' employment).[68] The British 1999 Act also makes 'effective management' the dominant test of legal bargaining units; and oddly imposes as the sole sanction against delinquent employers the best collective remedy it can think of, namely the arcane, discretionary order for 'specific performance' which it will be difficult juridically and socially for the High Court to apply.[69] As often elsewhere, the provisions for such sanctions on recalcitrant employers are a surrender to trepidation, and in the project for the legislation even the TUC had jettisoned any attempt to analyse the problem, which despite the decline in multi-employer bargaining might have built on past experience[70] by providing for *substantive* CAC awards endowed with inderogability as a meaningful sanction to enforce an obligation to bargain.[71] In addition to encouraging new voluntary agreements, the legal obligation extended collective bargaining to small groups of workers in 2001.[72]

Even the small jewel in the crown of the Act – an extension of remedies for unfair dismissal to employees dismissed by reason of their taking protected industrial action if dismissal takes place within eight weeks of the beginning of the action (a seemingly arbitrary limit) or later if the employee has stopped taking part or the employer has not taken reasonable procedural steps to resolve the dispute (Sched. 5 para. 3, s. 238A TULRCA 1992) – is vitiated by the employee being required to prove this

---

[67] See S. Engblom in 'Equal Treatment of Employees and Self-employed Workers' (2001) 17 Int. Jo. Comp. Lab. Law & Ind. Rels. 211; and on the *Albany* line of cases, below n. 152 and Sciarra, below, ch. 4.

[68] See M. Freedland, ch. 1, G. Amato, ch. 8, and S. Sciarra, ch. 10, in M. Freedland and S. Sciarra (eds.) *Public Services and Citizenship in European Law* (Oxford, 1998).

[69] See generally, but especially B. Simpson, 'Trade Union Recognition and the Law' (2000) 29 ILJ 193–222; also Wedderburn (2000) 29 ILJ 33–42; S. Moore, S. Wood, P. Davies (2000) 29 ILJ 406.

[70] See the remnant remaining in s. 185(5)(6) TULRCA 1992.

[71] See Wedderburn, 'A British Duty to Bargain – A Footnote on the End-Game' (1998) 27 ILJ 253. It had, however, been shown that proposals were not appropriate that advocated remedies stripping companies of limited liability (Wedderburn, rightly rejected by the *Donovan Report* (1968 Cmnd 3623) para. 253) or imposing officials in place of the board to act for the company in negotiating an agreement (K. Ewing (1990) 19 ILJ 209, 225). On substantive awards by the Labour Court under the Irish Industrial Relations (Amendment) Act 2001, see (2001) 330 EIRR 8.

[72] See 'Due Recognition' (2000) 712 IRS Emp. Trends 4: see CAC, *Applications and Decisions under Sched. A1 TULRCA 1992* (2001), and n. 65, above.

principal reason in the 'mind' of the employer, and now by the competence granted to a tribunal to adjourn the claim where proceedings for an interlocutory injunction have been launched to challenge the ballot or other ground of protection for the industrial action, a delay which may last months or years until all the interlocutory appeals have been exhausted.[73]

The new limitations on lawful trade union action introduced in the 1980s have been retained and not amended in any positive manner. It remains the case that from the point of view of their authors 'the very purpose of the laws was to disempower unions from distorting the labour market and causing unnecessary labour costs'.[74] The 1999 amendments relating to discrimination against trade unions and their members, after ss. 146–148 of TULRCA and the Law Lords' decision in the *Wilson* and *Palmer* cases,[75] constituted a tragic own goal. Worse, the government accepted an Opposition amendment (remarkably pleading lack of time to find the right form for alternative regulations) which emasculated s. 17 of the Act (giving power to the Secretary of State to make regulations to protect workers from discrimination for refusing to accept personal terms replacing a collective agreement). The amendment (now s. 17(4)) prevents effective regulations by excluding from the section payments or benefits where the contract of employment does not 'inhibit' membership of a trade union and the payments etc. are rendered under it and 'reasonably relate to services provided by the worker' under it. And still the strike constitutes a breach of employment contracts, and the mysteries of 'unlawful means' lie ready to apply new limitations to industrial action and social protest.[76] Still the class procedures of the interlocutory labour injunction continue unamended.[77]

---

[73] Employment Tribunals (Constitution and Rules of Procedure) Regulations 2001, Sched. 1 para. 9. No order of re-employment can be made until after the industrial action has ceased: s. 239(4)(a).

[74] J. Hendy, *Union Rights . . . and Wrongs* (2001) IER 23. Supporters can inexplicably still regard all this as a 'legal basis for fair trade unionism': Lord Haskel, Parl. Deb. HL 22.6.2001, col. 157.

[75] [1995] 2 AC 454 HL; see the argument in (2000) 29 ILJ at 18–20, and Novitz (2000) 63 MLR at 389–91.

[76] Contrast *Dept. of Transport* v. *Williams*, *The Times*, 7 Dec. 1993 CA, and *Michaels* v. *Taylor Woodrow* [2001] 2 WLR 224; cf. Clerk & Lindsell, *Torts*, 18th edn (London, 2000), ch. 24 'Economic Torts'.

[77] 'The Injunction and the Supremacy of Parliament' (1989) 23 Law Teacher 4; *ERBE*, ch. 7; cf. (2001) 30 ILJ 206–14 'Underground Labour Injunctions'; and now *R. M. T.* v *Midland Mainline Ltd.* [2001] IRLR 813, CA.

These defects in labour law have been compounded by the latest proposals of the official committee of timid practitioners, judges and academic lawyers on reform of company law, which aim to delete from
British law the duty imposed in 1980 on directors (now section 309,
Companies Act 1985) to consider the *interests of employees* 'as well as'
the interests of shareholders. In its place they propose a duty to consider
merely the interests of the company's shareholders and the company's
'business relationships, including those with its employees'[78] – an aston-
ishing step back towards the nineteenth century. The servants' interests,
individual or collective, are not to be the concern of the directors except
so far as their 'relationships' with the company are concerned. In themselves they are strangers and their interests do not rank. This is an odd
form of 'partnership' to propose in the year that deaths from workplace
accidents rose by over a third.

But it is in this general analysis that we find also the illustrations of a
special fundamental defect in our labour law. That defect inheres in the
extravagant individualism of our law. In the light of recent ILO Experts'
conclusions, that now appears in itself to lead to breach of ILO principles.
On occasion, the characterisation of workers' rights as 'individual' can,
it is true, assist in their effective enforcement.[79] What is more, except
in time of war neither English common law nor our statute law knows
of lawful worker-conscription as in the old French *réquisition* or current
Italian *precettazione*,[80] though whether 'market-failure' theorists would
blanch from introducing such measures if need arose is not entirely clear.
Authoritarian measures to limit still further the right to abstain from
labour cannot be ruled out in the foreseeable future.

But the obsession with individualism (and exclusion of sanctions at
collective level against employers) leads British law into absurdities. For

---

[78] *Final Report: Modern Company Law for a Competitive Economy,* Company Law Review Steering
Group (2001, URN/942 and 943, DTI), vol. I, Annex C, Schedule 2, para. 2, note 2: 'replacing
the obscure and ambiguous provision on employees' interests in section 309' Companies
Act 1985: 352, n. 318. See the positively Jesuitical discussion in *The Strategic Framework*
(1999) paras. 5.1.17–5.1.33; [and now see Wedderburn (2002) 31 ILJ 99].

[79] See *Kerry Foods* v. *Creber* [2000] IRLR 10 CA. ('individual' nature of the remedy of protective award under 190, 192 TULRCA 1992, served to preserve the worker's right under reg.
8 TUPE Regulations 1981: see too *Commission* v. *UK* (382, 383/92) [1994] ICR 664 ECJ).

[80] Code du Travail (2000) Art. L. 521-2, notes V 793-4; J.–C. Javillier, *Manuel: Droit du Travail,*
6th edn (Paris, 1998) 604; G. Orlandini in P. Pascucci (ed.), *La nuova disciplina dello sciopero
nei servizi essenziali* (Rome, 2000), 157–193, on the order for *precettazione* after the new
Italian law 83/2000; compare TULRCA 1992, s. 236.

no good reason, we lack a general concept of an *action de substitution*, allowing the union to enforce not merely *les intérêts collectifs de la profession* but also many *intérêts individuels* for workers in the courts.[81] Thus a new obligation for employers to inform and consult with a union declared by the CAC entitled to recognition about its policy on training of workers in the bargaining unit is ultimately, supposedly enforced in an action for compensation (of up to two weeks' pay) by *each* worker affected – and, just to get things straight, proceedings for such an award 'may not be commenced by a trade union' (s. 5; s. 70C(6)(b) TULRCA 1992).[82] Conversely, an employer's rejection of a union's request for recognition gives no remedy to prejudiced employees;[83] and even discrimination against an employee in the course of a union's recognition application affords no remedy for the union.[84] The ability of a union to institute judicial review proceedings[85] is no substitute for this juridical gap. The most important effect of this cultural genome is of course found in the normative provisions of collective agreements, which in virtually all other modern systems of labour law have an inderogable character as minimum conditions of employment. In Britain there is no such protection; the individual employment contract is dominant; and in the last resort the employer can 'negotiate' a new contract excluding such collective terms.[86] The question whether this should be so was raised for the New Labour government which robustly answered with a petulant stamp of the foot:

> The terms of agreements resulting from collective bargaining are normally incorporated into individual employees' contracts... and thus set minimum terms and conditions for all employees in the bargaining

---

[81] See G. Lyon-Caen, J. Pélissier, A. Supiot, *Droit du Travail*, 19th edn (Paris, 1998), 569–74. See too the right of the *délégué du personnel* to challenge improper inquiries by the employer into the employee's private life under the Law of 31 Dec. 1992.

[82] The pattern is common elsewhere, e.g. enforcement of rights to information and consultation in transfers of undertakings, TUPE Regulations 1981 SI 1794, reg. 11; we may contrast the exceptional penalty provision of the Transnational Information and Consultation of Employees Regulations 1999, regs. 20–22; and the criminal remedies in s. 193 TULRCA 1992, under which no prosecution has ever been brought (though some 4,000 notices are given annually: letter from Lord Sainsbury Under-Secretary of State, 30 May 2001).

[83] *Carrington* v. *Therm-A-Stor Ltd.* [1983] ICR 208 CA.

[84] TULRCA 1992, Sched. A1, paras. 156–165.

[85] *R.* v. *Sec. of Trade and Industry, ex parte TUC* [2000] IRLR 565.

[86] Or even dismiss and re-engage on terms less advantageous than the collective terms: *Whent* v. *Cartledge* [1997] IRLR 153, 157.

unit. Under existing law an employer and employee can agree different terms if they wish. Since the current law allows flexibility and works well, the Government sees no reason to change it.[87]

The evidence is that, even where unions are recognised, employers frequently do just that.[88]

Curiously, in the same period the Committee of Experts of the ILO expressed a view on the problem. On complaints concerning the Commonwealth Workplace Relations Act 1996 and a parallel Act of 1993 in Western Australia, relating to Convention 98 on the Right to Organise and Collective Bargaining, the Committee observed on the first:

> the Committee remains of the view that the Act gives primacy to individual over collective relations through the AA procedures . . . where the Act does provide for collective bargaining, clear preference is given to workplace/enterprise-level bargaining. The Committee, therefore, again requests the Government to take steps to review and amend the Act to ensure that collective bargaining will not only be allowed, but encouraged . . .

and on the second,

> The Committee also raised a concern that the Workplace Agreements Act 1993 as amended gives preference to individual agreements over collective agreements, thus not effectively promoting collective bargaining . . . in ratifying the Convention the government undertook to take appropriate measures to encourage and promote the full development and utilisation of machinery for the voluntary negotiation between employers and *workers' organisations* with a view to the regulation of terms and conditions of employment by *collective agreements.*[89]

It would appear from these carefully couched conclusions that preference for individually negotiated terms and conditions, and failure to provide inderogability *in peius*[90] for minimum terms collectively bargained, is in ILO terms a significant failure to provide fundamental rights

---

[87] *Fairness At Work* (May 1998, Cm. 5968, DTI) 42.

[88] See W. Brown, S. Deakin, M. Hudson and Cliff Pratten, *The Limits of Statutory Trade Union Recognition* (Cambridge, 2001).

[89] *Application: International Labour Conventions: Report of the Committee of Experts*, ILO 88th Session 2000, Report III (Part 1A) 223, 22 (emphasis in original).

[90] See 'Inderogability, Collective Agreements and Community Law' (1992) 21 ILJ 245 (*LLAF*, ch. 6); the best summary of the Italian concept is in L. Mariucci, *Le Fonti del Diritto del Lavoro* (Turin, 1988), 36–57.

to workers. Such protection is a commonplace in continental labour law systems; yet it has been a matter of little or no interest to the TUC, despite its recent tormented addiction to all things (it believes to be) 'European'.[91] An advance in this direction would no doubt be shocking to British conventional wisdom; but it would be the most fundamental advance in the British system for centuries and could not be undertaken without leadership which appreciated its character. In this and other respects, reform of domestic labour law is a task which in Britain engages the mind as part of the agonising issues of international labour law and the global market.

Yet paradoxically the English common law notion of individualism, based more on ideas of property than of citizens' formal equality,[92] has not given us any parallel protection for the dignity and privacy of the individual worker. Instead, it has to make do with limping notions of duties of 'mutual trust and confidence'[93] or 'privacy' concealed within notions of 'confidentiality'.[94] This is of mounting importance in an age of information technology – the 'information superhighway' about to become 'e-commerce', as Chomsky has remarked – where the freedom of the worker as a human being has been exposed to new dimensions of invasion and control,[95] from the old 'Videotex' that records the worker's every move, risking a return to treatment of the worker 'as part of a machine, regarded merely as eyes and hands' (Sinzheimer), to the new uses by employers of references, automated decision-taking

---

[91] The most remarkable illustration was its proposal, in the face of urgent need for improved union rights to consultation about closures in 2000–1, not for a new UK law but for a new EU Directive which would take many years to implement. On the new Directive, which will take some years to implement: EWC Bull 2001, no. 34, 1, 5–8, [and 2002, no. 38, 4–6].

[92] See B. Russell's account of Locke's concept, *A History of Western Philosophy* (London, 1948) 647–653. Cf. A. Fox, *History and Heritage: The Social Origins of the British Industrial Relations System* (London, 1985), 15–21.

[93] Consider the limitations in *Johnson* v. *Unisys* [2001] 2 WLR 1076 HL; *BCCI* v. *Ali* (No. 3) [1999] IRLR 508, and [2001] ICR 337 HL; *Macari* v. *Celtic FC* [1999] IRLR 787 CS; *National Grid Co.* v. *Mayes* [2001] IRLR 394 HL; *University of Nottingham* v. *Eyett* [1999] IRLR 87. The duty of 'trust and confidence' may have particular perils for the employee: *Neary* v. *Dean of Westminster* [1999] IRLR 238.

[94] Contrast Brooke LJ and Sedley LJ in *Douglas* v. *Hello! Ltd.* [2001] 2 WLR 992, paras. 50–102, 109–144. This seems to be the case even after the Human Rights Act 1988 establishing everyone's right to respect for private and family life (ECHR art. 8.1), though the position is unclear after *Halford* v. *UK* [1997] IRLR 475 ECJ; compare more optimistically, B. Hepple 'Human Rights and the Contract of Employment' (ELA, 2000).

[95] See the seminal article of S. Simitis 'Reviewing Privacy in an Information Society' 135 Univ. Penn. L. Rev. (1987) 707.

and CV scanning, aptitude and psychometric tests, automated performance monitoring (especially at call-centres), health records and practices including HIV/AIDS information, alcohol and drugs testing, genetic testing, criminal records (the Rehabilitation of Offenders Act 1974 having become a broken reed), fraud monitoring, e-mail interception,[96] 'intelligent' CCTV surveillance and international data transfers.[97]

It has always been an ambition of those who challenged the subordination of wage labour to achieve an 'emancipation' of the individual worker. Winstanley would have made employment of one man by another illegal.[98] Habermas linked Marx and Freud by their distinguishing 'interest in emancipation going beyond the technical and practical interest of knowledge'.[99] Ever since Henry Ford sent investigators to inspect employees' private lifestyles (an aspect of 'Fordism' often overlooked)[100] employers have increasingly encroached on what jurists claim to be the 'non-relevance' of the worker's private life to the establishment, performance and termination of the employment relation.[101] By late in the century, it was found that employers

> more than ever consider that systematically collected, continuously updated information on employees is an elementary condition for rational planning and successful monitoring of personnel.[102]

---

[96] For an 'e-mail filtering and monitoring' system offered to employers to avoid legal liability and 'improve productivity', see SuperScout 'Acceptable Usage Policy' *SurfControl* 2001: www.surfcontrol.com

[97] See the Personal Policy Research Unit *Report on Personal Data in Employment* (1999), esp. Table 1; and see part 5 and Appendix on the special risks for contract workers and agency workers.

[98] *Law of Freedom* (Harmondsworth, 1975 [1652]); see C. Hill, *A Nation of Change and Novelty* (London, 1990) ch. 7; *The World Turned Upside Down* (Harmondsworth, 1975).

[99] Jürgen Habermas, *Theory and Practice* (London, 1974) 9, quoted by D. Held, *Introduction to Critical Theory* (Berkeley, 1980), 323. On the destruction of human 'authenticity' in advanced capitalism, see E. Luttwak, *Turbo Capitalism* (London, 1999), ch. 13.

[100] A. Nevins, *Ford – The Man and the Company* (New York, 1954), 54.

[101] G. Giugni, 'Political, Religious and Private Life Discrimination' ch. 4, in F. Schmidt (ed.) *Discrimination in Employment* (Stockholm, 1968). On control in the modern US office, see Barbara Garson, *The Electronic Sweatshop: How Computers are Transforming the Office of the Future into the Factory of the Past* (New York, 1998).

[102] S. Simitis, 'Developments on the Protection of Workers' Personal Data', and ILO 10 *Conditions of Work Digest* (Geneva, 1991) 7–8, 14ff.; ILO, 'Workers' Privacy: Part II Monitoring and Surveillance in the Workplace' 12 *Conditions of Work Digest* (Geneva, 1993); and now 'Reconsidering the Premises of Labour Law' (1999) 5 Eur. L. J. 45–62. See also M. Ford's valuable 'Worker Privacy and Management Prerogative' (Doughty Street Chambers; Industrial Law Society paper, 19. 5.2001) which pushes the boundary of the discussion forward; see too n. 108 below.

In response, modern German constitutional law asserts the fundamental right that employment should not 'absorb the entire personality of the worker' and the German Works Council has powers of co-determination over the introduction and use of devices for monitoring employees' performance and behaviour.[103] The Italian Statuto dei Lavoratori 1970 protected the private opinions and beliefs of workers and made unlawful the use of audio-visual and 'distance' supervision of employees unless the consent of local union representatives or, in special cases, of the Labour Inspector had been obtained.[104] And the French Law of 1992 included strong protection for aspects of the worker's private life at the time of hiring and during employment, with remedies exercised through legal action and by workers' representatives.[105] British law has been by contrast poverty stricken and confused in concepts and in content;[106] and recent accounts of surveillance at work reveal practices which take little account of any such fundamental principle.[107] Recent regulations and codes[108] have shown contradictory attitudes and weak understanding of the principle, as the TUC put it, that: 'Workers should be able to carry out their duties in a dignified manner, with respect for

[103] T. Ramm, 'Diritti fondamentali e diritto del lavoro' (1991) 50 Giorn. DLRI 359, 364; Works Constitution Act 1972, art. 87(1)(6).

[104] Art. 4 (see *ERBE* 234, 265, from (1990) 19 ILJ 154; *LLAF* 314). On data protection, now Law 675, 31 December 1996.

[105] Law of 31 December 1992, no. 92-1446; now Code du Travail Art. L. 121-6 to -8. See J. Grisnir (1993) Droit Ouvrier 237, and especially the wide-ranging profound report preceding that Law: G. Lyon-Caen, *Les Libertés publiques et l'emploi* (1992, La documentation française no. 27, Paris).

[106] Consider private sexual orientation, private opinions or soft drug preferences: S. Deakin and G. Morris, *Labour Law*, 2nd edn (London, 1998), 349–53; 'Labour Law and the Individual' in Wedderburn, M. Rood, G. Lyon-Caen, W. Däubler, P. van der Heijden, *Labour Law in the Post-Industrial Era* (Aldershot, 1994), 40 (now *LLAF*, ch. 9); *The Worker and the Law*, 3rd edn (Harmondsworth, 1986), 349–353. Cf. *Adv.-Gen for Scotland* v. *Macdonald* [2000] IRLR 431 (CS IH). On European law, *Grant* v. *SW Trains* (C-249/96) [1998] ECR 1-621; N. Bamforth (2001) 63 MLR 694.

[107] See *McSherry* v. *British Telecommunications* [1992] 3 Med. L. R. 129, cited by M. Ford *Surveillance and Privacy at Work* (1998 IER London) 1.

[108] Consider the different and ambiguous policies in e.g. the Data Protection Act 1998 (see Ford, *Surveillance and Privacy at Work*, ch. 4), the Information Commissioner's Draft Code on Use of Personal Data in Employer-Employee Relationships 2000, Data Protection (Processing of Sensitive Personal Data) Order 2000 SI 417, and on rules on subject access 2000 SI 184 (UK financial and economic interests) 191, 413, 415, and 1865; and the Interception of Communications Act 1985, Regulation of Investigatory Powers Act 2000, Telecommunications (Lawful Business Practice) (Interception of Communications) Regulations 2000 SI 2699 (interceptions for purposes relevant to a business) and Crime and Disorder Act 1998.

their privacy and autonomy and without fear of constant monitoring.'[109] British business leaders have reacted with 'outrage' at proposals to regulate such control.[110] Nor have modest EU Directives transformed the British situation.[111] As Ford points out, individual enforcement rights are (once again) inadequate, and what is needed is a range of union powers to protect workers to enforce even the inadequate protections of the 1998 Act. Whether one sees this issue as resistance to 'colonisation' of the individual worker's behaviour[112] or as part of the simple principle of reassessing 'what is exchanged in the contract of employment, what is stipulated for by the employer and what is promised by the employee',[113] it is central today to fundamental rights at work. The question: who owns information? becomes part of the question: who owns how much of the worker? Even so, economic labour law theorists regard privacy as merely an 'intermediate good' or inefficient,[114] while the attitude of some corporate managers has remained: 'You already have zero privacy. Get over it.'[115] Beyond that, more sophisticated corporations try

> to change the beliefs of those who work for them . . . what they call an individual's sense of identification (in effect, changing preferences so that workers view their interests as coinciding with those of the firm) . . . a far more effective form of control device in organizational design than trying to change incentive structures.[116]

That is a consideration which affects the whole of our discussion.

---

[109] TUC, *Surveillance at Work: Sensible Solutions* (London, 2000) assessing the various regulations. It is still unclear how far the law on 'unfair dismissal' might now provide remedies; but that would not cover all ongoing employment abuses.

[110] *Financial Times*, 29 June 2001.

[111] Directives 95/46 OJ L281/31, and 97/66 OJ 1997 L 24/1. On the need for further European action: S. Simitis (1999) 5 Eur. L. J. 45; compare Council of Europe Convention for Protection of Individuals on Automatic Processing of Personal Data 1981; on effects in the USA: G. Shaffer (1999) 5 Eur. L. J. 419–437.

[112] S. Simitis, 'The Rediscovery of the Individual in Labour Law', in Rogowski and Wilthagen, *Reflexive Labour Law*, above n. 24.

[113] Lyon-Caen, *Les libertés publiques et l' emploi*, above n. 105, 12.

[114] See R. Posner, 'The Right of Privacy' 12 Ga. L. R. 393, 394 (1978).

[115] Scott McNealy, CEO, Sun Microsystems Inc, quoted in M. Froomkin, 'The Death of Privacy?' 52 Stanford Law Rev. 1461 (2000), n. 1 (generally giving an account of the extraordinary range of lawful and questionable privacy-destroying technologies in the USA and elsewhere, but challenging the conclusion of D. Brin, *The Transparent Society* (New York, 1998) that it is now impossible to control them by law).

[116] J. Stiglitz, *Challenges in the Analysis of the Role of Institutions in Economic Development*, Deutsche Stiftung für Internationale Entwicklung (Berlin, 2000), 7.

IV. Gobalisation and labour law

Increased cooperation in and integration of the world's economies does not necessarily produce disaster for the people involved. But the impact of mobile global capital in the world's markets, and its demand for entry into social relations via 'free trade' and entry into all countries' markets, have produced a very particular result. By 2000, 51 per cent of the world's largest budgets were budgets not of states but of multinational corporations or groups.

> Globalization is both an active process of corporate expansion across borders and a structure of cross-border facilities and economic linkages that has been steadily growing and changing. [It] is also an ideology whose function is to reduce any resistance to the process by making it seem both highly beneficent and unstoppable... One of the main objectives of TNC movement abroad has been to tap cheaper labor resources.[117]

It had long been suggested at national level that

> so long as investment decisions are made by the corporations, the locus of social control and coordination must be sought among them; government fills the interstices left by these prime decisions.[118]

As a British minister remarked in 1968, as the strength of the multinational corporations advanced, the nation states' governments could soon be reduced 'to the status of a parish council'.[119]

> These corporations have helped to create enormous wealth, but in the process they have broken down traditional community links and brought forth new problems whose solution requires protective and control mechanisms, private and governmental, local, national and international, that do not now exist.[120]

No doubt it is true that

> there exists no *logically necessary* incompatibility between interests in global capitalist planning and freedom of investment, need for

---

[117] E. Herman (1999) 7, 26 *New Politics* 1.
[118] H. Braverman, *Labor and Monopoly Capital* (New York, 1974), 269.
[119] T. Benn, see *LLAF* 237; 'Multinational Enterprise and National Labour Law' (1972) 19 ILJ 1.
[120] E. Herman, *Corporate Control, Corporate Power* (Cambridge, 1981), 301.

planning and renunciation of intervention, and independence of the state apparatus and dependency on individual interests.[121]

But it has since become a commonplace in experience to observe the gradual 'silent takeover' of the nation state[122] – and not just of state power, but of national culture: where, for example, the brand, that powerful tool in the markets, elevates trade mark law to primary relevance on employment displacement and therefore in labour law.[123] The essential character of the new economy has been said to be marked by a tripartite 'retreat of the state, globalization and computerization'.[124] In 2015, experts predict:

> States will continue to be the major players on the world stage but governments will have less and less control over flows of informa-tion, technology, diseases, migrants, arms, and financial transactions, whether licit or illicit, across their borders.[125]

For some, global capitalism is best seen as the 'latest phase of cap-italism', a renewal of that phase of the nineteenth century – transna-tional investment, after all, began long before the 1960s – but distin-guished by 'computers plus deregulated capital'.[126] For others, it is a 'kind of cyberspace in which money capital has reached its ultimate

---

[121] J. Habermas, *Legitimation Crisis* (1975) 64, cited in T. McCarthy, *The Critical Theory of Jürgen Habermas* (Cambridge, 1978) 367 (emphasis in original).

[122] See the journalistic account in N. Hertz, *The Silent Takeover: Global Capitalism and the Death of Democracy* (London, 2001); cf. G. Monbiot, *The Captive State: the Corporate Takeover of Britain* (London, 2000). But on the local state roots of many units of 'global' companies, especially through labour markets, see M. Scott, *Heartland: How to Build Companies as Strong as States* (London, 2001).

[123] T. Frank, *One Market Under God* (London, 2001), the dominance of the brand and 'market-populism'; and Naomi Klein, *No Logo: Taking Aim at the Brand Bullies* (New York, 2000). See especially the law on 'parallel imports' in the EU: *Silhouette* (C-355/96) [1998] ECR I-4799, *Zino Davidoff* v. *A & G Imports* [2000] Ch. 127, pending ECJ, but see 2000 SLT 683 C.S. (O.H.); J. Eaglesham and D. Hargreaves, *Financial Times*, 22 Jan. 2001 (on the Tesco-Levi litigation). Also *Arsenal FC* v. *Reed*, ref. to ECJ, 1 May 2001 Laddie J; and on the relation of trade marks to art. 30 of the Treaty, *Glaxo Group* v. *Dowelhurst Ltd* (No. 2) [2000] FSR 5291 (*contra* S. Hilton and G. Gibbons, *Good Business* [London, 2002]).

[124] E. Luttwark, *Turbo Capitalism* (London, 1999), 50.

[125] US National Foreign Intelligence Board, *A Dialogue about the Future with Non-Government Experts* (Washington, 2000) 8 ('in close collaboration with US Government specialists' and with RAND corpn., the CIA, and academic experts).

[126] M. Desai, 'Globalisation: Neither Ideology nor Utopia' (2000) xiv Camb. Rev. International Affairs 16, 22. Cf. S. Sassen *Globalization and its Discontents* (New York, 1998), ch. 9, 'Electronic space and power' (and now M. Desai, *Marx's Revenge* [London, 2002]).

dematerialization'.[127] The step from steam engine to chip was manifestly qualitative, and capital's need for labour to produce wealth is today reduced.[128] The magnitude of that step and that process is not lost on labour law. In face of such developments, it seems unlikely that a *Ya Basta* withdrawal into 'autonomous' activity alone can ever produce lasting resistance (though pressure from people in their guise as citizens or consumers, from Babymilk Action to Greenpeace, may make even the multinational react). That is why the active pursuit of human rights and the struggle for labour standards is crucial.

Some, like Kahn-Freund, concluded some decades ago that in these circumstances, when we have effective management but neither traditional government nor union power as an effective countervailing force,

> the entire basis of our thinking on collective labour relations and collective labour law is destroyed.[129]

But paradoxically the globalisation process has to some degree increased the importance of national laws. For example, trade unions' rights of sympathetic action to balance the right of capital to move freely across borders – rights for labour not merely to cross borders individually as in the EC, but to exercise collective pressure across the frontiers of states, which the EU does not afford – are critical; otherwise, as was clear in the same era, the social function of national laws is merely to 'assist in the fragmentation of the international labour and trade union movement'.[130] The increasing inability of the ITWF lawfully to use industrial action in UK and other jurisdictions against flag of convenience ship owners who exploit third world crews is a clear lesson on the point. What is more, state corporation laws granting the immunity of limited liability and the privilege of legal personality matter intensely to the international impact of labour law; and the structures on corporate governance, 'partnership' and workers' rights are of equal relevance, though it is surely early and rather extravagant to conclude that

---

[127] F. Jameson, 'Culture and Finance Capital' (1997), in M. Hardt and K. Weeks (eds.), *The Jameson Reader* (Oxford, 2000), 268.

[128] Lord Dahrendorf, Parl. Deb. HL 19.4.2000, col. 764, whose book on globalisation would be called, perhaps extravagantly, *Capital Without Labour*.

[129] 'A Lawyer's Reflections on Multinational Corporations' (1972) Jo. Ind. Relns. (Aus.) 351, 356.

[130] Wedderburn (1972) 1 ILJ 12–14 [*LLAF*, 243–4].

we already live in an era of workers' 'contingent control rights'.[131] In a forthright phrase, the TUC general secretary has said of the multinationals: 'They are the new medieval princes and we are the serfs.'[132] Workers collectively, despite European Works Councils and minimal consultation rights for their unions, have entered a new era of weakness as the coverage and power of their unions declines. This is not because of a lack of international trade union organisations[133] or even wholly of proposals for standard international collective agreements,[134] though suitable employers' organisations are sometimes hard to find.[135] But international, even transnational collective bargaining and industrial pressure have proved to be the most difficult activities to make effective. This is not because there are no issues of common interest to the world's workers – consider work safety and industrial disease, HIV/AIDS, medicines and the pharmaceutical companies, moving job markets, labour exploitation, child labour, poverty, ecological devastation: all crucial to the condition of the worker but often beyond collective reach by reason of false consciousness that sees their confrontation as 'protectionism' for some workers, or as furtherance of issues that is visionary. Few things are as important as discovering new ways of fostering 'countervailing workers' power' in pursuit of the fight against these common perils.[136]

Nor do regional groupings necessarily fare better than national laws. Certainly the EU has, despite street demonstrations, not seen a powerful

[131] J. Armour and S. Deakin, *Insolvency, Employment Protection and Corporate Restructuring* (Cambridge, 2001), discussing the 'TUPE Regulations 1981' and the position of employees in the United Kingdom as 'stakeholders'.

[132] J. Monks (TUC press release 19 January 2001) speaking to Vauxhall workers after General Motors' decision to close their plant (details, Parl. Deb. HC 6.4.2001, col. 671). For government reaction effectively ignoring global factors: S. Byers MP, Secretary of State for Trade and Industry, Parl. Deb. HC 13.12.2000, cols. 641–55.

[133] See the list of 'International Trade Secretariats' linking millions of workers sectorally throughout the world: (2000) 318 EIRR 29, (2000) 324 EIRR 26, (2001) 327 EIRR 31, and the multinational union councils, 32. The amount of transnational solidarity created has been useful but limited. On the 'contradictory and contingent' process of constructing international trade unionism, see H. Ramsay, ch. 8 in J. Waddington (ed.), *Globalization Patterns of Labour Resistance* (London, 1999); and on 'global social movement unionism' R. Lambert and A. Chan, ch. 4, 'Global Dance'.

[134] One of the best known is that proposed by the Intl. Fedn. of Building and Wood Workers, 'Model Framework Agreement with a Multinational'. Such agreements have mainly been made with Nordic-based multinationals such as IKEA: (2001) EIRR 327; and see EWC Bull 2001, No. 34, 15–17 (OTE, Telefonica, Carrefour).

[135] P. Marginson and K. Sisson, 'European Collective Bargaining: A Virtual Prospect?' (1998) 36 Jo. Common Market Studs. 505.

[136] See K. Klare, 'Countervailing workers' power as a regulative strategy', in *Legal Regulation of the Employment Relation*, ch. 3, above n. 6.

'European' trade union movement emerge in action, nor does 'labour law' within it effectively confront the multinationals, despite occasional hints at doing so.[137] That is why it is better to refer to collective 'labour law *in* the EU', rather than collective 'labour law *of* the EU'.[138] Repeated well-intentioned efforts to construct or 'find' fundamental labour and social rights in the EU have met with scant success in practice.[139] Where is the worker who has achieved a remedy for breach of his 'European' fundamental rights as such? This lack of fundamental social protection is associated with the very nature of the Community and the Union.[140] Federico Mancini made it clear that the foundation was and is the free market: 'upstream from enlightenment and welfare' and from workers' rights, there lay at the heart of the EC the 'conditions of competition', and provisions on labour law had to be seen within those priorities. Freedom of movement for workers was necessary to oust provisions which otherwise would distort freedom of competition. Labour protection was an adjunct to that freedom in its many forms.

> If a country can authorise redundancies on less stringent conditions than other countries its industry will be given an incalculable advantage.[141]

Again and again analysis of EC law has followed through this theme, that competition law and the law that promotes integration of the market dominate labour relations in the EC legal order.[142] Neither the Action

---

[137] For example, in the 'Vredeling' draft Directive: see C. Docksey (1986) 49 MLR 281; cf. B. Hepple (1987) 16 ILJ 77.

[138] See A. Lo Faro, *Regulating Social Europe: Reality and Myth of Collective Bargaining in the EC Legal Order* (Oxford, 2000); cf. (2001) 30 ILJ 136–143.

[139] See e.g. R. Blanpain, B. Hepple, S. Sciarra, M. Weiss, *Fundamental Social Rights: Proposals for the European Union* (Leuven, 1996); S. Deakin, N. Koistinen, S. Kravaritou, U. Muckenberger, A. Supiot, B. Veneziani, *Manifeste pour une Europe Sociale* (Brussels, 1996); B. Veneziani, *Nel Nome di Erasmo da Rotterdam: La faticosa marcia dei diritti sociali fondamentali nell'odinamento comunitario* (2000), Riv. Giur. di Lav. e della Prev. Soc. 779–840. For an extraordinary vision of future developments, C. Engel, 'The European Charter of Fundamental Rights' (2001), 7 Eur. L. J. 151–170; cf. J. Weiler, 'Does the EU truly need a charter of rights?' (2000) 6 Eur. L. J. 95.

[140] *LLAF*, ch. 10, 370–408; see too (2001) 30 ILJ 136–143.

[141] G. F. Mancini, 'Labour Law and Community Law' (1985) 20 Irish Jurist (n.s.) 1, 2, 12. The ECSC was, of course, materially different in structure.

[142] See P. Davies (1995) 24 ILJ 49–77 and ch. 10 in McCarthy, *Legal Interventions in Industrial Relations* (Oxford, 1992); Wedderburn (1991) 13 Dublin Law Journal 1, now *LLAF*, ch. 8; G. Lyon-Caen, 'L'infiltration du droit du travail par le droit de la concurrence' (1992) Droit Ouvrier 314. Sex equality (on pay) in the Treaty was, it is true, only in part a product

Programmes of the 1970s, the Social Fund nor later social programmes have altered this structural perspective;[143] and it is difficult to find practical, as against rhetorical proof that a 'social market ideology' has 'since 1989...gained ascendancy',[144] save perhaps in the international policy since 1998 of affording trade advantages to states which comply with principles of freedom of association, collective bargaining and prohibition of child labour (mainly not available by reason of their economies to least developed countries). The well-known ECJ decisions which support the dominance of the competition and commercial freedom articles in the Treaty[145] have not been affected by the 'social chapter' of the EU Treaty. Indeed, the exclusion from the social chapter procedures of a right to freedom of association and right to strike (art. 137(6))[146] reaffirms that philosophy. As for the new *Charter of Fundamental Rights of the European Union*,[147] even if in a spasm of activism the ECJ finds a way out of its 'non-binding' character (and what remedies for real people would that produce?), as it stands the Charter adds little to workers' rights to consultation, to negotiate collective agreements 'at appropriate levels' and to take strike action in cases of conflict of interests (a material limitation not found in UK law), for these are declared to be subject to 'national laws and practices'.[148] A forthcoming Directive on rights to information and consultation in enterprises of fifty workers or more will usefully complement but not expand the Charter; nor, it seems, will the Human Rights Act 1988 substantially affect it in Britain, when the Strasbourg Court has dealt so narrowly with the purported

---

of competition ideology: cf. the *Spaak Report* (1956) Part I, ch. 2, 63, cited in O. Kahn-Freund in E. Stein and T. Nicholson (eds.), *American Enterprise in the European Common Market* (Ann Arbor, 1960), 325–330.

[143] Contrast the view of P. Davies in S. Sciarra (ed.), *Labour Law in the Courts* (Oxford, 2001), 132–133.

[144] B. Hepple in S. Picciotto and R. Mayne (eds.), *Regulating International Business: Beyond Liberalization* (Basingstoke, 1999), 198.

[145] *Merci Convenzionali* (179/90) [1991] ECR I-5889; *Commission* v. *France* (265/95) [1997] ECR I-6959; see G. Orlandini (1999) 84 Giorn. DLRI 623–668 on Regulation 2697/98. *Cf. Job Centre* (C-111/94) [1995] ECR I-3361.

[146] If the Nice Treaty is ratified, it will be art. 137(5).

[147] OJ 2000 18.12.2000. C364/1; arts. 27, 28. Emiglio Gabaglio, Secretary of the ETUC, suggested to the writer in 2000 that the 'national law' limitation must be amended; at present this seems unlikely. It is sometimes forgotten that the right to strike in art. 6 European Social Charter 1961, revsd. 1996, is also limited to conflicts of interest.

[148] For a more up-beat interpretation of the Charter, see B. Hepple (2001) 230 ILJ 225, though it is there accepted that it creates no new rights, 227.

right to freedom of association in Article 11 of the Convention.[149] In contrast, concentration of capital in Europe has grown rapidly; competition laws have not effectively thwarted the consequent growth of power in the multinationals, and its institutions can doubtfully resist massive takeovers and mergers.[150] As before, however, where workers and unions aim to pursue effective remedies to protect their rights, for example for breach of rights to be consulted before restructuring, it is usually to effective national labour law systems and courts that they have to turn.[151] British workers at Vauxhall, Rover or Motorola had in reality no such opportunity.

Indeed, under the EC provisions collective agreements have escaped only by the skin of their teeth from themselves being subjected to the crushing weight of competition law under Articles 81 and 82 (ex arts. 85 and 86) of the Treaty,[152] and it is still unclear just how far the exception granting that status to this product of the permitted 'social dialogue' can extend.[153] Modern fashion may well concentrate on the need to 'ensure the competitiveness of self-employed workers as compared to other enterprises' and therefore give a narrow interpretation to the escape of collective labour law from market competition imperatives.[154] What the ECJ will do can be seen only darkly through Luxembourg glass. The British company collective agreement may be thought even less likely to be subjected to the Treaty's competition article, since the technical question of an 'undertaking' being created is less likely to arise; but any agreements extending outside the 'core' range of pay and conditions

---

[149] See the summary in K. Starmer, *European Human Rights Law* (London, 1999) 668–73; the Charter of 2000 is bound by this case law indirectly when EU law is in issue: arts. 51(1), 52(3).

[150] Price-fixing cartels are still active: *Financial Times*, 19 July 2001. See too the battle between EU Commission and the United States, with some American business interests joining the 'European' side, when the EU Commission banned the GE–Honeywell merger, 'the largest industrial takeover': *Financial Times*, 16 June–1 July, 2001, [and 10 April 2002].

[151] Consider the French cases on *Renault Vilvorde* (1997 12 EWC Bull. 15) and *Fédération CGT c. Soc. Marks & Spencer* T. de G. I. Paris, 9 avril 2001 (2001) Droit Ouvrier 156 n. F. Samarito (negation of right to be consulted before closures led to nullity of dismissal procedures). See too the French employer's duty to produce a 'social plan': Code du Travail Art. L. 321-4-1. On the use of the works councils procedures by the employer, see the dispute at Danone: (2001) 330 EIRR 24–26.

[152] *Albany Intl. BV* v. *Stichting Bedrijfspensioenfonds Textielindustrie* (67/96) [1999] ECR I-5751 ECJ; *H. van der Woude* v. *Stichting Beatrixoord* (C-222/98) 21 Sept. 2000 ECJ.

[153] See the diverse approaches of S. Vousden (2000) 29 ILJ 181, and S. Evju (2001) 17 Int. Jo. Comp. LLIR 165.

[154] For example, P. Ichino (2001) 17 IJCLLIR 185, 231.

into future employment plans or forms of joint control of managerial prerogative might be at greater risk of being subjected by the Court of Justice to competition law.[155] But competition law and freedom of movement for capital, goods and services are not the only inhibitions. Public procurement law[156] and the extent to which contract compliance can be used to maintain standards are outstanding issues for labour law under the law of the integrated single market.[157]

Some other regional arrangements, however, build in protections which may utilise national protections. The best example perhaps is the North American Free Trade Agreement (NAFTA) and its Labor Cooperation Agreement. Here effective enforcement with sanctions of some of the eleven recognised fundamental labour standards has been realised, so long as they fall within the three national systems, based upon 'the principle of labour rights trade linkage',[158] though how far this structure can be extended to more general North–South American arrangements is more uncertain. It is not right or helpful to see such measures as merely 'protectionist' for the workers involved.[159] On the other hand, reciprocal treaties enforced by established systems of inter-state arbitration, can contribute to massive penalties for third world countries at the suit of transnational corporations.[160]

---

[155] On an interesting inter-connection between inter-industry, sectoral and enterprise agreements in Belgium, see Annotation to *Aleene's* case (2001) 19 Intl. Labour Law Rep. 473, 474.

[156] See *Likenne Ab.* v. *Liskojarvi* (C-172/99) [2001] IRLR 171 ECJ; *Thompsons Lab. and Eur. Law Rev.* 2001, March 2 (UK reforms of the TUPE Regulations and redundancy consultation law are still awaited).

[157] See *LLAF*, 379–387; C. McCrudden in S. Arrowsmith and A. Davies, *Public Procurement: Global Revolution* (London, 1998); for the transposed Public Services Contracts Regs. SI 1993/ 2338 as amended, see (2001) Pub. Proc. L. R. 165. The uncertain meaning of *Geb. Beentjes BV* v. *The Netherlands* (C-31/87) [1988] ECR 4635 ECJ, is still of importance to labour law and employment schemes: E. Szyszczak, *EC Labour Law* (Harlow, 2000) 160–3.

[158] L. Compa, 'NAFTA's Labour Side Agreement Five Years On' (1999) 7 Can. Lab. & Empt. L. J. 1, 24; N. Keresztesi, 'Mexican Labour Laws and Practices come to Canada' 8 (2001) Can. Lab. & Empt. L. J. 411. See too, the proceedings in the United States against Chentex after Nicaraguan litigation was used to try to protect 'maquila' workers: *Financial Times*, 6 April 2001.

[159] It is inadequate merely to dismiss those who may lose jobs from free trade as 'special interests' protecting their 'rents': J. Stiglitz, 'Democratic Development as the Fruits of Labor' (Washington, DC, 2000), 18.

[160] See *American Manufacturing and Trading Inc.* v. *Zaire* (1997) 12 Intl. Arbn. Reps. A1 (award under the International Centre for Settlement of Investment Disputes), recovering compensation even for its subsidiary's losses: E. Gaillard and A. Hardin (1998) New York L. J., April 1. On the proposed Multilateral Agreement on Investment, and an 'open door to business', see S. Picciotto, in Picciotto and Mayne, *Regulating International Business*, 86 ff., above n. 144.

Given the conflicting aims of powerful multinationals and weakened states,[161] all means must be considered whereby fundamental labour standards and principles can be created, upheld and enforced in the global market.[162] At the centre of any such consideration, of course, stands the shining example of the International Labour Organisation. Without its many Conventions, Recommendations, and its Declarations and constant pressures through tripartite machinery, such international labour law as we have would be impoverished beyond measure, even if some react to its interventions by asking, as Stalin did of the Pope: 'How many divisions have they got?' Publicity in 2001 about slave ships carrying third world children off the Ivory Coast, forced labour in Burma (a WTO member) and conditions in Guatemala's Starbuck coffee fields renewed public interest in the ILO restatement of fundamental core rights on freedom of association, collective bargaining, compulsory labour, child labour and discrimination.[163] The ILO's modest objective has been

> to place social progress into a relationship with the economic progress expected from the liberalization of trade and globalization.

After all 'competition did not prevent the main industrialized countries of Europe from adopting the first labour laws'.[164] We should remember, however, that this was achieved not merely by enlightened public opinion, but by struggle.

By comparison, more limited protection is offered by 'Guidelines' of other institutions on employment and industrial relations practices, aiming to have enterprises 'conduct their activities in a competitive manner . . . within the applicable laws and regulations' in various countries and their 'science and technology policies and plans', but adopt a favourable policy towards trade unions.[165] World trade organisations

---

[161] B. Hepple, 'The Future of Labour Law' (1995) 24 ILJ 303, 320.

[162] See S. Gibbons, *International Labour Rights – New Methods of Enforcement* (IER, 1998); cf. B. Hepple, 'New Approaches to International Labour Regulation' (1997) 26 ILJ 353–66.

[163] ILO, *Declaration on Fundamental Principles and Rights at Work and its Follow-up* (Geneva, 1998); *Fundamental Principles and Rights at Work*, Report of Director General, ILO (Geneva, 2000).

[164] ILO, *International Labour Law* (ILO, Geneva, 2000) quoting ILO, *Standard Setting and Globalization* (1997).

[165] OECD, *Guidelines for Multinational Enterprises*, rev. edn (Paris, 2000), Parts. IV, VIII, IX, in its *Declaration on Investment and Multinational Enterprises*. Unions are able to obtain opinions from the committee for International Investment and Multinational Enterprise. But see the crushing indictment of 'OECD's Crocodile Tears' in *Flying Fish*, www.flyingfish.org.uk/articles/oecd/tears.htm.

have scarcely improved the position. The use of 'social clauses'[166] has not won a strong place in global regulation or practice, and the EU has largely

> thrown away the bases of an international commercial policy integrating respect for fundamental workers' rights, which would permit it to work coherently to render acceptable a social clause on a universal and multilateral level.[167]

Moreover, the view of many employers' groups, such as the Swedish Employers' Federation, has been implacably hostile to such a clause.[168] Generally, international recognition of labour standards has been set back notably by the refusal of the World Trade Organisation, the International Monetary Fund, GATT and the World Bank[169] to accept a linkage between such standards and trade, plus a disinclination to adopt policies towards developing countries which favour their free, social development with labour standards upheld.[170] Despite considerable rhetoric in many international circles, there has in practice, as natural resources and exploited workforces can testify, been only marginal response to the UN call:

> individually through your firm, and collectively through your business associations, to embrace, support and enact a set of core values in the areas of human rights, labour standards and environmental practices.[171]

After Seattle the world organisations dominated by global capital have more clearly become less part of the solution than part of the

---

[166] See the over-optimistic outlook in D. Chin, *A Social Clause for Labour's Cause: Global Trade and Labour Standards* (IER, 1998).

[167] A. Perulli, *Diritto del Lavoro e Globalizzaione* (Milan, 1999) 177, and see generally on social dumping and the contexts of such clauses, the detailed survey in his 'La Clausola Sociale nel Commercio Internationale' ibid. 1–177. Cf. M. Trebilcock, 'What Future for Social Clauses?' IIRA *Eleventh World Congress: Acts* (1998); also Wedderburn part 6(4), W. Sengenberger and D. Campbell, *International Labour Standards and Economic Interdependence* (Geneva, 1994).

[168] See H.-G. Myrdal in Sengenberger and Campbell, *International Labour Standards*, n. 167, 339–56.

[169] On problems thought to be inherent in replacing loans with grants: *Financial Times*, 20 July 2001.

[170] See J. Stiglitz, 'The Insider', *New Republic*, 17 April 2000 (previously chief economist and vice president of the World Bank) on the IMF's policies in the east Asian crisis, 1997. On the threat to welfare from tax competition, resource mobility and e-commerce: V. Tanzi, 'Globalization and the Future of Social Protection' (January 2000, IMF Working Paper WP/00/12).

[171] Kofi Annan, UN Secretary-General, *Address to World Economic Forum Davos*, 31 Jan. 2000 (UN/SG/SM/6881/Rev. New York) 1.

battleground. So too, useful international initiatives have been obs-tructed or killed off, as with the campaign which eventually down-graded the UN Centre for Transnational Corporations and its promising 'Code'.[172] Just as importantly, economic aid and steps towards 'elimi-nating poverty' make limited contribution to this goal in less developed economies unless they are based upon

> the overarching concern with the process of enhancing individual free-doms and the social commitment to help to bring that about.[173]

Just as on the national level all 'except the most devout free market economists' have long accepted 'the notion of *some* social responsibil-ity in the sense of incurring uncompensable costs for socially desir-able but not legally mandated action'[174] – even if only as part of the old CBI maxim that a public company should be 'a good citizen in business' or the belief of executives that: 'The best place to do busi-ness is a happy, healthy community'[175] – without solving the problems of corporate governance, or social responsibility, some multinationals have followed a similar, international course and established codes of conduct.[176]

Such developments could be of great importance, if they were effec-tive, especially in the light of the internal markets and the commodity chains created by transnational enterprises and associated enterprises. Unhappily, many of these codes do not contain all of the core labour standards, often the collective fundamental rights, and some codes were accused by union leaders of being a way to avoid unionisation. Nor is there any guarantee that such codes of conduct will be enforced, especially if the multinational enterprise comes across less profitable times. It is to be remembered that in respect of all international codes

---

[172] See S. Sheik and W. Rees, *Corporate Governance: Corporate Control* (London, 1995), 261–3.

[173] Amartya Sen, *Development as Freedom* (Oxford, 1999), 297–8, explaining successful de-velopment 'as a process of expanding substantive freedom that people have'. Contrast the common political approach which pays less attention to this aim or the obstruction of multinationals to it: UK Government, *Eliminating World Poverty: Making Globalisation Work for the Poor* (2000 HMSO Cm.5006).

[174] V. Brudney, 95 Harv. Law Rev. 597 (1982), 604–5.

[175] See Wedderburn, 'The Social Responsibility of Companies' (1985) 15 Melbourne Univ. L. Rev. 1, 12, 15.

[176] For a useful compilation of many such codes, see 'Multinational Enterprises and Social Challenges of the XXIst Century' (2000) 37 Bull. Comp. Lab. Relns (special number) and Appendices.

on labour standards, their main weaknesses have been identified by Hepple as:

> the absence of positive obligations on states to require TNCs to observe both core and core-plus standards . . . [and] the reliance that the international system places on national labour laws at a time when national governments have been disempowered by globalization . . . [Also] a major problem is that national labour laws are often not effectively enforced especially in developing countries.[177]

But much research continues into ways of finding mechanisms for the enforcement and improvement of labour standards, and given the difficulty of the enterprise, none of it should be discounted. In addition to traditional actors, the role of leading international firms and other 'drivers of globalisation' is seen by some scholars as crucial to a 'ratcheting' of labour standards, almost as it were by osmosis, setting in train a process of 'continuous improvements in the treatment of labour and the environment'.[178] By contrast, recent idealist and utopian thinking that owes more to Spinoza than to economic analysis suggests that the 'multitude', acting at an international – and emphatically not a national – level, will overturn the new 'empire'.[179] Such predictions are for the future to prove. More likely is the continuing need for decades of hardpressed struggle by workers and other groups in societies increasingly subject to the power of global capital without protection in reality for effective international standards of their fundamental dignity, decency and humanity. The ILO reported in 2001 that many millions suffered a 'decent work deficit' in the world, alongside those who had no work at all, and commented on the 'alarming' social protection gap and rights gap, its investigations having discovered a rise in child labour and trafficking in human beings on a world-wide scale.[180] It instituted a new investigation by 'a world commission of eminent personalities' into the

---

[177] B. Hepple, 'A Race to the Top? International Investment Guidelines and Corporate Codes of Conduct' (1999) 20 Comp. Lab. Law and Policy Jo. 347, 361–2.

[178] C. Sabel, D. O'Rourke and A. Fung, *Ratcheting Labor Standards: Regulation for Continuous Improvement in the Global Workplace* 23.2.2000, www.law.columbia.edu/sabel/papers/ratchPO.html.

[179] M. Hardt and A. Negri, *Empire* (Cambridge, MA, 2000).

[180] J. Somavia, Director-General, ILO, *Reducing the Decent Work Deficit – A Global Challenge*, www.ilo.org/public/english/standards/reports/report1.htm and working party report, www.ilo.org/public/english/standards/decl/publ/reports/report2.htm; (2001) 331 EIRR 30, 31.

social dimension of globalisation. While such moves maintain the centrality of the ILO in the international picture, it remains to be seen how effective ILO strategy will be in enforcing basic standards in the coming decades.

Despite the obstructions and the difficulties, however, our mood should not be one of unrelieved pessimism. History, which has not ended, has a habit of springing surprises whatever the power and authority that seems to determine it. The struggle for dignity and emancipation across the world and for fundamental rights for the bodies and minds of its people, has increased in its perceptions and zeal in recent years. The central challenge to the power of globalisation is the struggle for social rights, not least labour standards, in pursuit of freedom. Global labour law remains to be made. Each generation makes its own contribution to the task. None of us has a right to see the success of the venture. But we shall perhaps make our contribution better if we think and live as if we shall.

2

The interaction of the ILO, the Council of Europe and European Union labour standards

PAUL O'HIGGINS

The first point that needs to be made is that all international bodies setting international labour standards are subject to, or are influenced by, a common set of factors which have led in the past, and continue in a modified way in the present, to mould the necessity for and the contents of international labour standards. When the International Labour Organisation was established by the labour articles in the Treaty of Versailles in 1919, they followed a preamble which identified four reasons for the necessity of the adoption of international labour standards. As set out in the current preamble[1] of the ILO Constitution, they are

I am very grateful for help and advice from many friends and colleagues, in particular Catherine Barnard, Professor Brian Bercusson, Professor Lammy Betten, Regis Brillat, J. Courdouan, David Dror, Professor Keith Ewing, Robert Kissack, Professor Peter Muchlinski, Brigitte Napiwocka, Professor Niall O'Higgins, Niav O'Higgins, Peter Tergeist and Dr Philippa Watson.

[1] The full text of the preamble reads:

Whereas universal and lasting peace can be established only if it is based upon social justice:

And whereas conditions of labour exist involving such injustice, hardship and privation to large numbers of people as to produce unrest so great that the peace and harmony of the world are imperilled; and an improvement of those conditions is urgently required; as, for example, by the regulation of the hours of work, including the establishment of a maximum working day and week, the regulation of the labour supply, the prevention of unemployment, the provision of an adequate living wage, the protection of the worker against sickness, disease and injury arising out of his employment, the protection of children, young persons and women, provision for old age and injury, protection of the interests of workers when employed in countries other than their own, recognition of the principle of equal remuneration for work of equal value, recognition of the principle of freedom of association, the organisation of vocational and technical education and other measures;

Whereas also the failure of any nation to adopt humane conditions of labour is an obstacle in the way of other nations which desire to improve the conditions in their own countries;

as follows.

1. World peace depends upon social justice;
2. social injustice, hardship and deprivation undermine good order;
3. low labour standards in one country inhibit the adoption of decent labour standards in other countries;
4. humanity and decency require the adoption of minimum labour standards everywhere.

Historically,[2] the two most important reasons for the adoption of international labour standards have been fear of social disorder and revolution – what one might call the 'social revolution factor' – and the fear of lower labour standards in less developed countries leading to the undercutting of prices of goods and services in the more advanced industrialised countries – what one might call the 'social dumping factor'.[3]

Between 1919 and 1989 the 'social revolution factor' took the special form of the presence of the Soviet Union, offering a hope and/or threat of an economic system rivalling democratic capitalism in its promise of better conditions for workers. From 1945 onwards, the presence of powerful communist and left-wing socialist parties led to west European governments competing with those parties for the support of workers and trade unions. The threat presented by the Soviet Union and left-wing trade unions was often given by west European politicians as a reason for the adoption of the Council of Europe's Social Charter. At the signing ceremony for the Charter in Turin on 18 October, 1961, the vice-president of the Consultative Assembly explained that the objectives of the charter included the need 'to show the Communist World, and the Afro-Asian and Latin American countries how great was the protection which European countries afforded their workers . . .'.[4]

The High Contracting Parties, moved by sentiments of justice and humanity as well as by the desire to secure the permanent peace of the world, and with a view to attaining the objectives set forth in this Preamble, agree to the following Constitution of the International Labour Organisation.

[2] See John W. Follows, *Antecedents of the ILO* (Oxford, 1951).

[3] Cf. Elaine Vogel-Polsky, 'What Future is There for a Social Europe Following the Strasbourg Summit?' 19 ILJ (1990), 65, at 72: 'Labour is concerned not only with the reconciliation and compatibility of the respective rights and interests of employers and employees, but also with its guiding object of fixing common rules for enterprises which have resorted to the labour market, so as to ward off unfair competition between business in the form of dumping.'

[4] I am indebted for this quotation to Patricia Conlon's LL.M. thesis for the National University of Ireland in 1985 entitled 'The European Social Charter: Implementation of International Economic and Social Rights: Ireland'.

The 'social dumping factor' has played a consistent role in the policy of many governments, especially that of the United States under President Bill Clinton, and in the European Community, where Article 94 (ex art. 100) EC Treaty[5] has been used in a number of cases, such as the Council Directive of Collective Redundancies[6] because of the unfair competitive advantage enjoyed by British industry in virtue of its lower labour costs in cases of large-scale redundancy.

With the demise of the Soviet Union and of the threat of communism and communist parties, 'the social revolution factor' may have lessened in significance. A new major operator in this field is represented by the numerous non-governmental organisations, evidenced by events such as the anti-globalisation protests in Seattle in September 1999. As we shall see, the non-government organisations have already achieved a significant influence over the activities of the OECD. It has been suggested that consumers may also have an important role to play. Consumer activity so far has contributed to the adoption by many corporate businesses of codes of conduct 'regulating labour standards in the Third World countries upon whose factories and workers many multi-national enterprises depend for the supply of the goods they sell'.[7] Labour law still remains a tug-of-war between unions and business. Because of the decline in the membership of trade unions they may be less effective as a countervailing force when faced with an increase in the power and influence of business corporations and, in particular, multinational enterprises.[8]

The ILO was the first international organisation to set labour standards,[9] which include, in particular, ILO conventions, recommendations, and, above all, the ILO Constitution itself, of which the Philadelphia Declaration of 1944 is an integral part. The Philadelphia Declaration, adopted by the General Conference of the ILO, reaffirmed

---

[5] 'The Council shall, acting unanimously on a proposal from the Commission, issue directives for the approximation of such provisions laid down by law, regulation or administrative action in Member States as directly affect the establishment or functioning of the common market.'

[6] 75/129/EC. There are, of course, other examples of this use of art. 100.

[7] See generally Naomi Klein, No Logo (London, 2000).

[8] Following ILO practice, I use the term *multinational enterprise* (MNE) as opposed to several alternative labels commonly used, such as *transnational corporation* (TNC), and so on.

[9] There were, of course, several earlier bilateral agreements between states – there were even a few multilateral agreements – setting labour standards, but the ILO was the first permanent standard-setting body.

'the fundamental principles on which the organisation is based, and, in particular, that:

    (a) labour is not a commodity;[10]
    (b) freedom of expression and of association are essential to sustained progress;
    (c) poverty anywhere constitutes a danger to prosperity everywhere;
    (d) the war against want requires to be carried on with unrelenting vigour within each nation, and by continuous and concerted international effort in which the representatives of workers and employers, enjoying equal status with those governments, join with them in free discussion and democratic decision with a view to the promotion of the common welfare.'[11]

In 1945, the leading role of the ILO as a standard-setter was reaffirmed through its becoming a specialised agency of the United Nations, which is itself an important setter of labour standards (albeit sometimes obliquely, as in its Universal Declaration of Human Rights, December 1948). Article 19 of the Universal Declaration of Human Rights guarantees the right of freedom of opinion and expression (always important in labour disputes and, in particular, picketing). Article 20 guarantees the right to freedom of peaceful assembly and association (picketing again, and trade union membership), with the express rider that 'No one may be compelled to belong to an association.'

Largely inspired by the UN's Universal Declaration, the Council of Europe adopted the 1950 European Convention for the Protection of Human Rights and Fundamental Freedoms.[12] Article 10 guaranteed the right of freedom of expression. Article 11 guaranteed the right of an individual to freedom of peaceful assembly and to freedom of association with others, including the right to form and to join trade unions for the protection of his/her interests. Articles 10 and 11 may be subjected only to such restrictions as are (i) prescribed by law, and (ii) are necessary in a democratic society and (iii) are necessary to protect certain values. It does not appear that the ILO played any direct role in formulating or influencing the contents of these two articles.

---

[10] See P. O'Higgins, ' "Labour is not a Commodity" – an Irish Contribution to International Labour Law', 26 ILJ (1997), 225–34.
[11] For the role of Edward J. Phelan in the adoption of the Philadelphia Declaration, ibid., 230.
[12] Signed 4 Nov. 1950: in force 3 Sep. 1953.

In the Treaty of Rome of 1957, which set up the European Economic Community, there were a few articles directly setting labour standards.[13] Articles 48 to 51 (now arts. 39 to 42 EC) dealt with migrant workers, including the prohibition of discrimination based on nationality as regards terms and conditions of employment. Article 117 (now art. 136) dealt with the harmonisation of working conditions and living standards. Article 118 (now art. 140) promoted cooperation between member states in the social field, particularly in matters relating to employment, labour law and working conditions, vocational training, social security, occupational accidents, diseases and hygiene, and the right of association and collective bargaining. Article 119 (now art. 141) dealt with equal pay for men and women. Article 120 (now art. 143) dealt with the maintenance of 'the existing equivalence between paid holiday schemes'. Article 121 (now art. 144) authorised the Council of Ministers to assign to the Commission tasks 'in connection with the implementation of common measures, particularly as regards social security for migrant workers'.

Again, it does not appear that the ILO had any direct role in formulating or influencing the content of these articles.

The next important development as regards labour standards was the Council of Europe's Social Charter.[14] This Charter, which is the counterpart of the European Convention on Human Rights in the sphere of economic and social rights, lays down in some detail a considerable body of minimum labour standards. The only Treaty text referred to in the Preamble to the Social Charter as influencing the content of the Social Charter is the Council of Europe's Convention for the Protection of Human Rights and Fundamental Freedoms and its 1952 Protocol. The omission of any reference to the ILO is somewhat surprising. The initiative for a charter, which seems to have come from a Council of Europe's Secretariat, was unanimously approved in 1953 by the Consultative Assembly. The Committee of Ministers then proceeded to produce a draft, which was examined by a Tripartite Conference at Strasbourg in December 1958, convened by the ILO under the general agreement between the Council of Europe and the ILO. Delegations at this conference were composed, following the ILO pattern, of government, employers'

---

[13] See International Labour Office, 'Social Aspects of European Economic Cooperation', *International Labour Review* 74 (1956) 99 et seq. ('The Ohlin Report').

[14] Signed 18 Oct. 1961; in force 26 Feb. 1965.

and workers' delegates.[15] 'What is new in the Charter is partly the formulation in terms of human rights of many undertakings found in ILO
conventions and recommendations and partly their assembly, usually
in more general terms, in a single document.'[16] Under Article 26 of the
Charter, the ILO may send a representative 'to participate in a consultative capacity in the deliberations of the Committee of Experts', which
is charged under Articles 24 and 25 with the examination of national
reports on the implementation by states of their obligations under the
Charter. It is significant that when member states submit national reports on their compliance with their obligations under the Social Charter, they are permitted to provide instead copies of any reports they may
have addressed to the ILO on the application of ILO conventions to the
extent that they cover the same field as their Social Charter obligations.
This facility has now been extended to allow Social Charter member
states to submit copies of other relevant reports they may have submitted to the European Union, the United Nations and the Council of
Europe.[17]

In 1974 the Council of the European Communities adopted by resolution its Social Action Programme.[18] The Council resolution refers
to neither the ILO nor the Council of Europe. In January 1989, eleven
of the twelve member states of the European Communities adopted the
Single European Act, including a Community Charter of the Fundamental Social Rights of Workers. The list of fundamental rights covers
social rights for workers comprising freedom of movement, pay, living
and working conditions, social security, freedom of association and collective bargaining, vocational training, equal treatment for men and
women, worker consultation and participation, health and safety, and
protection of the young, the elderly and disabled persons. The Preamble
to the Single European Act refers specifically to the European Convention on Human Rights and Fundamental Freedoms and the Council
of Europe's Social Charter. The preliminary words to the Community
Charter of the Fundamental Social Rights of Workers state that: 'Inspiration should be drawn from the Conventions of the International
Labour Organisation and from the European Social Charter of the Council of Europe.' This seems to be the first example of labour standards

---

[15] For background to the Charter, see David Harris, *The European Social Charter*
(Charlottesville, 1984), ch. 1.
[16] Ibid., 10–11.   [17] Council of Europe Document T-SG(97) 16.   [18] 74 C13/01.

adopted by the European Union being inspired by the ILO. The Council Directive on the Protection of Young People at Work in its Preamble indicates that 'Account should be taken of the principles of the International Labour Organisation regarding the protection of young people at work, including those relating to the minimum age for access to employment or work.'[19] More recently, a Council Directive implementing a sectoral agreement on the working time of seafarers concluded by the European Community Shipowners' Association and the Federation of Transport Workers in the European Union was adopted. This agreement reflects the provisions of the ILO Convention concerning Seafarers' Hours of Work, No. 180 (1996).[20] A Council Directive implemented the 'European Framework Agreement on Part-time Work'. The Agreement was much influenced by the ILO Convention on Part-Time Work, No. 175 (1988).[21]

The 1992 Maastricht Treaty or Treaty on European Union[22] contains a Protocol and Agreement on Social Policy.[23] These further implement the 1989 Social Charter by encouraging dialogue between 'management and labour'. No reference is made to either the Council of Europe or the ILO as a source of inspiration.

Late in autumn 2000 came the adoption by the European Union of a draft Charter of Fundamental Rights of the European Union.[24] Article 5 prohibits slavery and forced labour. Article 11 guarantees the right to freedom of expression. Article 12 guarantees the right to freedom of assembly and to freedom of association 'at all levels, in particular in political, trade union and civic matters, which implies the right of everyone to form and join trade unions for the protection of his or her interests'.[25] The Preamble to this Charter derives inspiration from 'the constitutional traditions and international obligations common to the member states, the Treaty on European Union, the Community Treaties, the European Convention for the Protection of Human Rights and Fundamental Freedoms, the Social Charters adopted by the Community and by the Council of Europe and the case law of the Court of Justice of the European Communities and of the European Court of

---

[19] Council Directive 94/33/EC; OJ 1994, L 216/12.
[20] Council Directive 99/63/EC, supplemented by Council Directive 99/95/EC.
[21] Council Directive 97/81/EC.   [22] OJ 1992, C/224.
[23] The United Kingdom was exempted from the Protocol and Agreement.
[24] See K. Ewing, *The Charter of Fundamental Rights of the European Union: Implications for Trade Unions* (London, 2001).
[25] Art. 12, para. 1.

Human Rights'. There is no explicit reference to the ILO, but since 'international obligations of the Member States' include the Constitution of the ILO and the Philadelphia Declaration, regard must surely be had to these in the interpretation of the European Union's Charter of Fundamental Rights.

Some degree of formal relationship was first developed between the ILO and the European Communities in 1958. In 1989 an exchange of letters between the two bodies provided for the Community, represented by the Commission, to be invited to meetings of the ILO's International Labour Conference and of the Governing Body. In return, the Commission would invite ILO representatives to its meetings 'at service level dealing with social and labour matters likely to be of interest to the ILO'. Provision was also made for consultation on possible cooperation between the two bodies and for the exchange of information or assistance in areas of shared interest. In an exchange of letters between the two bodies in May 2001, it was recognised that in a time of globalisation both would benefit from increasing cooperation in the promotion of labour standards, employment, social dialogue, social protection and development, 'notably with a view to strengthening the social dimension of development, while also collaborating at the operational level in the service of sustainable development'.[26] It is understood that the European Union had wished to become a member of the ILO, but as it is not a state this was not possible. Even if membership had been possible, it is not clear how the European Union could produce employers' and workers' representatives for its delegation.

The Council of Europe adopted the Revised Social Charter in 1996, providing for more detailed social rights, for more detailed labour rights and for their better enforcement.[27] There is no reference in the revised Charter's Preamble to the ILO.

It may be worth looking at the differing interpretations of labour standards adopted by the European Commission and Court of Human Rights, and at the decisions given by the European Court of Justice interpreting labour standards of the European Union. The European Court of Justice has attached great significance to the European Convention on Human Rights and Fundamental Freedoms. As Francis Jacobs and Robin White summarise the situation:

[26] OJ 2001, C 165/23.   [27] Signed 3 May 1996; in force 1 Nov. 1999.

> The cumulative effect of the case-law of the [European] Court of Justice is that the Court must have regard to national constitutions and to international instruments, especially the European Convention [on Human Rights and Fundamental Freedoms]. The Convention is not formally binding on the Community, but its provisions can and must be given effect as general principles of Community law. The result is much the same as if the Community were bound by the Convention . . . [28]

Surprisingly, there is little evidence of the willingness of the European Court of Justice to give effect to an older human rights instrument as part of European law, namely the Constitution of the ILO (1919) and the Philadelphia Declaration, with its basic rule that 'labour is not a commodity'. It would seem to be impossible that the European Court of Justice could have reached the conclusion it did in *Jenkins* v. *Kingsgate (Clothing Productions)*[29] had it had regard to this basic legally binding principle. Should not at least the ILO's core of fundamental labour rights not be part of the law administered by the European Court of Justice? Given that *all* member states of the International Labour Organisation have committed themselves to respect, promote and give effect to the principles in the ILO's *Declaration on Fundamental Principles and Rights at Work and its Follow-up*,[30] what obstacle should there be to the Court giving effect to these principles as part of the law of the European Communities?

In the European Court of Human Rights, decisions on freedom of association under Article 11 of the European Convention, such as the *Young, James and Webster* case[31] and the *Sigurjonsson* case[32] establishing a right not to associate, seem inconsistent with the approach of the ILO, not to mention the *travaux préparatoires* to the European Convention itself. In the *National Union of Belgian Police* case[33] Article 11 was found not to oblige an employer to consult with unions. In the *Swedish Engine Drivers' Union* case,[34] the Court took the view that Article 11 does not oblige an employer state to enter into collective agreements with unions. In

---

[28] Francis G. Jacobs and Robin C. A. White, *The European Convention on Human Rights*, 2nd edn (Oxford, 1996), 413.

[29] (1981) ECR 911.

[30] International Labour Office, *Your Voice at Work* (Geneva, 2000), 1.

[31] *Young, James and Webster* v. *UK* (1982) 4 EHRR 38.

[32] *Sigurdur A. Sigurjonsson* v. *Iceland* (1993) 16 EHRR 462.

[33] *National Union of Belgian Police* v. *Belgium* (1979–80) 1 EHRR 578.

[34] *Swedish Engine Drivers' Union* v. *Sweden* (1979–80) 1 EHRR 617.

the *Schmidt and Dahlstrom* case,[35] the Court held that the right to join a trade union in Article 11 did not imply a right to strike. In a case involving the denial by the United Kingdom government of the right to belong to a trade union to civil servants employed at GCHQ, the European Human Rights Commission denied that there had been a violation of Article 11.[36] This must be contrasted with the approach of the ILO Governing Body's Committee of Freedom of Association in the same case, which took the view that clearly there had been a violation of the right to belong to a trade union under Article 2 of the ILO Convention, No. 87.

The European Court of Justice has had to consider the relationship between ILO standards and those of the Treaties of the European Communities in a number of cases. In the *Stoeckel* case[37] the Court carefully avoided facing up to a potential conflict between the ILO's Convention, Night Work (Women) Convention, No. 89 (1948) and the provisions of Community law. In *Opinion 2/91*[38] the Court considered the relationship between the ILO Chemicals Convention, No. 170 (1990) and Community law. 'The Court . . . distinguished between two situations. On the one hand, it said that in the areas where the Community had laid down only minimum requirements and those standards were inferior to those set by the ILO the Member States had competence under Article 118a(3) to adopt more stringent measures. On the other hand, the Court said in those areas where the Community had harmonised rules . . . the Community alone had competence.'[39]

The *Albany International* case[40] and, in particular, the opinion of the Advocate General deserves careful examination for implications it may have for an extended scope for workers' rights to association, collective bargaining and strike action.[41]

An interesting area of labour standard setting is to be found in the field of multinational enterprises (MNEs). The story begins[42] in the early 1970s. Less developed countries were seeking a change in the balance of world economic power through the adoption of a New International

---

[35] *Schmidt and Dahlstrom* v. *Sweden* (1979–80) 1 EHRR 67.
[36] *Council of Civil Service Trade Unions and others* v. *UK* (1987) 50 DR 228.
[37] [1991] ECR I-4047.   [38] [1993] ECR I-1061.
[39] Catherine Barnard, *EC Employment Law*, 2nd edn (Oxford, 2000), 69.
[40] Case C-67/96, judgment of 21 Sept.
[41] For discussion, see Barnard, *EC Employment Law*, Ch. 8, Part B. See also Ch. 5 below.
[42] This story is told in Peter Muchlinski, *Multinational Enterprises and the Law* (Oxford, 1995), Ch. 16.

Economic Order under the auspices of the United Nations. The UN Economic and Social Committee was persuaded in 1974 to set up a commission on transnational corporations to draw up a legally binding code of conduct. The United Nations Conference on Trade and Development (UNCTAD) started negotiations on codes of conduct, on transfer of technology and on restrictive business practices, and the ILO began to draft a set of principles on multinational enterprises and social policy. 'To counter these developments, the OECD ministers, urged on by the US government, decided to adopt their own policy on MNEs, which it was hoped would influence the UN's attempts at "codification" to move away from the highly regulated position of "MNE control".'[43] The efforts of certain governments to head off legally binding rules was successful. The OECD adopted in 1976 Guidelines for Multinationals, including a section on employment and industrial relations. A weak system of 'enforcement' allowed the OECD Committee on Investment and Multinational Enterprises to give clarification on issues arising under the Guidelines. Some of the issues before the Committee involved consideration of labour standards, but no reference seems to have been made to standards other than those in the Guidelines themselves.[44] The Guidelines were revised in 2000. Following the collapse of the Multilateral Agreement on Investment, brought down principally by an alliance of non-governmental organisations, not to mention the French government, in 1998,[45] NGOs were invited to express their views on a draft, as was the ILO. The preface to the revised *OECD Guidelines for Multinational Enterprises*, paragraph 8 reads:

> Governments are co-operating with each other and with other actors to strengthen the international legal and policy framework in which business is conducted. The post-war period has seen the development of this framework, starting with the adoption in 1948 of the Universal Declaration of Human Rights. Recent instruments include the ILO Declaration on Fundamental Principles and Rights at Work, the Rio Declaration on Environment and Development and Agenda 21 and the Copenhagen Declaration for Social Development.[46]

[43] Ibid., 578.

[44] See John Robinson, *Multinationals and Political Control* (London, 1983), for a study of the 'case-law' of the Committee on Investment and Multinational Enterprises.

[45] At a public meeting in 1998, before the collapse of the MAI, a government minister was asked to express his views on the MAI. He said that he had not heard of it.

[46] *OECD Guidelines for Multinational Enterprises* (Paris, 2000), 16.

The OECD's Committee on Investment and Multinational Enterprises, as a result, is now empowered to invoke the aid of the ILO Declaration on Fundamental Principles and Rights at Work in its clarifications. The ILO adopted in 1977 a tripartite Declaration of Principles on Multinationals and Social Policy, which is more detailed than the relevant provisions of the OECD's Guidelines. It should be noted, however, that the Commentary to the OECD's Guidelines asserts that the ILO tripartite declaration can be of use in understanding the Guidelines 'to the extent that it is of a greater degree of elaboration'.[47]

Professor Muchlinski has drawn my attention to the possibility that as both the ILO and the OECD have trade union representation within their structures, there might arise the possibility for informal discussions between members of the OECD's Trade Union Advisory Committee and the union delegates in national delegations to the ILO Conference. As we shall see later, members of the OECD Trade Union Advisory Committee are already taking part in joint action with the International Confederation of Free Trade Unions and the International Trade Secretariats.

The UN eventually gave up on the adoption of a Code of Transnational Corporations.[48]

The UN Commission and Centre on Transnational Corporations have been closed down.

Stephen Neff has used the phrase 'the policemen of capitalism' to describe three organisations which could have a vital impact on labour standards, particularly in the third world, namely GATT (now the World Trade Organisation), the World Bank and the International Monetary Fund.[49] The World Bank 'has slowly begun to accept that it must take a stance on child labour and prison labour, [but] it has not shifted on other labour standards'.[50] As regards the World Trade Organisation, there is now an alliance consisting of the International Confederation of Free Trade Unions, the International Trade Secretariats and the Trade Union Advisory Committee of the OECD to persuade the World Trade Organisation to guarantee respect for core labour standards.[51]

---

[47] Ibid., 45, para. 20.   [48] Muchlinski, *Multinational Enterprises*, 592–7.

[49] Stephen Neff, *Friends But No Allies: Economic Liberalism and the Law of Nations* (New York, 1990), Ch. 6.

[50] Public Services International, *Report of Activities 2000* (Geneva, 2001), 12.

[51] Ibid. For fuller discussions of the role that trade unions could play see Madeleine Bunting, 'A new role for unions', *Guardian*, 10 September 2001, and K. D. Ewing and Tom Sibley, *International Trade Union Rights for the New Millenium* (London, 2000).

In the light of all this, one might ask how seriously regional organisations such as the European Union and national governments regard international labour standards, particularly those authoritatively formulated and interpreted by the ILO. The European Union has shown an increasing willingness to embrace ILO standards. There still remains, however, the possibility of a conflict between ILO standards and those of the European Union, particularly as regards the exercise of the right to strike. The European Court of Human Rights has tended to interpret the Convention on Human Rights and Fundamental Freedoms in a way which is more restrictive than the parallel rights under the ILO. On the whole, the Committee of Experts under the Council of Europe's Social Charter tends to adopt an approach similar to that of the ILO. This is not surprising given the presence of an ILO observer at their proceedings.

How far do member states fulfil their existing obligations in relation to international labour standards? It is sobering to consider the latest Report of the European Committee of Social Rights, which considered the extent to which the United Kingdom complied with its obligations under Articles 1, 5, 6, 12, 13, 16 and 19 of the Council of Europe's Social Charter.[52] Of the twenty-three obligations binding on the United Kingdom, the Committee was satisfied in only ten instances that the United Kingdom was fulfilling its obligations. The Committee deferred judgement on four of the obligations but in nine instances it found that the United Kingdom was in breach of its obligations. But, even more significantly, the Committee was unable to find that the United Kingdom was in compliance with any of the obligations contained in Article 6, which lays down the simplest and most elementary rights in the spheres of collective bargaining and collective action.

What of the practice followed by international organisations, such as the European Union and the Council of Europe, in regulating relations with their own staff? After all, here, there would appear to be no threat to international peace through lack of social justice, and no fear of social dumping. On the other hand, lack of fairness might give rise to strikes and other forms of disorder. Would a philanthropic sense of justice not seem to point to the desirability of implementing generally recognised international labour standards? The picture is not a happy one. There

---

[52] *European Social Charter: European Committee of Social Rights – Conclusions XV-1, Vol. 2* (Strasbourg, 2000), Ch. 16, 684.

have been strikes by international civil servants belonging to a number of organisations. It must come to anyone, as it did to me, as a shock that no UN body, with the single exception of the ILO, recognises a trade union to which its employees belong and with which it engages in collective bargaining. Even in the case of the ILO, the first agreement of this kind is dated 27 March 2000.

It is interesting to look at the terms of some of the recent ILO agreements. There are currently five such agreements in force. Their Preambles show a surprising variation in the standards recognised by the parties to be applied in their relations. The principal agreement, the *Recognition and Procedure Agreement* between the International Labour Office and the ILO Staff Union, reads:

> Whereas the [International] Office and the [the ILO Staff] Union recognise that, so far as it has authority to do so, the Office, as an employer, should promote the principles and rights embodied in the Freedom of Association and Protection of the Right to Organise Convention, 1948 (No. 87), the Right to Organise and Collective Bargaining Convention, 1949 (No. 98), the Labour Relations (Public Service) Convention, 1978 (No. 151), and Article 20 of the Universal Declaration of Human Rights...

One hopes that the reference to the authority of the 'Office, as an employer' refers only to authority to negotiate and not to authority to promote relevant labour standards.

The Preamble to the Collective Agreement on a Procedure for Recruitment and Selection provides that the procedure

> will be conducted in accordance with due process, fair procedures and natural justice having regard to relevant international law, including international labour standards and the ILO Declaration on fundamental principles and rights at work.[53]

In conclusion, one has to say that there is considerable confusion between the differing standard-setting bodies that we have looked at. In my opinion, one needs some means of ensuring the primacy of standards set by the ILO. This would require some overall supervisory body,

---

[53] Identical words are used in the *Agreement on a Procedure for the Resolution of Grievances*. Similar is the *Agreement on the Prevention and Resolution of Harassment-related Grievances*, but with the omission of any reference to international law.

preferably a court, where authoritative interpretations can be given resolving any potential conflicts. Far too many areas are still subject to codes of practice of a non-legally binding character.[54] It is true that a voluntary code of practice may be a preliminary to the establishment of a legally binding standard, but in some areas the adoption of a voluntary code may merely be the means of heading off legally binding obligations and advancing the public relations image of the institution concerned.[55] More important, perhaps, would be the adoption by the ILO of legally binding rules for the regulation of the industrial relations and employment law practices of multinational enterprises. There is sadly little realistic prospect of this happening.

---

[54] See Klein, *No Logo*, 430–7. For a very important discussion of codes of practice, see *International Union Rights*, 8, 3 (2001), which is largely devoted to codes of practice.

[55] See also Ch. 10 below.

II

The potential of fundamental social rights
in the European Union

3

The politics of the EU Charter
of Fundamental Rights

MANFRED WEISS

I. Introduction

At a point very early in the development of the European Community fundamental rights had become an issue. When the jurisdiction of the European Court of Justice (ECJ) destroyed any doubts about the supremacy of Community law over the law of the member states, this position was questioned by those states that had a constitution containing fundamental rights. In particular the German Federal Constitutional Court was not willing to accept this dogma of supremacy as long as there was no guarantee that the level of fundamental rights as provided by the German constitution would be respected by the ECJ.[1] Since the EC Treaty mainly focused on the freedom of movement of capital, goods, services and workers in order to optimise market conditions, it was not at all clear what its position was towards fundamental rights. Therefore the danger of the deconstruction of the platform of fundamental rights at national level could not be excluded. It soon turned out, however, that fears of this kind were unjustified. By referring to the European Convention for the Protection of Human Rights and Fundamental Freedoms and to the constitutional traditions of the member states the ECJ established a jurisdiction which was, and still is, based on fundamental rights.[2] An informal collaboration between the European Court of Human Rights (ECtHR) and the ECJ has been established. A safeguard has thereby been brought into existence to make sure that the ECJ's interpretation does not run in conflict with the position of the ECtHR. In view of this development the German Federal Constitutional Court gave up its opposition

[1] Federal Constitutional Court, Judgement of 29 May 1974, BVerfGE 37, 27.
[2] For this development see J. H. H. Weiler, *The Constitution of Europe* (Cambridge, 1999), 107.

and declared that it would respect the supremacy of European Community law as long as the ECJ follows this path.[3] The ECJ not only maintained but even strengthened its efforts to build its jurisdiction on the sound basis of fundamental rights.[4] All this is well known and uncontested.

The practice of the ECJ is now confirmed by the Treaty on European Union (TEU). According to Article 6 paragraph 2 'the Union shall respect fundamental rights, as guaranteed by the European Convention for the Protection of Human Rights and Fundamental Freedoms signed in Rome on 4 November 1950 and as they result from the constitutional traditions common to the Member States, as general principles of Community law'. And Article 46(d) TEU stresses that the ECJ is empowered to enforce Article 6 paragraph 2 TEU 'with regard to action of the institutions, insofar as the Court has jurisdiction under the Treaties establishing the European Communities and under this Treaty'. In addition Article 136 paragraph 1 of the Treaty establishing the European Community (EC Treaty) in laying down the objectives of social policy refers to 'the fundamental social rights such as those set out in the European Social Charter signed at Turin on 18 October 1961 and in the 1989 Community Charter of the Fundamental Social Rights of Workers'.

In view of this situation the question arises why one should bother at all about a charter of fundamental rights. Isn't it sufficient to leave everything as it is? A closer look clearly shows the deficiencies of the present state of affairs.

The reference system is vague, confusing and not at all enlightening. It is unclear in what way the European Convention, the constitutional traditions of the member states, the European Social Charter and the Community Charter of the Fundamental Social Rights of Workers are to be observed by the Community.[5] In particular the wording of Article 136 paragraph 1 EC ('having in mind') leaves open whether the two charters to which the article refers are only meant to be a very unspecific point of orientation or whether it means that each part of

---

[3] Federal Constitutional Court, Judgement of 22 October 1986, BVerfGE 73, 339.

[4] See for this development with reference to fundamental social rights B. Hepple, 'The Development of Fundamental Social Rights in European Labour Law', in A. Neal and S. Foyn (eds.), *Developing the Social Dimension in an Enlarged European Union* (Oslo, 1995), 23.

[5] Europaeische Kommission, *Die Grundrechte in der Europaeischen Union verbürgen. Bericht der Expertengruppe 'Grundrechte'* (1999), 18.

these charters is to be applied directly. The latter is very unlikely. It has to be kept in mind that the Governmental Conference establishing the Amsterdam Treaty was confronted with the demand that a catalogue of fundamental social rights be integrated into the Treaty in order to make the Community's social profile transparent for everybody.[6] This request evidently was not met, not least for the reason that fundamental social rights might have implied additional costs for the Community and for its member states. Therefore the mere reference to the two charters has to be interpreted as representing an alternative to such a catalogue of fundamental social rights, merely referring to the underlying values of those charters in a very unspecific way. If the reference to the charters in Article 136 paragraph 1 EC signifies that they would really have to be integrated into the Treaty to their full extent, it is not possible to explain why in Article 137 paragraph 6 EC the Community's power to legislate in the areas of 'pay, the right of association, the right to strike or the right to impose lock-outs' is denied. The exclusion of legislative powers with reference to 'the right of association' also shows that the reference to the ECHR does not mean that the latter is fully integrated into the system of the Treaties. There, after all, the right of association is guaranteed.[7] And of course the most unspecific part is the reference to the constitutional traditions of the member states. It is extremely difficult to specify what this may mean. These constitutional traditions are very different. Some countries do have written constitutions, others don't. Some constitutions contain a bill of rights, others don't. The fundamental rights guaranteed by these constitutions differ significantly. Is the mention of the constitutional traditions of the member states a reference to a specific constitutional tradition or rather to the average, to the top or to the bottom? This remains unclear.[8] Finally, the question arises whether other international treaties containing fundamental rights – as for example the ILO conventions – are to be excluded for the mere fact that there no reference is made to them. The result of this sketchy analysis turns out to be frustrating: it remains unclear what fundamental rights form the basis of the EU and to what extent they are guaranteed. The citizens of the EU are unable to recognise these rights. There is no transparency whatsoever. It therefore becomes evident that

---

[6] For details of this discussion see M. Weiss, *Fundamental Social Rights for the European Union* (Amsterdam, 1996), 7 et seq.

[7] See art. 11, para. 1.

[8] For a profound discussion of this problem see Weiler, *The Constitution of Europe*, 109.

there is an urgent need to specify the rights which are considered to
be the basis for the Community and which define its specific profile.
There is no other way but to draw up a comprehensive catalogue of such
rights and to make it visible to everyone by integrating it into the Treaty.
In this respect the Charter of Fundamental Rights of the European Union
as accepted at the Nice summit in December 2000 is a first important
step. The more difficult part – the integration of this Charter into the
Treaty – still remains a task to be fulfilled.

This chapter discusses the broad lines of the genesis of the Charter as
well as its main structure and its implications for the EU. And it *tries*
to speculate on the probability its being integrated into the Treaty in a
foreseeable future.

II. The genesis and the content of the Charter

In order to influence the Governmental Conference elaborating the
terms of the Amsterdam Treaty the Commission of the European Communities set up a group of experts, the so-called 'comité des sages',
to analyse the state of affairs concerning fundamental rights and to
make recommendations. The group presented its report in March 1996,
strongly pleading for the integration of a catalogue of fundamental rights
into the Treaty.[9] The recommendations suggested by the comité des sages
were supported, further elaborated and strengthened by a second group
of experts on fundamental rights which presented its report in February
1999.[10] Even if the recommendations of the comité des sages were ig-
nored by the authors of the Amsterdam Treaty the comité des sages kept
alive the discussion on this very issue. By establishing the second group
of experts the Commission was able to increase the pressure to overcome the weaknesses and inconsistencies of the Amsterdam Treaty as
sketched above. The ground thereby was prepared for further action in
promoting fundamental rights.

During the German presidency of the EU the summit in Cologne in
June 1999 took the decision to establish a body, the so-called concilium,[11] to draw up a text for a Charter of Fundamental Rights. At the

---

[9] European Commission, Directorate-General for Employment, Industrial Relations and
Social Affairs, *For a Europe of Civic and Social Rights*, Report by the Comité des Sages (1996).
[10] See Europaeische Kommission, *Die Grundrechte in der Europaeischen Union verbürgen*, 13.
[11] The UK delegates, however, rejected this label and insisted on using 'convention'.

summit in Tampere, Finland, in October 1999 the composition of the concilium was determined, with the intention that this drafting body should enjoy utmost legitimacy. This requirement was met by the fact that almost three quarters of the members of the concilium were members of a parliament: of the sixty-two members of the drafting body thirty came from national parliaments and fifteen from the European Parliament. Each government of the fifteen member states and the Commission were represented by one person, while the concilium was chaired by the former president of the Federal Republic of Germany, Roman Herzog. The concilium not only enjoyed a remarkable democratic legitimacy but was in addition supposed to perform its activities as transparently as possible and to include in its deliberations the opinions of different groups of society. Not only was each of the final fifty versions of the draft put on the Internet but also the various suggestions for amendments. The Internet became a pool for extensive discussion, providing important feedback to the concilium. It should be stressed that the concilium also established very fruitful and efficient communications with representatives of the candidate countries to the EU. Parallel to the activities of the drafting body quite a few conferences were set up in the different member states to discuss the matter and to familiarise as many people as possible with the problems arising in the context of elaborating the Charter. This ongoing discourse was a very important element in improving the chances of the acceptability of the result as presented by the concilium. It seems that the composition of this body as well as the manner of its proceeding has sharpened the awareness throughout Europe of the deficiencies of the more or less clandestine proceedings of the representatives of governments in the context of the different amendments of the Treaty. It will be difficult to return to this former route. The concilium has thus become somehow a model of how to proceed in shaping the future face of the EU.

The concilium had to fulfil its task under a very severe restriction imposed on it by the decision taken at the summit in Cologne: the Charter should not lead to an extension of the legislative powers of the Community. The existing framework should be maintained. As far as the content of the catalogue of fundamental rights was concerned, there was from the very beginning full agreement that it was necessary to integrate into this catalogue all the rights contained in the ECHR. The question was of what to add in order to meet new challenges and to really provide a Charter of Fundamental Rights for the society of today and tomorrow. These deliberations led among others to the inclusion of the right to the protection of personal data (art. 8) and of the right to education and to have access to vocational and continuing training (art. 14), to mention just two prominent examples. The chapters on dignity (arts. 1 to 5), on freedoms (arts. 6 to 19), on equality (arts. 20 to 26), on citizens' rights (arts. 47 to 50) and on access to courts and to effective remedies under the label of 'justice' (arts. 47 to 50) turned out to be relatively unproblematic, at least in principle. The controversies arising in the context of these chapters mainly referred to details and to the wording of the different provisions, in an attempt to make sure that the rights included do not remain as merely wishful thinking but really are rights to be challenged in court or to establish an obligation for the Community to be respected and met by its organs. The real battle was on the inclusion of the so-called fundamental social rights, which are now listed up in the 'solidarity' chapter (arts. 27 to 38).

III. Civic versus social fundamental rights

The background

The debate on the inclusion of fundamental social rights in the Charter of Fundamental Rights has to be reflected in view of the history of the Community social policy. When in 1957 the Rome Treaties were concluded, it was the prevailing philosophy of the founding fathers of the European Economic Community (EEC) that there was no need for the EEC to have a social policy of its own. Even if there was an awareness of the danger of 'social dumping' between the member states, there was a stronger belief that the merger of the economies in a single European market would lead automatically to a gradual harmonisation of social policy throughout the Community. Therefore the focus was almost exclusively on the framework necessary to establish a common market: free movement of workers, freedom of establishment, freedom to provide goods and services and free movement of capital. Of course free movement of workers does have implications for social policy. But it is understood to be first of all a necessary precondition for the common market. The Community's powers to establish rules in the area of social policy were almost non-existent. In the Preamble to the Treaty the intention continuously to improve living and working conditions was mentioned. According to Article 117 the member states were encouraged to develop progressively the living and working conditions, and according to Article 118 the Commission was given the task of promoting cooperation between the member states in the area of social policy. There was only one exception: according to Article 141 paras. 1 and 2 (ex art. 119) EC the member states were supposed to respect the principle of 'equal pay for equal work' for men and women. This provision, however, was merely meant to prevent social dumping by using women as cheap labour. There was no social consideration. In short and to make the point: the original EEC Treaty contained only a minimalist approach to social policy.[12]

It is important to remember that the Community made progress in the area of social policy not because of but in spite of the Treaty. In view of the increasing unemployment of the early 1970s the politicians of the member states increasingly gained the insight that progress in social policy is by no means an automatic implication of the establishment of a common market. Therefore the summit of 1972 in Paris urged the Community to take energetic steps in the area of social policy. This led not only to a detailed social action programme but to a whole range of directives based on Article 94 (ex art. 100) EC which empowers the Community to legislate in order to fight distortion of competition or on Article 308 (ex art. 235) EC which establishes an accidental competence for the Community in case the specific legislative powers are not sufficient to reach the Treaty's goals. Both articles evidently have no specific link to social policy. Nevertheless they were used as a basis for the Directives on equal opportunities for men and women[13] as well as for the Directives on protection of workers in case of collective redundancies,[14] in case of transfer of undertakings[15] or in case of the insolvency of the employer.[16] It was no problem that these steps only could be taken by unanimous decision of all member states: the unanimous compassion of all member states was the driving force.

---

[12] See Weiss, *Fundamental Social Rights*, 1.

[13] In particular the Directive 76/207/EEC of 9 February 1976 on the Implementation of the Principle of Equal Treatment for Men and Women as regards Access to Employment, Vocational Training and Promotion, and Working Conditions (OJ 1976, No. L 39/40).

[14] Directive 75/129/EEC of 17 February 1975 (OJ 1975, No. L 48/29).

[15] Directive 77/187/EEC of 14 February 1977 (OJ 1977, No. L 61/27).

[16] Directive 80/987/EEC of 20 October 1980 (OJ 1980, No. L 61/27).

This pragmatic approach to social policy, however, turned out to be very fragile. It totally broke down when in 1980, due to the change of government in the United Kingdom unanimous decision-making was no longer a realistic option. The vulnerability of the social policy side of the EU became particularly evident when in 1989 the United Kingdom refused to sign the Community Charter of Fundamental Social Rights of Workers[17] and when the United Kingdom opted out of the Maastricht Social Protocol. This possibility of opting out clearly demonstrated that social policy was not yet considered to be an essential part of the Community's overall policy equal in importance to economic policy. Therefore it was no surprise that the request for fundamental social rights for the EU became a burning issue. The integration of fundamental social rights into the Treaty was understood to be a tool to guarantee the social profile of the Community and to make sure that the possibility of opting out in this particular area no longer was available.[18] However, as already indicated, the different attempts to promote this issue failed. The only modest result was the already mentioned, very unspecific reference to the European Social Charter and to the Community Charter in Article 136 paragraph 1 EC.

The category of fundamental social rights

In view of the emphasis given to fundamental social rights in the preceding discussion it was pretty clear that the Charter of Fundamental Rights to be elaborated was supposed to contain a chapter on fundamental social rights. The comité des sages, as well as the second group of experts on fundamental rights stressed in their respective reports the need to put fundamental social rights within the Charter on the same footing as the classical civil liberties. This position, however, met strong resistance throughout the deliberations of the concilium. Until the very end it was not at all clear whether fundamental social rights would remain included.

The arguments pushing back fundamental social rights are well known. They either are considered to be rights of a minor importance

---

[17] Reprinted in R. Blanpain, *Labour Law and Industrial Relations of the European Community* (The Hague, London, Boston, 1991), 211.

[18] See R. Blanpain, B. Hepple, S. Sciarra and M. Weiss, *Fundamental Social Rights in the European Union* (Leuven, 1996).

compared to the classical political rights or – even worse – they are considered not to be fundamental rights at all.[19] They are denounced as not being rights because they first of all impose obligations on the political actors to built up a framework in order to allow individuals to enjoy these rights. If for example the access to social security and social assistance is guaranteed (see art. 34), it is evident that the political actors first have to provide an infrastructure for such services. The same applies to the right to a high level of human health protection (art. 35), to the right of access to services of general economic interest (art. 36), to the right to a high level of environmental protection (art. 37) and to the right to a high level of consumer protection (art. 38). Provisions such as these are categorised as being merely defining political goals, thereby creating illusions and expectations which cannot be met.[20] The inclusion of such goals is supposed to delegitimise all the rest of the Charter. Therefore, only judiciable rights should be admitted to the category of fundamental rights.

The doubts about fundamental social rights are mainly to be explained by the late discovery of these rights in comparison with the classical set of human rights and civil liberties.[21] The arguments, however, are not convincing at all. First it has to be stressed that nowadays it even has become questionable whether the traditional categorisation still is valid. Formerly it was appropriate to categorise the classical fundamental rights as the rights of the individual to defence against the state, protecting an individual's position against state intrusion. Fundamental social rights, to the contrary, were understood as rights aiming at the provision of services by the state. This view, however, no longer can be supported. The original concept of classical fundamental rights as mere defence rights has changed dramatically. To take only the German constitutional doctrine: there the classical fundamental rights to a greater and greater extent are redefined as being not merely rights of defence against the state but rights of meaningful participation in society.[22] To give an example: the constitutional guarantee by which all persons are

---

[19] See e.g. H. Huber, 'Soziale Verfassungsrechte?' in E. Forsthoff (ed.), *Rechtsstaatlichkeit und Sozialstaatlichkeit* (Darmstadt, 1968), 11.

[20] See in particular D. Merten, 'Entwicklungsperspektiven der sozialen Dimension in der EG: Funktionen sozialer Grundrechte' in D. Merten and R. Pitschas (eds.), *Der europaeische Sozialstaat und seine Institutionenen* (Berlin, 1993), 63.

[21] See Europaeische Kommission, *Die Grundrechte in der Europaeischen Union verbürgen* 23.

[22] For an overview on this approach see E. Denninger, *Staatsrecht*, II (Hamburg, 1979), 162.

to be treated equally is no longer understood merely as a formalistic defence right but as a right to equal opportunities. Article 141 paragraph 4
EC actually is inspired by the same spirit. This means that classical fundamental rights in the meantime also are focusing on services provided
by the state, therefore the distinction between the two categories has
become much more difficult to make than in the past. This lack of a
clear-cut borderline is reflected by the content of the Charter, where
outside the chapter on 'solidarity' rights are established which by no
means are mere defence rights against the state, but establish an obligation to provide services and infrastructures. To give just some examples:
if according to art. 14 'everyone has the right to education and to have
access to vocational and continuing training', it is pretty evident that the
precondition for being able to enjoy such a right is an education system
which provides such services. This system and the respective services are
to be established and provided. The same applies if children are guaranteed 'the right to such protection and care as is necessary for their
well-being' (art. 24 para. 1) or if 'the rights of the elderly to lead a life of
dignity and independence and to participate in social and cultural life'
(art. 25) are to be respected.

It is certainly correct that it is a characteristic of fundamental social
rights to be judiciable only to a limited extent and mainly to formulate
goals to be met by the state, or in the case of the EU Charter, by the
Community. Quite often there is not, or at least not yet, an individual's
right to be directly enforced, but first of all an obligation to be fulfilled
by the political authorities. This, however, does not say anything against
these rights' quality as fundamental rights. In this context it is important
to understand that fundamental rights reflect the value system on which
a society is based. This perception of fundamental rights as an expression
of basic values has in Germany led to the concept of the horizontal
application of fundamental rights: the underlying values of fundamental
rights are not only to be applied in the relationship between citizens and
state but also in the relationship between citizens themselves.[23] They
define the profile of a society as a whole, and therefore have to be the
pillars of the system in all respects.

It is wrong to categorise fundamental social rights as of minor quality
compared to the classical fundamental rights. The guarantees of freedom

---

[23] Ibid., 151.

and equality only can be enjoyed in a substantial way if there is a social structure allowing the individual to make use of such rights. Anatole France's famous statement that the rich and the poor have the same right to sleep under bridges demonstrates impressively the distortion which classical freedom rights would suffer without a social structure supporting them. Therefore classical fundamental rights and fundamental social rights are two sides of the same coin. They cannot be separated, but have to be integrated. Or, as the report by the comité des sages puts it: 'The civic and social side of the building of Europe cannot remain its poor relation, for it would increasingly become a source of weakness, whereas it should and can become a source of progress, a goal to be attained.'[24] It was this very insight which finally led to the inclusion of fundamental social rights in the Charter.

It has to be stressed that of course not only the rights as listed in the chapter on 'solidarity' have an impact on the social sphere, in particular on the employment relationship. There is a whole set of such rights of the utmost importance in the social context. To give just some examples: the prohibition of forced labour (art. 5), the protection of personal data (art. 8), the freedom of thought, conscience and religion (art. 10), the freedom of expression and information (art. 11), the freedom of association, which implies the right of everyone to form and to join trade unions for the protection of his or her interests (art. 12), the already mentioned right to education and to have access to vocational and continuing training (art. 14), the right to engage in work and to pursue a freely chosen or accepted occupation (art. 15), the comprehensive prohibition of discrimination (art. 21), the guarantee of equality between men and women (art. 23), the right of persons with disabilities to benefit from measures designed to ensure their independence, social and occupational integration and participation in the life of the community (art. 26), and the citizen's right to freedom of movement (art. 45). All these rights do have a social side which cannot be separated from the remaining content. This shows again that it is difficult to draw the borderline between so-called classical fundamental rights and fundamental social rights. It is no longer possible to define fundamental social rights as a specific category. In any event they comprise much more than what is contained in the chapter on 'solidarity'.

---

[24] See *For a Europe of Civic and Social Rights*, 25.

The chapter on 'solidarity'

The chapter on 'solidarity' contains twelve provisions of a very different nature. The articles referring to health protection (art. 35), to environmental protection (art. 37) and to consumer protection (art. 38), as well as the right of access to services of general economic interest (art. 36) are mainly defining goals for the politics of the EU in a very broad and unspecific sense. However, the article on health care as well as the article on services of general economic interest at the same time establish an individual right to services under the conditions established by national law and practices. The provision referring to social security and assistance (art. 34) abides exclusively to the latter pattern and establishes an individual right in the framework as established by national laws and practices as well as by Community law. Article 33 on the protection of family life contains in its first paragraph an institutional guarantee but also a very vague and unspecific political goal (art. 33 para. 1) as well as an individual right (para. 2). Prohibition of child labour and protection of young people at work is guaranteed as an individual right (art. 32). The same is true for the rights of access to a free placement service (art. 29) and to protection against unjustified dismissal (art. 30), as well as to the right to fair and just working conditions (art. 31). The rights of collective bargaining and collective action are guaranteed as subjective rights either for workers and employers or for their respective organisations (art. 28). Finally, Article 27 provides for a subjective right for either workers or their representatives on information and consultation.

It may well be doubted whether this mixture in the same chapter of political goals and subjective rights is a strategy to be supported. As has been already mentioned and explained, the inclusion of political goals is inevitable. However, they should be strictly separated from subjective rights in order to make sure that they signify different things, otherwise the effect of delegitimising subjective rights cannot be excluded. It is becoming difficult for the reader of the Charter to distinguish the different significance of provisions all put together in the same chapter and – as shown above – sometimes even in the same article.

In specifying the freedom of association as guaranteed already by Article 12 paragraph 1 the Charter provides for the right to negotiate and conclude collective agreements and for collective action 'at the appropriate levels' (art. 28). This of necessity includes the Community level. However, there is a dramatic inconsistency. The right embedded in Article 28 only is guaranteed 'in accordance with Community law and national law and practices'. And Article 51 paragraph 2 stresses expressly that the Charter 'does not establish any new power or task for the Community or the Union, or modify powers and tasks defined by the Treaty'. This has to be related to Article 137 paragraph 6 EC which denies the Community's power to legislate in respect of 'the right of association, the right to strike or the right to impose lock-outs'. The consequence is evident: the Community is obliged by the Charter to promote a right for which it has no legislative competence whatsoever. This is a contradiction which might lead to the conclusion that the guarantee as provided by Article 28 is not meant to be taken seriously. Such an inconsistency certainly is not very helpful for the Charter's legitimacy. Therefore, and in spite of Article 51 paragraph 2 of the Charter, it is necessary to reach consistency by eliminating paragraph 6 of Article 137 EC in order to empower the Community to build up a legal framework for transnational collective bargaining including transnational collective action.

The wording of Article 28 ('collective action to defend their interests, including strike action') might be misleading. It repeats the wording of Article 6 paragraph 4 of the European Social Charter. There this passage has led to enormous controversies on the question whether only the right to strike is guaranteed or also the right to lock-out, a controversy which up to now has not been resolved in a satisfactory way.[25]

The fact that after quite a bit of resistance the workers' or workers representatives' right to 'information and consultation in good time' has been included (art. 27) is important. Thereby a development is supported and further strengthened which in the meantime is shaping the social face of the EU: the focus is on participation and cooperation instead of conflictual antagonism. This development has begun with the establishment of workers' participation with reference to specific subjects (collective redundancies, transfer of undertakings, health and safety), has reached a new dimension by means of the Directive on European Works Councils and has been further elaborated by the recent model of workers' participation in the context of the European company.[26]

---

[25] For this discussion see M. Mitscherlich, *Das Arbeitskampfrecht der Bundesrepublik Deutschland und die Europäische Sozialcharta* (Baden-Baden, 1977), 86.

[26] For this development see M. Weiss, 'Workers' Participation in the European Union', in P. Davies et al., *European Community Labour Law – Principles and Perspectives* (Oxford, 1996), 213.

However, it would have been better to formulate the text in a more open-ended way, to make provision for the accommodation of future developments. Whereas the Charter limits the workers' or workers representatives' right to information and consultation, the second expert group on fundamental rights went further by including 'co-determination'.[27] And even existing Community law goes further. Article 11 paragraph 2 of the framework Directive on health and safety[28] provides that 'workers shall take part in a balanced way, in accordance with national law and/or practices', which certainly is not confined to information and consultation and which for example in the German context definitely includes codetermination. Therefore, it would have been better to talk in Article 28 of the Charter of workers' participation in its broadest sense.

At least the authors of the chapter on 'solidarity' did not repeat the mistake made in previous drafts: to include the programme of social policy as a whole. They – at least in principle – succeeded in not confusing the fundamental rights with the instruments necessary to promote the values expressed by such fundamental rights. However, there are still parts to be eliminated. To give just one example: the guarantee contained in Article 31 paragraph 2, according to which 'every worker has the right to limitation of maximum working hours, to daily and weekly rest periods and to an annual period of paid leave', does nothing other than specify the guarantee provided by paragraph 1 of the same article, the right 'to working conditions which respect his or her health, safety and dignity'. Such specifications do not belong in a charter of fundamental rights. They refer to the instruments by which health, safety and dignity of working conditions are to be achieved. If they are confused with fundamental rights, this might well lead to the delegitimation of the Charter as a whole or at least of the chapter on 'solidarity'.

It might well be doubted whether the 'right of access to a free placement service' (art. 29) belongs in such a catalogue of fundamental social rights or whether this is not merely what is implied by the 'right to engage in work and to pursue a freely chosen or accepted occupation' as guaranteed by Article 15 paragraph 1 of the Charter. In addition it might well be doubted whether this 'fundamental right' corresponds

[27] See Europaeische Kommission, *Die Grundrechte in der Europaeischen Union verbürgen*, 26.
[28] Directive 89/391/EEC of 12 June 1989 on the Introduction of Measures to Encourage Improvements in the Safety and Health of Workers at Work (OJ 1989, No. L 183/1).

to a fundamental need of workers, given the fact that already specific groups of job-seekers in the upper levels of the job hierarchy are not at all interested in a free placement service. Such an example shows that more weight should be given to the question of what is fundamental in fundamental rights.

There is a very interesting inconsistency in the chapter on 'solidarity'. As already indicated, the Community is obliged to ensure a high level of human health protection, a high level of environmental protection and a high level of consumer protection. However, a high level of employment as a political goal to be achieved is not envisaged by the Charter. This discrepancy is difficult to understand.

It would have been very helpful and would have improved the interpretation of the text if the Charter had made it perfectly clear that nationals of third countries who are authorised to reside in the territories of the member states are covered by the fundamental social rights to their full extent. The Charter, however, contains different references to nationals of third countries in different places. In Article 15 paragraph 3 nationals of third countries who are authorised to work in the territories of the member states 'are entitled to working conditions equivalent to those of citizens of the union'. This certainly covers also the job-seeking procedure and thereby the guarantee contained in Article 29. However, it is not at all clear whether this also refers to the collective rights as contained in Articles 27 and 28. One might assume that the reference should be understood in this way, but it would have been better to spell it out more clearly. As far as social security and social assistance are concerned, 'everyone residing and moving legally within the European Union' is included (art. 34). Such a reference, however, is lacking in the context of health care, of services of general economic interest, of environmental protection and of consumer protection. It may well be questioned why nationals of third countries authorised to reside in the territory of the EU are excluded from these fundamental social rights. If fundamental rights are at stake it should be clear that every person residing legally in the EU is entitled to enjoy them. Otherwise the character of those rights as fundamental rights is put into question, representing another threat to the ligitimacy of the Charter.

In spite of the deficiencies mentioned above, it should be stressed that the mere fact that a whole chapter of the Charter has been devoted to fundamental social rights in itself signifies important progress. It is the result of a very controversial debate during which compromises were reached. It cannot therefore be surprising that the chapter does not contain an ideal structure and a fully coherent concept. And for the same reason the existing inconsistencies and deficiencies should not be overestimated. They might disappear in the course of integrating the Charter into the Treaty. It should not be forgotten, however, that the existing compromise was only possible in view of the fact that as a concession to fundamental social rights 'the freedom to conduct a business' (art. 16) is now recognised in the Charter. This means that a balance will always have to be found between the fundamental social rights and this freedom to conduct a business. In this respect lessons can be drawn from the jurisdiction of the German Federal Constitutional Court. The German constitution has a similar structure: fundamental social rights are competing with the employers' fundamental right to conduct a business. The Constitutional Court's efforts to establish a fair balance can be studied in the abundant case law material.[29]

IV. The implications of the Charter for the EU

The Charter is an expression of the fact that the EU is a Community based on values. The mere awareness of this orientation towards values may help to overcome the legitimacy crisis within the EU. All powers given to the Community – be they legislative, executive or judicial – are to be performed respecting these fundamental values. The set of values contained in the Charter means for the population of the EU a new possibility to identify itself with the European project. And it has to be understood that a signal is sent to the candidate countries to ensure that respect for these values is a precondition for joining the EU.

Fundamental rights as contained in the Charter will significantly facilitate the role to be played by the ECJ. As already mentioned, the ECJ has contributed in an impressive way to introducing fundamental rights into the Community by referring to external sources such as the European Convention of Human Rights and to internal sources such as the constitutional traditions of the member states. However, it cannot be expected that the ECJ should develop a holistic and coherent concept of fundamental rights by itself. This would endanger the ECJ's

---

[29] The reports of the Federal Constitutional Court's judgements has already exceeded a hundred volumes. For a very interesting example in this context see the judgement of 1 March 1979 on the constitutionality of the Act on Co-Determination (BVerfGE 50, 1).

legitimacy, because the Court would have to play a role which is not that of a judiciary. The Charter takes pressure off the ECJ by providing for it a reference system within which it can maintain its proper role. This does not mean that the ECJ will no longer be important in the context of fundamental rights, just the reverse: the ECJ's legitimate and challenging function will be to interpret and clarify the vague notions of the Charter, thereby acting as a true constitutional court.[30] The Charter, of course, only will lead to this effect to its full extent, if it is embedded in the Treaty. However, the ECJ has already shown that it refers to an increasing extent to the Charter as supported and adopted by all member states, even if in a legally non-binding version.

In spite of the reservation made in Article 51 paragraph 2, according to which the Charter 'does not establish any new power or task for the Community or the Union', there is no doubt that the Charter will increase the pressure to add new areas of Community politics in order to make sure that the requirements as established by the Charter can be met. Of necessity the Charter initiates a momentum which no longer can be stopped by national thinking in terms of sovereignty. Already the 1989 Community Charter of the Fundamental Social Rights of Workers – not really containing fundamental rights but merely describing a programme of social policy – has played a significant role in extending the Community's powers in the area of social policy. The same will be even more true of this comprehensive Charter for all areas of politics related to it.

The mere fact that the Charter in one and the same text combines classical fundamental rights and fundamental social rights means that greater emphasis is given to the relevance of social policy within the Community. Social policy no longer can be understood as merely a marginal annex to EU politics: now it definitely has become an essential part of it. At least as important is the signal given by the content of the chapter containing the fundamental social rights. They include collective rights and insist on the Community's and the member states' responsibility for providing job security, for providing working conditions which respect the worker's health, safety and dignity and for protecting young people at work. They furthermore insist on measures to make family and professional life compatible and to provide social security as well as social assistance. Taken all together it becomes pretty evident that this is a concept which would be incompatible with mere

---

[30] Whether and how far the ECJ is to be restructured in order to be able to cope with this challenge is a difficult question, not to be dealt with here.

deregulation, decollectivisation and de-institutionalisation.[31] Or to put it in broader terms: it would be incompatible with a strict neoliberal approach. Thereby the chapter on 'solidarity' reconfirms the European social model and strengthens it. This also is an important message to the candidate countries where the ideology of pure individualism and anti-collectivism still is rather widespread. Of course: whether this model on the long run will survive in the global context, is an open question. It, however, has to be stressed that the Charter's focus on the quality of work and working conditions is in line with the efforts made by the ILO in promoting 'decent work'. This shows that at least the EU has a powerful global ally in its attempt to rescue and promote a social profile.

V. Integration of the Charter into the Treaty

The question should no longer be whether the Charter is to be integrated into the Treaty on the European Union but rather when, how and by what procedure. For the Charter not to become part of the Treaty would mean that the member states are sending out a dramatically wrong signal, indicating that they have not meant the Charter to be taken seriously. This would destroy everything which was built up by elaborating the Charter. The whole concept of a Community based on fundamental values would be put into question. Therefore, there is no alternative to the integration of the Charter into the Treaty.

Integration means that the Charter as a whole has to become part of the Treaty's text. In order to provide the utmost transparency it certainly would not be sufficient simply to refer to the Charter somewhere in the Treaty.[32] Merely by reading the Treaty should the European citizen have the opportunity of seeing the whole catalogue of fundamental rights. Only the integration of the full text corresponds to the importance fundamental rights are to be given in the EU project. Or to phrase it even more clearly: the future core of the Treaty has to be the catalogue of fundamental rights.

Unfortunately in Nice no specified agenda for proceeding further was approved; everything still is open. However, there should be no doubt that the process of integration of the Charter into the Treaty has to be

---

[31] For an in-depth discussion of these concepts see B. Hepple, 'Economic Efficiency and Social Rights', in R. Blanpain (ed.), *Law in Motion* (Brussels, 1997), 868.

[32] See Europaeische Kommission, *Die Grundrechte in der Europaeischen Union verbürgen*, 24.

organised in a way which at least corresponds to the process by which the Charter was elaborated. The transparency and democratic legitimacy achieved by the concilium has now become the least that can be expected. This implies that the future of the Charter is not to be left to the mere discretion of the traditional mechanism of a governmental conference. The legitimacy base has to be much broader.[33] In view of the importance of this catalogue of fundamental rights for the future of the European project it seems essential that the population of the EU is made as aware as possible of the contents of the Charter and that a broad discussion is initiated throughout the Community. The consciousness of the crucial function of the fundamental rights to be embedded into the Treaty has to be spread. Since acceptability and legitimacy in this case are of the utmost importance, it might be advisable to put the Charter to a referendum. This referendum should take place in all the member states at the same time, thereby demonstrating that the EU population as a whole is giving its vote and that the Charter in essence is the people's Charter. Such a proceeding would certainly facilitate the implementation afterwards. The risks of such a proceeding should not be underestimated. First, it might be time-consuming and thereby delay the integration of the Charter into the Treaty. Secondly, the danger that the referendum will be a failure cannot be excluded. Balancing the advantages and disadvantages of such a proceeding, however, it seems to be clear that the advantages prevail. In view of the merits of a broad public discussion and of a referendum, the possible delay as a factor should not be overestimated. And the risk of failure of the referendum could be minimised by careful preparation. It will be important to communicate the content of the Charter as well as its function in a way which can be understood by everybody and which will make it possible for the population to identify itself with this project.

VI. Problems of implementation

Once the Charter has been integrated into the Treaty, problems of implementation will remain. As already indicated, the ECJ will play an important part in giving effect to the fundamental rights by judicial

---

[33] For such a strategy see E. Denninger, 'Anmerkungen zur Diskussion um Europäische Grundrechte' (2000) KritV 149.

interpretation. It will have to make sure that 'the institutions and bodies
of the Union . . . and the Member States . . . when they are implementing
Union law' (art. 51 para. 1) respect the fundamental rights. However, as
indicated above, particularly in the context of fundamental social rights
it is only goals that have to be met by EU policies. These provisions will
be legally binding like any other provision. They establish an obligation for the institutions and bodies of the EU to develop strategies to
meet these goals and thereby to fulfil these obligations. There has to be
a monitoring mechanism to make sure that the necessary measures are
undertaken and that the wording of the Charter is not without effect. The
structure as provided in the context of the Directive on the protection of
individuals with regard to the processing of personal data and the free
movement of such data could be a model.[34] There the Council is supposed to establish an independent supervisory body for the purpose of
monitoring the application of the Directive (art. 286 para. 2 EC). Such
an independent, democratically legitimised body would have to have
investigative powers. In discovering deficiencies it should be possible
for such a body to publish its findings, to make recommendations and
thereby to put pressure on the authorities of the EU. In the context of the
fundamental social rights it might be advisable to establish a structure
according to which such an independent body closely cooperates with
the social partners. Such a model could to a certain extent follow somehow the logic of the chapter on employment (arts. 125–30 EC), even if
an analogy only can be drawn in a very limited range. The function of
such a supervisory system in any case should be to put pressure on the
responsible actors and to force them to justify why they do not fulfil their
obligations in a satisfactory way. The proceedings of such a body would
have to be as transparent as possible. Thus the independent supervisory
body could initiate and stimulate public discussion and thereby spread
and promote public consciousness of the need for political measures as
implied by the fundamental rights.

In view of the fact that the ECJ and the European Court of Human
Rights (ECtHR) will have to apply what are in context the same fundamental rights, the question arises of how to organise the relationship between those two bodies. The Charter at least gives an indication

[34] For this analogy see Europaeische Kommission, *Die Grundrechte in der Europaeischen Union
verbürgen*, 22.

of how to proceed by stating that 'nothing in this Charter shall be interpreted as restricting or adversely affecting human rights and fundamental freedoms as recognised . . . by Union law and international law . . . , including the European Convention for the Protection of Human Rights and Fundamental Freedoms' (art. 53). This of course also means that what is guaranteed by the jurisdiction of the ECtHR is to be respected. In order to guarantee the consistency of the jurisdiction of the two courts it may be doubted whether the already existing pattern of informal cooperation is sufficient. It might be advisable to establish a mechanism eliminating different approaches. For questions already decided by the ECHR it might be sufficient to make the ECtHR judgements binding on the ECJ. For questions not yet decided by the ECtHR the system could be developed according to the model as provided by Article 234 EC: the ECJ might be allowed or even obliged to present to the ECtHR for a preliminary ruling the questions referring to fundamental rights as contained in the European Convention on Human Rights, in order to guarantee utmost consistency.[35] Whatever system is chosen, fundamental rights which are identical in the context of the EU and in the context of the Convention have to be interpreted the same way. Otherwise the danger of destroying their authority cannot be denied.

VII. Conclusion

The Charter as a coherent and comprehensive structure provides a new quality to the EU's process of constitutionalisation. It has to be integrated to its full extent. However, corrections to detail still are necessary, and the further destiny of the Charter should be subject to a transparent process, involving to a significant extent the population of the EU. In this way the catalogue of fundamental rights could become a people's charter, providing the most complete legitimacy. The process of elaboration in this case is as important as the end result. The discussion on the integration of fundamental rights into the TEU might lead – to take up the notion introduced by Jürgen Habermas into the German context – to something like a 'constitutional patriotism' for Europe, thereby

---

[35] This proposal had already been presented as a possibility in the report of the expert group: see Europaeische Kommission, *Die Grundrechte in der Europaeischen Union verbürgen,* 21.

becoming an important safeguard against any form of nationalism within the Community.

In addition it should be perfectly clear that the EU cannot now fall behind the stage which has already been reached in integrating civic and social fundamental rights, otherwise it would risk an enormous loss of legitimacy which might endanger the European project as a whole.

4

Market freedom and fundamental
social rights

SILVANA SCIARRA

I. How to defend the rationale of labour law and its function
as a legal discipline: re-forming

This chapter is built around a linguistic *escamotage*, which should lead
me to argue that labour law continues to play a very central role in
the current academic debate on European integration as well as in the
legislative implications at a national and supranational level. 'Re' as a
prefix repeated in the words appearing in the subheadings of this chapter
indicates that an intellectual effort is behind what may appear to be a
mere linguistic exercise. Labour lawyers place themselves in a leading
position, trying to act upon a complex procedure whereby economic
priorities should be dealt with in harmony with national legal traditions
and with the maintenance of a role for the social partners.

It will be argued in this chapter that the visible inclusion of labour
law reforms in supranational macro-economic policies, while accentu-
ating the fear of the gradual disappearance of this discipline from the
core of European law, might also have the effect of favouring innovative
discourses. The discourse on social rights, far from being a rhetorical exercise, is presented in this context as an opportunity to broaden the angle
of labour law analysis and link it to the ongoing discussion of new legal
methods which can be successfully associated with political reforms.

European labour law's best and most widespread heritage has been
reformist. This assertion reflects a well-established legal point of view,
which can be traced in both common and civil law countries. Since
the beginning of the twentieth century, passing through the – at times
dramatic – changes in legal regimes, it has been maintained that a free
choice would be the core of the contract of employment, similar in this

facet to other contracts.[1] Interpretation stemming from civil law was centred more frequently on maintaining and supporting formal equality between the contracting parties. This meant liberating the notion of 'subordination' from all negative values and allowing the employees to be part of the productive process.[2]

Labour law later on developed its own original tools to sharpen legal rationality and make it more functional in terms of the combined needs of employers and employees. On the one hand employers aimed at standardising production processes as well as rules to be strictly observed inside the enterprise. On the other hand one of the tasks of labour law became to provide guarantees for the individual employee, linked to his contractual obligations and aimed at creating participatory institutions at factory level.[3]

The common law's approach was masterfully and critically outlined by Kahn-Freund, who warned several generations of foreign and domestic interpreters on how little attentive British judges were to the implications of the contract of employment.[4] His comparative sensitivity and the many insights he offered on different legal systems brought

---

[1] A recent historical analysis, mainly centred on Italy, is in L. Mengoni, 'Il contratto individuale di lavoro' (2000) DLRI, 181 ff. The Spanish legal system is given a comparative analysis by A. Baylos, *Derecho del Trabajo: Modelo para armar* (Madrid, 1991). See also G. Lyon-Caen, 'Défense et illustration du contrat de travail' (1968) 13 Archives de philosophie du droit, 59–69; and B. Veneziani, 'The Evolution of the Contract of Employment' in B. Hepple (ed.), *The Making of Labour Law in Europe: A Comparative Study of Nine Countries up to 1945* (London, 1986), 31 ff. In relation to pre-war German labour law, O. Kahn-Freund wrote that it was 'a mixture of liberal–individualist and conservative–welfare legal ideas': see 'The Changing Function of Labour Law', in R. Lewis and J. Clark (eds.), *Labour Law and Politics in the Weimar Republic* (Oxford, 1981), 166.

[2] Mengoni, 'Il contratto' 184.

[3] H. Sinzheimer is the lawyer who best theorised the role of works councils in democratising the workplace in a similar manner to what occurred at state level during the Weimar Republic. His writings were collected by T. Ramm, *Arbeitsrecht und Politik.Quellentexte 1919–1933* (Berlin, 1966). They were also translated into Italian and collected, together with contributions by other authors, by G. Arrigo and G. Vardaro, *Laboratorio Weimer: Conflitti e diritto del lavoro nella Germania prenazista* (Rome, 1982). See in particular the introduction by G. Vardaro, 'Il diritto del lavoro nel "laboratorio Weimar" ', 7 ff., which exemplifies once more the need for European labour lawyers to go back to their roots.

[4] O. Kahn-Freund, 'Blackstone's Neglected Child: The Contract of Employment' (1978) 93 Law Quarterly Review, especially at 512–16 and 519–23; idem, *Labour and the Law* (London, 1977), at 22, states that the common law ignores the disequilibrium in the contract of employment. See also Wedderburn, *Labour law – From here to autonomy? A Franco-British Comparison*, in *Employment Rights in Britain and Europe: Selected Papers in Labour law* (London, 1991) especially at 109–11.

to the attention of a far-reaching and differentiated academic community a rich field of legal analysis, while emphasising the peculiarities of the British system. Methodological indications, as well as the author's personal choices in the selection of a lawyer's priorities, were very openly put forward: 'Law is a technique for the regulation of social power. This is true of labour law, as it is of other aspects of any legal system. Power – the capacity effectively to direct the behaviour of others – is unevenly distributed in all societies.'[5]

It is not the purpose of this paper to describe how this debate contributed to the flourishing of European comparative labour law. Neither can we investigate how postwar legal systems, which had opened up a significant space for collective labour law, were later confronted with sophisticated challenges resulting from comparative research.[6] The point to be made is that through the understanding of the social and economic function of individual contracts of employment, as well as of collective agreements, the discovery of further elements of legal innovation began.[7]

Reformism, possibly a characteristic strengthened by early comparative studies, was a key to disclosing labour law's potential in interacting with social forces and creating a specific role for collective actors.

Reformism was also the key which opened up a new scenario when, following the economic turbulence of the mid-1970s, labour law had to review some of its methods and learn how to adapt its own institutions to reduced economic resources. Comparative indications were once more drawn from the British system, affected by drastic changes which occurred under Conservative governments. The kind of reformist agenda set in those years by critics of a 'control by the market' is still

---

[5] Kahn-Freund, *Labour and the Law*, 3.

[6] A good example is G. Giugni's seminal book *Introduzione allo studio dell'autonomia collettiva* (Milan, 1960), 95 ff., in which the Italian notion of 'autonomy' of collective bargaining is confronted with Kahn-Freund's description of 'industrial autonomy' in the 'British System (Legal Framework)', in Allan Flanders and H. A. Clegg (eds.), *The System of Industrial Relations in Great Britain: Its History, Law and Institutions* (Oxford, Blackwell, 1954). It was in 1960 that Lord Wedderburn started to teach labour law at Cambridge, as he reminds us in Ch. 1 of this book.

[7] This is also one of the arguments which has emerged in S. Simitis's comparative analysis. See in particular his 'The Case of the Employment Relationship: Elements of a Comparison' in W. Steinmetz (ed.), *Private Law and Social Inequality in the Industrial Age: Comparing Legal Cultures in Britain, France, Germany, and the United States* (Oxford, 2000), 181 ff. For a critical assessment of the distinction between the legal significance and the social utility of the contract of employment, see Mark Freedland, *The Contract of Employment* (Oxford, 1976).

a valid starting point from which to evaluate current developments in several European countries.[8]

During the 1970s reformism in labour law had to come to terms with anti-inflationary mechanisms and with means of controlling wage bargaining. Later on the accent was put on labour market reforms: this too was a test bed for legal reformism, which had to redefine the entire scope of the discipline.[9] This discussion was carried on essentially at national level, since internal political compromises were far more pressing than supranational ties. In the current phase of European integration the same crucial issues are ingrained in broad macro-economic policies and are part of multi-level policy-making, which requires the active participation of several actors.

Two arguments must be put forward before proceeding to the next sections of this paper. One has to do with the autonomy of labour law from economic strategies when it comes to establishing and consolidating its own fundamental principles.[10] The second argument is that labour law is capable – and it always has been – of adapting to a broad economic framework in which the market and its regulatory methods seem to be dominant and exclusive. It is historically proven – and references provided earlier confirm such a statement – that, starting from the beginning, labour law has been fully permeated by industrial culture and has combined efficiency with the achievement of social goals.

Efficiency – as a leading Italian labour lawyer, commenting on national legal developments in the 1980s, has written – is not 'a principle for the settlement of social disparity';[11] it is a regulatory principle, a rule of the game, essential but not exclusive in setting a common point of reference for the conflicting parties. If we take efficiency as a starting point

---

[8] See the introduction by P. Davies and M. Freedland to O. Kahn-Freund, *Kahn-Freund's Labour and the Law*, 3rd edn ed. P. Davis and M. Freedland (Stevens, London, 1983).

[9] It was only in the early 1990s that international organisations discovered 'that it was no longer inflation, but employment which was now the crucial issue' as indicated by R. Dore, 'Introduction', in R. Dore, R. Boyer, Z. Mars (eds.), *The Return to Incomes Policy* (London and New York, 1994), 16. The book presents an interesting selection of national cases.

[10] For example, after a careful consideration of the function of labour law in supporting a social democratic or democratic socialist constitution, Keith Ewing concludes that 'The case for labour law...remains essentially a political one, though clearly the shape and content of labour law at any time will be determined to a large extent by economic and social constraints': K. Ewing, 'Democratic Socialism and Labour Law' (1995) 24:2 ILJ, 103–32, at 131, reference omitted.

[11] G. Giugni, 'Il diritto del lavoro negli anni "80"', in G. Giugni, *Lavoro, legge, contratti* (Bologna, 1989), 334.

and even as a shared value, we then have to find ways in which elements of compatibility with the consolidation of social rights can be established.

II. A market without a state in the EU: re-balancing

When presenting a dilemma such as market rights versus social rights we have to bear in mind the unusual institutional set-up which has characterised the European Community since its early days. The market followed its own path of integration without a state[12] and adapted all essential freedoms around its own fundamental values. When regard for social law was shown, it was oriented towards measures which would functionally interact with market efficiency.[13] Contrary to what happened within most national legal systems, in which labour law was, as much as possible, kept autonomous and apart from other state interventions, Community labour law from the beginning was by definition intertwined with market principles.[14]

Re-balancing is the technique national legislators have adopted over the years whenever labour law reforms were under threat, either because drastic reorganisation occurred in government or in conformity with a changed equilibrium among the social partners. Later on, during the years following the Maastricht Treaty, national re-balancing also became part of a new strategy of European integration, which strengthened market principles in view of new, prominent objectives.[15] The principle of coordination in economic and monetary policies (now in art. 99 of the EC Treaty, as amended by the Amsterdam Treaty) in accordance with the principle of 'an open market economy with free competition' (art. 98 EC) inspired national governments in all fields which fell under

---

[12] C. Joerges, 'The Market without the State? The "Economic Constitution" of the European Community and the Rebirth of Regulatory Politics', European Integration On line Papers 1997, n.19, available at http:/eiop.or.at/eiop/texte/1997-019 a.htm; P. Davies, 'The Emergence of European Labour Law', in W. McCarthy (ed.), Legal Intervention in Industrial relations: Gains and Losses (Oxford, 1992).

[13] G. F. Mancini, 'Effect of EC Law on Member States' Employment Law' in G. F. Mancini, Democracy and Constitutionalism in the European Union (Oxford, 2000), in particular at 114 ff.; G. and A. Lyon-Caen, Droit social international et européen (Paris, 1993).

[14] S. Deakin, 'Labour Law as Market Regulation: The Economic Foundations of European Social Policy' in P. Davies et al. (eds.), European Community Labour Law: Principles and Perspectives (Oxford, 1996).

[15] P. Beaumont and N. Walker (eds.), Legal Framework of the Single European Currency (Oxford, 1999).

the scrutiny of the Council of Ministers. Soft law measures, such as the Council's broad guidelines, demonstrated their effectiveness in reaching all targets and in monitoring subsequent economic performance.[16]

From then onwards, European labour lawyers have perceived the potential collision between market freedom and social rights as an intangible and yet existing threat to domestic traditions. Early steps towards monetary union echoed the academic and political discussion on asymmetric shocks and pointed to the centrality of labour market reforms and anti-inflationary wage policies.[17]

When the European Central Bank (ECB) started to be fully operative it soon became evident that while achieving price stability and pursuing statutory objectives, other areas could be informally addressed, either through the media or through the ECB's internal documents.[18] The practice of informal communications, be it through press conferences or speeches delivered by leading officials in the ECB, proved that, even in the absence of formal powers, political pressure can be put on governments and consequently on the social partners engaged in negotiations. This again may be seen as an element of innovation in national collective bargaining machinery, if negotiators choose to take seriously supranational monetary policies and translate them into national variables to be discussed at the bargaining table.[19]

Under these circumstances, economic stability in the monetary union, similarly to what has been said for the efficiency of the market, can easily be pictured as a dogmatic principle. Self-restraint by the central banks, a good practice as well as an essential element of equilibrium in national

---

[16] For references to the impact of such measures on collective bargaining see S. Sciarra, 'Collective Agreements in the Hierarchy of European Community Sources', in Davies et al., *European Community Labour Law*, 189 ff.

[17] P. Pochet (ed.), *Monetary Union and Collective Bargaining in Europe* (Brussels, 1999); C. Crouch, 'National Wage Determination and European Monetary Union', in Crouch (ed.), *After the Euro* (Oxford, 2000), 203 ff.

[18] See, for example, 'Developments in and structural features of the euro area labour markets', *ECB Monthly Bulletin*, May 2000, which urges 'further substantial improvements in the functioning of the labour markets'. Wages are, paradoxically, kept out of community competence (art. 137(6) EC).

[19] One interesting case is Finland, where EMU 'buffer funds' have been proposed to finance temporary reductions of payroll taxes in case of asymmetric shocks in the economy. See P. Holm, J. Kiander and P. Tossavainen, 'Social Security Funds, Payroll Tax Adjustment and Real Exchange Rate: The Finnish Model', Government Institute for Economic Research, 1999; P. J. Boldt, 'EMU and the labour market. The Finnish case', in T. Kauppinen (ed.), *The Impact of EMU on Industrial Relations in the European Union* (Helsinki, 1998), 62 ff.

industrial relations, should, on the contrary, still be pursued. Particularly at the EU level, industrial relations are characterised by the unevenness of institutional powers. The inclusion of the social partners in several committees and the granting to them of a consultative role even on matters of macro-economic policy cannot be compared to the practice of collective bargaining, neither has it the same political implications.

Notwithstanding the complexity of this policy-making apparatus and the uneven distribution of powers among social and political actors, the dilemma suggested at the beginning of this section of a sharp contrast between market freedom and social rights could be formulated in less drastic terms. Equilibrium among different regulatory sources inside the market is the correct notion to elicit. As Deakin and Wilkinson argue:

> Social rights, far from being inimical to the effective functioning of the labour market, are actually at the core of a labour market in which the resources available to a society, in the form of the potential labour power of its members, are fully realised.[20]

The argument labour lawyers have refined over the years is that legislation, both of a protective and an auxiliary denomination,[21] is not against the market but adds a different dimension to it. In the most consolidated and widespread reformist traditions originating in the 1970s, ranging from the Nordic systems of industrial democracy to the French, Italian and Spanish legislative support to trade unions, market-driven integration has never been perceived as a synonym for anarchy, neither has it implied disregard for democracy. Accordingly, not only is it possible to make an economic case for social rights – namely, that they operate as an input to the functioning of the market, by correcting

---

[20] Simon Deakin and Frank Wilkinson, 'Capabilities, Spontaneous Order and Social Rights', ESRC Centre for Business Research, University of Cambridge, Working Paper No 174 (2000).

[21] A lot could be said on this terminology. The notion of protective legislation, developed in civil law systems, reflects the unequal bargaining power of individual parties to the employment contract, '*sous le signe de l'ordre public*' as G. Lyon-Caen reminds us ('Défense', at 61). See P. Davies and M. Freedland, 'Labour Markets, Welfare and the Personal Scope of Employment Law' (1999) Comparative Labour Law and Policy Journal, 232, who criticise the terminology 'employment protection', imported into the United Kingdom from Scandinavia in the 1970s, and use instead the expression 'safeguarding the welfare of workers'. The notion of auxiliary legislation outlined by O. Kahn-Freund (for instance in *Labour Law, Old Traditions and New Developments* (Toronto, Vancouver, 1968), 29 ff.), influenced legislators and academics in continental Europe, particularly during the 1970s and predominantly in the area of collective labour law.

market failure;[22] in addition, it is arguable that diverse national systems of labour and social law across the member states of the EU enhance the competitiveness of the EU as a whole, provided core labour standards are maintained.[23]

The European common market was founded on rational choices of the member states, which very often reflected their specific economic interests.[24] The common market – as has been pointed out in many different ways and contexts – was not built around social values, but those inspiring national labour law systems were not endangered, nor were they diminished by the wording of Article 117 of the Rome Treaty, which, on the contrary, aimed at amplifying the role of the market as 'the principle vehicle of harmony',[25] namely upward harmonisation.

A stereotypical notion of economic rationality, which does not include social rights among the factors leading towards innovation, simply does not reflect the choices of the same member states at domestic level, spread across the many facets of legal intervention both of a protective and supportive kind.

Re-balancing indicates that some of the achievements brought about by reformist labour law may be under threat in the EU at a time in which we can envisage an even further consolidation of market principles. It also implies that labour lawyers should now exploit the instinctive capacity they showed in the past to reinvent their own thinking and to engage in a constructive dialogue with courts and legislators.

I maintain that in an open and fair comparison between competition law and labour regulations, scholarly work can play a crucial role in

---

[22] See Simon Deakin and Frank Wilkinson, 'Labour Law and Economic Theory: A Reappraisal' in G. de Geest. J. Seegars and R. van den Bergh (eds.), *Law and Economics and the Labour Market* (London, 1999). Compare Catherine Barnard's observations that the justification for EU social legislation should no longer be confined to the issue of addressing market failure or dealing only with matters having a transnational dimension: C. Barnard, 'Regulating Competitive Federalism in the European Union? The Case of EU Social Policy' in J. Shaw (ed.), *Social Law and Policy in an Evolving European Union* (Oxford, 2000), at 65.

[23] As Deakin and Reed argue, in the context of the debate over the European social model and regulatory competition between the member states, 'it should not be the aim of harmonisation to remove Member States' autonomy in the social field . . . Rather, the goal of harmonisation should be actively to preserve diversity at Member State level' so as to prevent a diminution of rights by means of a 'race to the bottom': S. Deakin and H. Reed, 'The Contested Meaning of Labour Market Flexibility: Economic Theory and the Discourse of European Integration' in Shaw, *Social Law and Policy*, n. 22, above, at 83.

[24] A. Milward, *The European Rescue of the Nation-State* (London, 2000).

[25] S. Simitis and A. Lyon-Caen, 'Community Labour Law: A Critical Introduction to its History', in Davies et al., *European Community Labour Law*, at 5.

influencing both fields[26] and lead towards successful cross-fertilisation. If we go back once more to Weimar and quote Kahn-Freund, we discover how an audible struggle among legal principles produced results which have been rediscovered later on and have come to be regarded as characteristic of the construction of European labour law. On the one hand the state had to establish a role for conflict and shape it around legal principles which were not to be confused with class struggle. On the other hand collectivism had to be nourished by an equilibrium between employers and employees.

> There is here a certain affinity between the legal system of collectivism and that of free competition. Both start from the premise that a struggle takes place within the framework of the legal system, and that this struggle, as a conflict between parties of potentially equal strength with potentially equal opportunities, produces a result which is susceptible to legal regulation.[27]

The dilemma we wanted to help solve is gradually fading away. Labour law's theoretical foundations are compatible with market economies, and legislative developments have not been driven by principles addressed to frustrating market performances. The history of European labour law proves, on the contrary, that markets at a national and supranational level acquire different dynamics when competition rules are balanced against social rules.

Collective bargaining is the most consolidated and powerful institution contributing to bringing some equilibrium to unbalanced economic situations. In national legal systems, collective agreements have been traditionally framed within a democratic design, which contributed towards the expansion of social goals, in parallel with other political achievements.

Looking at the supranational level, it has been insinuated that such an institution is part of a 'regulatory crisis' embedded in the Community. Collective bargaining would be nothing but a 'regulatory technique' deprived of constitutional roots, such as freedom of association and

---

[26] Lord Wedderburn, *Labour Law and Freedom* (London, 1996), 370–91.

[27] O. Kahn-Freund, 'The Changing Function of Labour Law', in Lewis and Clark, *Labour Law and Politics*, 172. This writing was later considered by the author almost 'an obituary notice', written under the influence of the deflationary measures taken by the Brüning government in 1930, which led to instances of severe interference with autonomous collective bargaining. See Kahn-Freund's postscript, ibid., 198.

the right to strike.[28] Similarly, the role of the social partners would only be instrumental to the overall objectives of supranational collective bargaining and lack real autonomy in the overall decision-making mechanism.[29]

Ways in which to transform collective bargaining into a 'regulatory and legitimacy resource'[30] have been indicated in legal research and are now part of a different discussion which includes several political options. Such a discussion has preceded the adoption of the Charter of Fundamental Rights and will no doubt continue in years to come, due also to the challenges coming from the case law of the European Court of Justice (ECJ).[31]

In this stage of renewed dialogue between courts and reformers – be they national or supranational or both – re-balancing means consolidating European labour law's constitutional roots and letting them expand in the same humus in which market freedom is developing. European competition law, unlike labour law, grew around a coherent set of rules directly applicable in national legal systems, and relied significantly on the role of national independent agencies. The European Commission's White Paper on the modernisation of antitrust rules indicates the need to specify further such a coherent approach, empowering national competition authorities to apply Articles 81 and 82 EC (ex arts. 85 and 86).[32]

An analogy can be drawn with a different field in which law can play a similar role, through mechanisms of direct enforcement. In order to combat organised crime, public authorities should be reintroducing rules in the market, and should create order and oppose it to the disorder introduced by illegal associations.[33] Institutions, in such a context,

---

[28] A. Lo Faro, *Funzioni e finzioni della contrattazione collettiva comunitaria: La contrattazione collettiva come risorsa dell'ordinamento giuridico comunitario* (Milan, 1999) (available in English as *Regulating Social Europe: Reality and Myth of Collective Bargaining in the EC Legal Order* (Oxford, 2000). See also Sciarra, 'Collective Agreements in the Hierarchy of European Community Sources', in Davies et al., *European Community Labour Law*, 13; J. Aparicio Tovar, 'Contrattazione collettiva e fonti comunitarie', in A. Baylos, B. Caruso, M. D'Antona and S. Sciarra, *Dizionario di diritto del lavoro comunitario* (Bologna, 1996), 173 ff.

[29] Lo Faro, *Regulating Social Europe*, 135.   [30] Ibid., 138 ff.   [31] See below, section III, 105–14.

[32] C. D. Ehlermann, 'The modernisation of EC antitrust policy: a legal and cultural revolution' (2000) CMLR, 537 ff. The White Paper on Modernisation of the Rules Implementing Articles 85 and 86 of the EC Treaty of May 1999 is in OJ 1999, C 132/1. It remains to be seen what the role of national judges will become and how national legal systems will deal with the controversial issue of introducing specialised courts.

[33] C. Donolo, *Disordine. L'economia criminale e le strategie della sfiducia* (Rome, 2001).

would be required to bring about transparency as opposed to hidden rules, to use prevention and support instead of punishment.

Institutions engaged in the social field – if we continue to draw this analogy – would be the ones to improve transparency in the labour market. One can think of the way in which the hidden economy should emerge and become visible as part of a healthy competitive system. It is reassuring to see that such measures are among the targets indicated by the Commission in planning employment policies.[34] The European social agenda approved at Nice, while stressing 'the role of social policy as a productive factor', also points out that the economic and monetary union is bringing about 'greater transparency in the comparison of costs and prices'.[35]

If these points reflect specific policy commitments, the reformist approach running through labour law and pervading its most solid institutions should be confirmed and supported at the European level.

III. Before and after *Albany*: re-establishing

It has been argued so far that at the beginning of labour law as well as during its recent history collective bargaining has been hinted at as the institution best suited to bring about equilibrium in the market and prevent unfair competition among social actors. Both a symbolic and a sound establishment in Western democracies, collective agreements are perceived as a dynamic factor of change as well as a conveyor of stability in the labour market.

After the ECJ's decision in *Albany*,[36] collective bargaining is also at the centre of a difficult intersection of disciplines and at times of conflicting points of view. A close examination of the Court's case law leads to the conclusion that re-establishing fundamental social rights within the European legal order is a necessary step in this critical phase of European integration. Re-establishing also indicates that this is not a completely

---

[34] As part of a strategy to combat undeclared work, member states are being urged, under Pillar II of the Employment Guidelines (Developing Entrepreneurship and Job Creation), to reduce and simplify the administrative and tax burdens on small and medium-sized enterprises: Council Decision of 19 January 2001 on Guidelines for Member States' employment policies for the year 2001 (OJ L 22/18), 2001/63/EC.

[35] European social agenda (2001/C 157/02), OJ C 157/4, 30.5.2001, respectively points 9 and 19.

[36] Case C-67/96, *Albany International BV* v. *Stichting Bedrijfspensioenfonds Textielindustrie* [1999] ECR I-5751.

new start. The patrimony of national constitutional traditions is a sound one, and many are the echoes coming from other international sources external to the EU.[37] Such a variety of approach increases the exigency of finding solutions directly generated inside the European legal order and to do so urgently, when the process of integration is in a mature state and the single currency is widely perceived as a positive factor of economic stability.

Re-establishing thus implies making use of procedures and norms, which go to the core of traditions, while emphasising recent and controversial developments.

In *Albany* the ECJ held that pension funds, set up by collective agreements to which affiliation was made compulsory by the Dutch public authorities for all workers in that economic sector, are undertakings within the meaning of Article 81 (ex art. 85) et seq. EC. The ECJ also ruled that granting an exclusive right to the fund for the purpose of managing a pension scheme does not infringe competition rules and does not imply abuse of a dominant position.

Within the Dutch pension funds discussed in *Albany* a collective agreement creates the scheme under which supplementary pensions are negotiated and guaranteed to all parties covered by the agreement itself in a given economic sector. In the Dutch system enforcing mechanisms are built around the power of the Minister of Social Affairs and Employment, at the request of a sectoral trade organisation which he regards sufficiently representative, to make the affiliation to the sectoral pension fund compulsory. His decision is assisted by injunctions against parties reluctant to pay.[38] The minister carries out careful investigations before externalising this very specific function; he consults the Insurance Board and the Social and Economic Council before adopting guidelines on exemptions from the fund,[39] paying special attention to the safeguarding of workers' rights.

---

[37] See Ch. 10 below; S. Sciarra, 'From Strasbourg to Amsterdam: Prospects for the Convergence of European Social Rights Policy', in P. Alston (ed.), *The EU and Human Rights* (Oxford, 1999).

[38] See para. 9 of the Court's decision.

[39] Workers who were already affiliated to a pension fund or had entered a life insurance scheme six months before the request made by a sectoral pension fund to the minister are not required to join the fund. It is also important to underline that such ministerial function runs parallel to the enforcement of legislation on pension funds which includes provisions on the Insurance Board's power of supervision.

These preliminary technicalities are not so marginal in the Court's judgement, which devotes attention precisely to the public authority's conferral on the pension fund of the exclusive right to manage pension schemes, without infringing Articles 82 and 86 (ex arts. 86 and 90) EC. Selecting criteria, adopting guidelines, guaranteeing the protection of individual rights can be described as a 'public' function of the minister, almost a continuation of state prerogatives. The minister relies on a collective and voluntary source and yet exercises his autonomous power.

An analogy can be drawn with all cases in which the extension of collective agreements through state measures – be they laws or decrees – or through judge-made law comes to express a functional link between different actors in the game. It does not affect the autonomy of collective parties, neither does it diminish their power to resort to lawful collective action. Law and collective agreements become in such cases interchangeable, while maintaining their own peculiarities. The latter are integrated by the former only for pursuing the effect of stability, which is inherent in the very notion of extension of the agreement *erga omnes*. In such a way, labour law has conceived one perfect way to harmonise market and social values and to combine market efficiency with respect for the autonomy of social institutions.

While proceeding through the narration of the Court's arguments, almost unexpectedly reference is made to Article 4(2) of the Social Policy Agreement (now art. 139 EC) and to the possibility management and labour have at Community level to apply to the Council for the implementation of an agreement.[40] It is a parallel drawn by the Court in order to justify further the decision of the Dutch public authority to make affiliation to a sectoral pension fund compulsory, without infringing competition law. It is difficult to understand why such different species of collective agreements, each based on its own legal order – one national, one supranational – should be offered as examples to be interpreted along similar lines of thinking. One justification could be that the Court is seeking to reinforce its own arguments by letting such collective roots penetrate as deeply as possible in Community law.

This point reflects the attempt made by Advocate General Jacobs in his Opinion when trying to establish that 'under normal circumstances'

---

[40] Para. 67 of the Court's decision.

there is a public relevance of collective agreements framed in the EC Treaty provisions.[41] The idea of 'normality' recurs in Jacob's contention that collective agreements are kept immune from competition law. Community law is treated as a public order, which should never be imperilled by unpredictable social factors. One of the reasons given for confirming the exemption from competition rules – in a rather intricate way – is that 'collective agreements between management and labour prevent costly labour conflicts, reduce transaction costs through a collective and rule-based negotiation process and promote predictability and transparency'.[42]

This static definition of a dynamic process which has been crucial in the construction of postwar European labour law cannot be totally convincing for labour lawyers, and might have negative implications in future interpretations of Community law. The result is to have only a very cautious definition of collective agreements: 'normal' when they deal with 'core subjects... such as wages and other working conditions'.[43] Furthermore, the immunity from competition law does not rely on subject matter only, but also on the 'framework' in which the agreement is concluded, namely a bilateral negotiation in good faith.[44]

References made so far to the Court's decision and to the Advocate General's monumental Opinion are meant to show that, when spoken outside its context, the language of labour law acquires different accents. In a national context it would be hard to imagine that a request put by management and labour to make compulsory the affiliation to a sectoral pension fund could be attacked as an agreement between undertakings. And yet the language of European competition law illustrates the reasoning of cross-frontier business against the national rules enforceable in one economic sector.

Jacobs makes the point that no general exemption from competition law can be suggested for the social field, but collective agreements can be given a special status.[45] This is a difficult conclusion to reach, since the EC Treaty only goes as far as encouraging collective bargaining, without

---

[41] Para. 185 Opinion.   [42] Para. 181 Opinion.   [43] Para. 178 Opinion.
[44] Para. 191–2 Opinion.
[45] Subsequently in *Pavlov* (Joined Cases C-180/98 to C-184/98, *Pavel Pavlov and Others* v. *Stichting Pensioenfonds Medische Specialisten*, [2000] ECR I-6451) Jacobs indicated that 'special immunity for collective agreements between management and labour cannot be extended or applied by analogy to other types of agreements or decisions,' para. 99 of the Opinion. The pension fund in this case was set by members of a profession.

mentioning any specific individual or collective right.[46] Nor can the ECHR be quoted as an external source to refer to, since the Strasbourg Court interpreted Article 11 very narrowly.[47] The implication behind this very learned journey through national and international labour law is that the inclusion of fundamental rights within the European legal system would not be a mere repetition of existing rights. It would rather serve the purpose of creating a collective area strong enough to interact with competition law.

Although labour lawyers reading *Albany* gain reassurance from the Court's decision exempting collective agreements from antitrust law, they have to come to terms with the idea that a pension fund is an undertaking within the meaning of European competition law. Since a collective agreement is behind the setting up of such a compulsory pension scheme, the fear cannot be completely removed that to be classified as an undertaking may add a totally unknown and unforeseeable dimension to the collective parties which are signatories to it.

And yet we have to acknowledge that in holding the pension fund compatible with competition law, the Court opens up the field of analysis to social law. 'A system ensuring that competition in the internal market is not distorted' (art. 3(1)(g) EC) – it is stated in an important passage of the Court's arguments – is included in the activities of the Community. 'A policy in the social field' (art. 2 EC) is part of such activities too.[48] This confirms the idea that 're-establishing' can be viewed as an indication if not a method in the Court's arguments and as an open process driven by judicial awareness of different and not conflicting objectives included in the treaties.

---

[46] Paras. 130 ff. with reference to the right to join a trade union or an association of employers, the right to resort to collective action.

[47] See paragraphs 144–145 and onwards of the Advocate-General's Opinion, which include the analysis of leading human rights cases, such as *Swedish Engine Drivers' Union* v. *Sweden* (6 February 1976, Eur. Court HR Rep., Series A, 20 (1976)) and *Gustafsson* v. *Sweden* (25 April 1996, RJD, 1996-II, No 9). See also S. Sciarra 'Individuals in search of fundamental social rights. Current proposals in the EU', in Dieter Simon and Manfred Weiss (eds.), *Zur Autonomie des Individuums. Liber Amicorum für Spiros Simitis* (Baden-Baden, 2000).

[48] See in particular paras. 60 and 75 of the decision. The mild language of the Treaty 'to promote throughout the Community a harmonious and balanced development of economic activities' and 'a high level of employment and of social protection' is inspiring for the Court in underlining social principles against competition rules. This point is followed by the Court in *van der Woude*; see below, n 61.

Despite the attention paid to Article 2 EC and the fact that collective agreements emerge from the Court's decision as institutions immune from competition law, the right to bargain collectively remains without a precise legal standing at Community level. This explains the complication of this case and at times some involutions in the presentation of legal arguments. It also explains why it gained the attention of both competition and labour lawyers for reasons of symbolic as well as of technical relevance.[49]

Re-establishing, as suggested, finds a concrete opportunity in the itinerary that labour law is designating within the EU. This also explains why *Albany* has been indicated as a demarcation point in the attempts made recently by the Court to stand at the crossroads of competition and labour law.

Before *Albany* two sides to the Court's rulings can be observed. One may be seen as an early defence of the territory occupied by competition law and as a defeat of social rules. *Merci Convenzionali*[50] became emblematic of a strong and painful contraposition between different sets of legal principles. It aroused the unconscious fears of labour lawyers who spoke of the 'infiltration' of competition law[51] and of 'vigilance' in the surveillance of national labour law.[52]

Poucet et Pistre,[53] followed by *Fédération Française des Sociétés d'Assurance*,[54] showed the Court's more 'solidaristic' face, whereas *Höfner*[55] and *Job Centre*[56] again put social values at the centre of a contested terrain. Both sides of this case law are characterised by a very careful adoption of concepts familiar to labour law and still extraneous to competition law.

Solidarity, when framed – as in *Poucet* – within a mandatory scheme and enacted between active and retired workforce, leads towards a

---

[49] Indicative of this combination of reasons is N. Bruun and J. Hellsten (eds.), *Collective Agreement and Competition in the EU* (Uppsala, 2001).

[50] Case C-179/90 *Merci Convenzionali Porto di Genova SpA* v. *Siderurgica Gabrielli SpA* [1991] ECR I-5889.

[51] Gerard Lyon-Caen, 'L'infiltration du droit du travail par le droit de la concurrence' (1992) Droit Ouvrier 313–21.

[52] A. Lyon-Caen, 'Droit social et droit de la concurrence: Observations sur une rencontre', in *Orientations Sociales du Droit Contemporain: Ecrits en l'honneur du Pr. Jean Savatier* (Paris, 1992), 343.

[53] Joined Cases C-159/91 and C-160/91 *Poucet et Pistre* [1993] ECR I-637.

[54] Case 244/94 *Fédération Française des Sociétés d'Assurance* [1995] ECR I-4013.

[55] Case C-41/90 *Höfner and Elser* v. *Macroton GmbH* [1991] ECR I-1979.

[56] Case C-55/96 *Job Centre* [1997] ECR I-7119.

reassuring confirmation of states' prerogatives in the social field, far from the notion of undertaking suggested in Article 81 (ex art. 85) EC. In *Fédération Française* the optional nature of old-age insurance, albeit operated under strict public control, and the principle of capitalisation to which it was inspired, offer a different ground for the Court's reasoning. There is an undertaking behind this different social function, even though the Court does not go as far as indicating that there is also abuse of a dominant position. Payment mechanisms – capitalisation as opposed to 'pay as you go' – not surprisingly become central to ascertain the nature of the social institution in question and so can become the non-profit qualification of the same.[57]

However, in an area in which national traditions often make a sensible differentiation in assigning the social label to institutions active in the field, to establish objective criteria becomes a difficult task. This is also why the 'principle of solidarity', evoked to explain the functioning of the sectoral pension fund,[58] is represented very distinctively in *Albany*, as previously pointed out, due to the fact that fundamental labour law principles are at stake. Reference to *Poucet et Pistre* is promising in establishing what is already a path in the Court's case law and in building on it. However, solidarity, referred to as a leading idea, not as a legal principle, is not strong enough to deprive the sectoral pension fund of its status as an undertaking within the meaning of the competition rules of the EC Treaty.[59]

No safety net is provided for the Court's arguments in *Höfner* and in *Job Centre*.[60] Controlling competition law's congenital capacity to invade other territories is too difficult a task when social functions are accomplished by institutions active in the labour market. It is most evident in

---

[57] As underlined by S. Giubboni, 'Social Insurance Monopolies in Community Competition Law and the Italian Constitution: 'Practical' Convergences and 'Theoretical' Conflicts' (2001) ELJ, at 72–76.

[58] In para. 75 of the Court's judgement mention is made of the fact that all workers are accepted without prior medical examination, there is entitlement to pension rights even in cases of incapacity to work, the calculation of pension rights is made by reference to an average salary.

[59] Jacobs dealt with a similar issue in *Pavlov* (above, n. 45), arguing that the pension fund set by members of a professional association, ruled by capitalisation principles, is an undertaking, but does not abuse its dominant position in the market. The Court decided along similar lines, at paras. 82 and 128 of the Court's decision.

[60] S. Sciarra, '*Job Centre*: An Illustrative Example of Strategic Litigation', in S. Sciarra (ed.), *Labour Law in the Courts: National Judges and the European Court of Justice* (Oxford, 2001), at 241 ff.

Job Centre that the Court's notion of solidarity does not rely on an autonomous notion of collective and diffuse interests to be addressed, but rather depends on whether the efficiency of the market is maintained. In the Court's reasoning solidarity does not mirror state priorities, neither can it operate as a regulatory principle affecting the social goals of a given society. One has to wonder whether relying on more visible fundamental social rights inside the European legal order would have guided the Court through these still fairly unknown territories of social law.

It was suggested that *Albany* marked a divide in the Court's rulings. A series of cases following it can be positively evaluated from the point of view of labour law. In *Van der Woude*[61] the Court held collective agreements concerning voluntary supplementary health insurance to be compatible with Articles 81 and 82 (ex arts. 85 and 86) EC. Advocate General Fennelly quotes the relevant passages in *Albany*[62] and leads the Court to a judgement moving a step forward. It is argued that the scope of collective agreements can be expanded as to the inclusion of health insurance within the legitimate 'core subjects', without breaching competition rules. It is established that core working conditions are subject to an extensive interpretation and that even the link with a third party – another insurer – for the implementation of the collective agreement is compatible with competition law.

The leading argument is that a dominant position should not automatically be termed an abuse and that such a decision should be left to national judges. Such an argument, well introduced by the Advocate General's Opinion and present in the Commission's written observations, frees the Court from competition law technicalities and leaves more space to the interpretation of collective agreements. It is not irrelevant that at the hearing the United Kingdom had asked the Court to clarify whether the '*Albany* exception' should apply to enterprise-level agreements; the positive, albeit interlocutory, answer given by Fennelly is yet another promising sign.[63]

In another recent Opinion delivered by Advocate General Jacobs, *INAIL*,[64] the Italian public law body in charge of compulsory insurance

---

[61] Case C-222/98, *Hendrik van der Woude* v. *Stichting Beatrixoord*, ECR [2000] I-7111.
[62] Paras. 19 ff.   [63] Opinion para. 14.
[64] Case C-218/00 *Cisal di Battistello Venanzio & C. Sas* v. *INAIL – Istituto Nazionale per l'assicurazione contro gli Infortuni sul Lavoro*, Opinion of Advocate General Jacobs delivered 13 Sept. 2001 [Judgement of the Court, 22 Jan. 2002].

against accidents at work and occupational diseases has not been considered an undertaking for the purpose of competition rules.[65] Jacobs is extremely careful in offering a different classification for such a body. He maintains that the 'mission' provided by the Italian Constitution in Article 38, whereby the tasks to insure workers in the above-mentioned cases must be assigned to bodies set up by the state, should not 'influence its classification' because 'competition rule must apply uniformly throughout the Community'.[66] Once more, state priorities must be excluded from the line of reasoning followed by the Court, to ensure the supremacy of competition law.

The presentation of the Court's case law in an area crossing the borders of two legal disciplines indicates that there are ways to reconcile apparently conflicting points of view. The suggestion is that such a reconciliation is already taking place in the Court's rulings, but is jeopardised by unbalanced premises in the treaties. The reason why such a lacuna appears incomprehensible now – as opposed to the early days of the EC – has to do with the unpredictable and original ways in which integration is materialising. The market is still without a state, but much stronger elements of unification have occurred both in the market and in the EU as a whole. Even the Court's attitude to acting as a quasi-federal court has indicated ways in which to integrate further national legal systems.

If we try to draw some conclusions from the key ideas brought forward in the Court's rulings, we discover that we are dealing with principles – such as solidarity – which have inspired most constitutional traditions of the member states and have given ground to the construction of welfare states. If we move to the notion of undertaking, we face a different legal reality: not a principle, but simply an adaptable legal entity, shaped by judicial interpretation in order to fit market necessities. The principal aim thus becomes to strengthen the notion of an undertaking in such a way that it should not depart from a well-accepted interpretation of Articles 81 and 82 EC.

The discussion under way on the modernisation of antitrust policy indicates very clearly that the main issue at stake is the redistribution of powers between national and European authorities, including national

---

[65] At para. 29 of the Advocate General's Opinion. S. Giubboni, above at n 43 comments on the preliminary reference made by an Italian court, which is the basis for this case.

[66] Para. 47 of the Opinion.

courts.[67] Article 81(3) EC is central in such a discussion; this confirms that we are dealing with exceptions rather than with principles. Although both are subject to interpretation, the former reflect the results of market adjustments, the latter address legal policies in many different fields. Whereas agreements, decisions and concerted practices constitute specific points of equilibrium in economic transactions, solidarity is at the core of social justice and of related mechanisms of distribution of resources.

IV. Two different legal devices, the Employment Title and the Charter of Fundamental Rights: re-thinking

In framing all that has been argued so far in an historical perspective we can see how the history of social policies since the beginning of the Community has been characterised by the lack of institutional premises, due mainly to decision-making mechanisms.[68] The long-lasting debate on unanimity vs qualified majority voting within the Council has marked the origin of European labour law and has indicated the way forward for opening up larger spaces to social issues.

Re-formists have maintained that constant steps forward have been made in different areas of social policies, notwithstanding slow and at times contradictory institutional choices, which showed from time to time the proclivity of economic manoeuvres to pre-empt other fields.[69]

Re-thinking in this case means discovering an inclination of labour lawyers to apply a non-traditional legal method when dealing with new legal devices. Such a capacity is magnified in recent developments of European law. The apparent paradox is to transform the weak sides of a process still *in fieri* into permanent, albeit not always very powerful, gains.

The two examples chosen to illustrate 're-thinking' are very different and yet they both address the issue of empowering the European legal order with new underpinnings. Broadening the legitimacy of the

---

[67] See Ehlermann, 'Modernisation of EC antitrust policy', who underlines the much stronger responsibility of national courts, should art. 81(3) be subtracted from the Commission's monopoly.

[68] S. Sciarra, 'European Social Policy and Labour Law. Challenges and Perspectives', in *Collected Courses of the Academy of European Law*, IV, Book 1 (The Hague, 1993).

[69] See generally Shaw, *Social Law and Policy* n. 22 above.

European legal system is an underlying issue in both cases, be it through the involvement of the social partners in national and supranational employment policies, or through consultation of civil society during the drafting of the Charter.[70]

The Employment Title is based on a very flexible infrastructure of Council guidelines; it aims at stimulating voluntary choices by the member states, which should then be coordinated in a broader institutional frame.[71] The geometry is that of a circle, around which decisions are taken without being necessarily implemented by the initial decision-makers. They are channelled through successive filters, which leave sufficient space to national prerogatives without removing power from the central institutions. They then go back to the starting point in the circle: Article 128 EC deals with the Council's obligations to issue guidelines each year, to be then taken into account by member states in their employment policies.

The interesting side of this circular geometry is that there are no sanctions to assist the European institutions, if member states perform poorly or if they don't follow the guidelines at all. However, moral sanctions, possibly linked to market sanctions, seem to induce member states to move towards a convergence of their choices, possibly helped by the Commission's continuous efforts to bring forward indicators on employment and on labour markets.[72] Nevertheless, as Diamond Ashiagbor argues, the flexibility of this infrastructure and the absence of hard law mechanisms means that there is a risk that employment creation and macro-economic policy objectives continue to have priority over social rights.[73] A similar note of caution is sounded by Deakin and Reed, who suggest that:

> As long as there is no institutional means by which the harmonisation
> of social rights can be built into the employment strategy, there is a
> danger that the kind of convergence to which the Employment Title

---

[70] See now, as an example of what appears to be an indication spreading across different sources, art. 14 of Council Directive 2000/78/EC, OJ L303/16, establishing a general framework for equal treatment in employment and occupation, in which 'dialogue' with NGOs having an interest in fighting against discrimination and promoting equal treatment is suggested.

[71] Erika Szyszczak, 'The Evolving European Employment Strategy' in Shaw, *Social Law and Policy*, at 197 ff.

[72] For the latest employment indicators see Commission of the European Communities, *Joint Employment Report 2001*, Brussels, COM(2001) 438 final.

[73] D. Ashiagbor, 'EMU and the Shift in the European Labour Law Agenda: From "Social Policy" to "Employment Policy" ' (2001) 7:3 European Law Journal, 311–30.

will give rise is one based on the kinds of 'structural adjustment' which are envisaged by EMU – or, in other words, deregulation.[74]

There is no fundamental 'right to work' behind this procedural effort to bring together criteria and evaluations of employment policies. Neither can we talk in terms of individual rights to be enforced under such procedures. The circle we described is an institutional one, linking together member states and European institutions, but the unemployed or the under-employed or those seeking employment are located somewhere else, outside the decision-making mechanism. They are also left with their own ways of seeking relief from their state of being the underprivileged or less privileged in the labour market. In this sense, one could say that even on these matters the European market is without a state, although national markets are asked to seek further ways of integration through co-ordination.[75] This in itself is a challenging task, which forces labour lawyers to re-think their realm of intervention.

The Nice Charter,[76] the second example chosen to illustrate 're-thinking', despite its weak standing as a non-binding legal source, aims at inspiring more prescriptive and uniform legal choices. Even in fields outside the competence of the EU the provisions of the Charter can be viewed as 'the expression of common values against which Union institutions and Member States could not make s stand, even if they do not have to implement them'.[77]

Social rights are spread across various chapters of the Charter: mainly concentrated in the chapter entitled 'solidarity', they are also included among fundamental freedoms[78] and are present among rights on equality and non-discrimination.[79] Even though the language adopted may sound at times not too accurate, it can be maintained that the intention

---

[74] Deakin and Reed, 'Contested Meaning', at 97.

[75] S. Sciarra, 'Integration through coordination: the Employment Title in the Amsterdam Treaty', [2000] Columbia Journal of Economic Law, 209 ff.

[76] Charter of Fundamental Rights of the European Union, OJ 2000/C 364/01. See also the Presidency Conclusions, Cologne European Council, 3 and 4 June 1999, SN 150/99 and the indication to make fundamental rights' 'overriding importance and relevance more visible to the Union's citizens'.

[77] Editorial comments [2001] Common Market Law Review, 4.

[78] Art. 12 deals with freedom of assembly and freedom of association and spells out that the right to form and join trade unions is implied. This appears to be a compensation for the exclusion of such freedom from EC competence (Art. 137(6)), but could also be seen as a contradiction.

[79] Art. 21 adopts a wide notion of non-discrimination; art. 23 includes employment in the areas in which equality between men and women must be guaranteed.

of the Charter is to expand the field of equality. Albeit in a very indirect way, a link is established between a fundamental right and policy orientations previously developed in a specific field, such as employment. A 'pillar' (namely, equal opportunities) in non-binding guidelines addressed to member states is also made visible as a fundamental principle in a non-binding Charter, thus providing an interesting source of inspiration for the ECJ. The process of open coordination is in this way mirrored in another soft legal mechanism of integration. A similar thing can be said for the concept of mainstreaming and the incorporation of equality considerations into other areas of law-making.[80]

In the chapter on solidarity the choice has been made to enshrine fundamental rights – both individual and collective – which are closer to labour law traditions of the member states. Whereas some of them, such as the right to health care and the right to benefit from medical treatment (art. 35), go beyond the scope of labour law, some others, such as the protection against unjustified dismissals (art. 30), are closely related to the contract of employment. The inclusion of this latter issue among the areas in which the Council should act unanimously (art. 137(3) EC) has not led so far to legislative initiatives. This has alarmed some observers who fear that the Charter is allowing the inclusion of 'new' rights, not covered by EC directives.[81]

Similarly alarming is the expansion of other rights, such as those to information and consultation, which are dealt with in secondary legislation, but never were ranked as fundamental and served purposes somehow dependent on the exercise of other rights.

The most strident contradiction is the mention of the right to take collective action, including strike action (art. 28), otherwise excluded from EC competence in Article 137(6) EC. As for the right of access to free placement services (art. 29), one could relate this to well-established national legislative traditions aimed at protecting weaker subjects in the labour market. This particular example of solidarity, when opposed to criteria of market efficiency, has been submitted to the ECJ in some cases previously mentioned.[82]

---

[80] M. Bell, 'Mainstreaming equality norms into European Union Asylum Law' (2001) ELRev, 20.

[81] B. Hepple, 'The EU Charter of Fundamental Rights' (2001) 30 ILJ, at 227, reports the fears of the Engineering Employers' Federation (EEF) which represents a large number of British companies.

[82] See above section III, in particular *Höfner* and *Job Centre*.

Even at a first glance, one can observe that fundamental social rights included in the Nice Charter have been organised around very unconventional criteria. The lack of a specific *sedes materiae* and the decision to scatter them in several chapters, however arguable, shows that social rights may be approached in many ways. Whereas the right to equality between men and women only needed to have its constitutional relevance confirmed and specified, even with a reference to affirmative action, rights which are closer to expectations or aspirations needed to be exposed to 'positivisation'.

In this sense the idea – first signalled by the 'Simitis Report'[83] and then reaffirmed in the Charter's Preamble – of making rights visible in order to increase the chances of their justiciability, seems a successful one. Non-justiciable social rights, criticised because they would be nothing but mere objectives to be pursued by the states, are proposed in the framework of the Charter as the original basis of a supranational legal order undergoing modifications.

Solidarity, often regarded as a concept and as a philosophical design, now stands up as a political programme central to the process of integration through coordination. At the same time solidarity is the connective thread keeping together a number of social rights crucial for acquiring an internal balance to the process of integration.

The image reflected through the analysis of such different legal instruments – a Title in the TEC and a Charter placed outside the Treaties – is that of the European legal order as an open process in a state of constant transformation. Labour lawyers observing such a process never cease to seek deeper levels of integration. In a way similar to what they have done in the past, acting at a national level, they tend to go beyond market integration, without being against the market.

Both examples were chosen in order to prove that attempts have been made to balance provisions in the EC Treaty. As the single currency – a most visible sign of the delegation of national prerogatives to a centralised institution – has been described as a metaphor of integration,[84]

---

[83] *Affirming Fundamental Rights in the European Union: A Time to Act*, Report of the Expert Group on Fundamental Rights, chaired by Professor Spiros Simitis, Office for Official Publications of the EC (Luxembourg, 1999).

[84] F. Snyder, 'EMU – Metaphor for European Union? Institutions, Rules and Types of Regulation', in R. Dehousse (ed.), *Europe After Maastricht: An Ever Closer Union?* (Munich, 1994), 63–99; see also F. Snyder, 'EMU Revisited: Are We Making a Constitution? What Constitution Are We Making?' in Paul Craig and Gráinne de Búrca (eds.), *The Evolution of EU Law* (Oxford, 1999).

we can propose social law as its opposite, namely a fair 'description' of current attempts to create a common core of rights. In its messages social law often lacks 'prescriptions', therefore it appears as a weak instrument, particularly as compared with other ways of insinuating European law into national legal systems.

In a still descriptive phase, while future developments are being envisaged, procedural norms – such as the ones in the Employment Title – stand as a counterpart to monetary policies. Soft law needs to prove once more its usefulness in an overall social law strategy which should bring closer together all elements of market integration.

Whereas in monetary policies states have directed the powers of national central banks towards a supranational institution, in social policies states are retaining as many powers as they can, while at the same time defending national traditions, be they constitutional or based on customs and practices, even at decentralised levels. In this context the Charter represents a reminder of possible scenarios.

In *BECTU*[85] Advocate General Tizzano, after quoting extensively international sources external to the EU, refers to the Charter of Fundamental Rights as 'an even more significant' source, despite its non-binding nature, due also to the fact that it includes statements which reaffirm rights 'enshrined in other instruments'.[86] The ECJ in its ruling states that the improvement of workers' safety – which lies at the origin of this case dealing with rights to paid annual leave – is not to be 'subordinated to purely economic considerations'.[87] Even though no reference is made to the Charter, in line with a self-restraint that the ECJ has chosen to adopt while the political discussion on this contested document occupies the scene, this judgement is a relevant and inspiring one.

In *Schröder*[88] and in *Sievers and Schrage*,[89] all of which were cases decided before the proclamation of the Charter and dealt with indirect

---

[85] Case C-173/99, *R* v. *Secretary of State for Trade and Industry, ex parte: Broadcasting, Entertainment, Cinematographic and Theatre Union (BECTU)* [2001] ECR I-4881.

[86] Opinion of Advocate General Tizzano, delivered on 8 Feb. 2001, paras. 26 and 27. See also para. 22 in which Tizzano places the issue of paid annual leave 'in the wider context of fundamental social rights'. See the commentary to this case by G. Ricci (2001) 30 ILJ 401–408. In Case C-133/00 *J. Bowden and Others* v. *Tuffnells Parcels Express Ltd* (Opinion delivered on 8 May 2001) the same argument is developed by Tizzano.

[87] Para. 59 of the Judgement.

[88] Case C-50/96 *Schröder* [2000] ECR I-0743. Advocate General Cosmas elegantly argued in his Opinion (delivered on 8 Oct. 1998, para. 80) that the principle of human dignity needs to be recalled when dealing with equality between men and women.

[89] Joined case C-270/97 and C-271/97 *Sievers and Schrage* [2000] ECR I-0929.

discrimination, the ECJ went as far as to say that the social aim pursued by Article 141 (ex art. 119) EC, to be regarded as a 'fundamental human right', is primary when compared with eliminating distortions in competition between undertakings in different member states.

The language adopted in such recent cases is such that there are indications that it is possible to see a very open attitude towards the understanding of social law as an evolving subject. The process of integration is open to inputs from all institutional and non-institutional actors and is capable of assimilating the language of fundamental social rights as a powerful vehicle for making various initiatives more cohesive.

V. Conclusions

The linguistic *escamotage* referred to at the beginning of this chapter has not been suggested as part of an old-fashioned rhetoric of labour law. It wants to communicate the fear that the rationale of labour law as a discipline can be brought into question when discussing fundamental social rights in an evolving European legal system. It is also meant to stimulate the search for innovation in labour law regulatory techniques, particularly when they need to be adapted to supranational and multiple levels of policy-making.

The main challenges to such an adaptation seem to come from European competition law. This observation is not made – and the examination of leading ECJ cases is intended to prove this point – from a subordinate position, as if there were an inferior angle of observation of the social and economic issues at stake.

The analysis here suggested, while emphasising the need to reestablish social priorities, also accentuates elements of compatibility with market principles. The tension between market freedom and social rights is not irreconcilable. Unequal starting points were set in the Treaties for two regulatory techniques, which, if not corrected, could perpetuate an unbalanced equilibrium. This would bring about, as has been suggested in this chapter, negative consequences for market efficiency and would imperil the role of national social institutions.

It appears contradictory – and once more not very effective – to accept that the social partners may play a major role at national level, even in the implementation of European law, while maintaining a critical position at supranational level, because of the feeble institutional premises set in the Treaties.

In order to imbue European labour law with the same re-formist aspirations present as a common element in the majority of member states and confirmed in different historical phases, institutional changes need to be under way. The suggestion to European re-formists at work is to allow themselves sufficient imagination. Labour lawyers can generously contribute to envisaging the 're-discovery' of national traditions and witness the 're-birth' of a legal discipline, which over the years has so notably expanded the breadth of European legal culture.

5

Corporate governance, European governance and social rights

CATHERINE BARNARD AND SIMON DEAKIN

I. Introduction

The quality of European governance has long been a running sore in the EU, with concerns being widely expressed about a democratic deficit and a lack of legitimacy, transparency and accountability. Recognising this, the European Commission has decided to make 'better European governance' its top strategic priority. This led to the publication of the White Paper on European governance in July 2001[1] which is based on the premise of 'opening up the policy-making process to get more people and organisations involved in shaping and delivering EU policy' and promoting 'greater openness, accountability and responsibility for all those involved'.[2] More generally, the White Paper explains that European governance concerns 'rules, processes and behaviour that affect the way in which powers are exercised at European level, particularly as regards openness, participation, accountability, effectiveness and coherence'.[3]

While the European governance debate, certainly as currently conceived, is of a rather recent origin, the corporate governance debate is of much longer standing. Corporate governance concerns 'the system by which companies are directed and controlled'.[4] This includes the

---

We are grateful to participants at the conference, and in particular to the discussant, Paul Davies, for comments on an earlier draft.

[1] COM(2001) 428. For the working document 'European governance' see SEC(2000) 1547/7 and the website http://europa.eu.int/comm/governance/index_en.htm.

[2] COM(2001) 428, 3.   [3] COM(2001) 428, 8.

[4] This definition was offered by Sir Adrian Cadbury at the time of the Cadbury Report in 1991 and was adopted by the Hampel Committee on Corporate Governance in its report in 1998. A Combined Code, consolidating the work of the Cadbury, Greenbury and Hampel reports,

management of companies, the financial regulation of companies' activities and the accountability of directors to the shareholders. More broadly, it is about the role accorded by the law to the different 'stakeholder' groups who have vital interests tied up in the success or failure of the corporate enterprise.[5] As such, it is vitally concerned with the scope and strength of social dialogue and other processes of worker involvement in corporate decision making. The European governance agenda also envisages a greater role for the 'new players' in Europe, in particular 'civil society'.[6] According to the White Paper, civil society 'plays an important role in giving voice to the concerns of citizens' and delivers 'services that meet people's needs'.[7] *Primus inter pares* of these new actors (at least to date) have been the social partners[8] who, as we shall see in section III, are involved in decision making at all levels. As the Economic and Social Committee has argued, 'It is impossible for good European governance to exist without the genuine involvement of the social partners and the third sector; but such involvement in turn creates a genuine responsibility for civil society.'[9] Therefore, civil society must itself demonstrate good internal governance in terms of accountability and openness.[10]

Thus the role envisaged for the social partners in both the European governance and corporate governance agendas suggests a convergence of the two debates. However, any such alignment disguises the fact that the two agendas have different origins: the European governance agenda arises from the need to address problems of democracy and legitimacy

---

was published in 1998 (*The Combined Code: Principles of Good Governance and Code of Best Practice* (London, 1998). See J. Parkinson and G. Kelly, 'The Combined Code on Corporate Governance' (1999) 70 Political Quarterly 101.

[5] See generally S. Deakin and A. Hughes (eds.), *Enterprise and Community: New Directions in Corporate Governance* (Oxford, 1997), also published as a special issue of the Journal of Law and Society (24, 1(1997)).

[6] According to the Governance White Paper COM(2001) 428, civil society includes the following: trade unions and employers' organisations ('social partners'); non-governmental organisations; professional associations; charities; grass-roots organisations; organisations that involve citizens in local and municipal life with a particular contribution from churches and religious communities: see COM (2001) 428, 14. For a more precise definition of organised civil society, see the Opinion of the Economic and Social Committee on 'The role and contribution of civil society organisations in the building of Europe', OJ C329, 17.11.99, 30.

[7] COM (2001) 428, 14.   [8] COM (2001) 428, 14.

[9] Economic and Social Committee own-initiative opinion on simplifying rules in the single market CES 1174/2000.

[10] COM(2001) 428, 15.

in the EU; the corporate governance agenda has its origins in the need to secure economic efficiency. Even here, the waters have been muddied. At Lisbon the European Council set the 'strategic goal' for the Union: to become 'the most competitive and dynamic knowledge-based economy in the world capable of sustainable economic growth with more and better jobs and greater social cohesion'.[11] This strategy was to be achieved by 'improving the existing processes, introducing a new open method of coordination at all levels, coupled with a stronger guiding and coordinating role for the European Council'; and it was envisaged that the social partners would have a significant role, especially in respect of modernising the European social model.[12] The Lisbon European Council also made a 'special appeal' to 'companies' corporate sense of social responsibility regarding best practices on lifelong learning, work organisation, equal opportunities, social inclusion and sustainable development'.[13] In its subsequent Green Paper on corporate social responsibility, the Commission argued:

> By stating their social responsibility and voluntarily taking on commitments which go beyond common regulatory and conventional requirements, which they would have to respect in any case, companies endeavour to raise the standards of social development, environmental protection and respect of fundamental rights and embrace an open governance, reconciling interests of various stakeholders in an overall approach of quality and sustainability.[14]

Thus part of the European governance agenda is to be deployed to help achieve the Union achieve the economic objectives set at Lisbon.

The aim of this chapter is to examine the interplay between these two different dialogues concerning governance. For corporate governance, a vital issue is whether the shareholder-oriented model which is associated with US and (to a degree) British practice comes to be more widely adopted within the EU. This is bound up with issues of political governance, since the form of regulation and, more specifically, the leeway allowed to regulatory competition may have profound implications for

---

[11] Presidency Conclusions, Lisbon European Council, 23 and 24 March 2000, para. 5.
[12] Presidency Conclusions of Feira European Council, 19 and 20 June 2000, para. 33 and Annex I of the Nice Presidency Conclusions, paras. 15 and 11. See also the Commission's Social Policy Agenda, COM(2000) 379 final.
[13] Presidency Conclusions, Lisbon European Council, 23 and 24 March 2000.
[14] *Promoting a European Framework for Corporate Social Responsibility*, COM (2001) 366, 3.

the substance of corporate governance rules in the member states. There is a possibility that certain key institutional features of continental company law systems will be called into question by judicial interventions in the area of the law relating to the single market, in particular the *Centros* case.[15] As a result of this process, European corporate governance may come to be shaped by a form of competitive federalism akin to the US 'Delaware effect'. For reasons we explain in more detail below, this is likely to weaken legal support for stakeholder voice in favour of giving greater priority to shareholder value.[16] This would have negative implications for the European social model and would undermine the anticipated role for the social partners in the European governance agenda. In this scenario, social rights would be needed in order to channel the market for legal rules in such a way as to avoid a destructive race to the bottom. Another possibility is that European models involving worker participation will retain their legitimacy at national level and will come to influence the debate over corporate governance and corporate social responsibility within EU law. If this occurs, the two dialogues on governance – European and corporate – will begin to dovetail. However, we shall argue that even here social rights will have an important role to play as a framework defining the parameters within which the social dialogue can evolve. Further uncertainty concerning the social partners' involvement arises from the 'open method of coordination' (OMC). Once again there is a need for social rights to ensure that the social partners have guarantees of participation and engagement at all levels in the decision-making process.

First, however, we begin by examining the development of European corporate governance.

II. The evolution of European corporate governance

The company law harmonisation programme

EU company law has its roots in provisions of the EC Treaty protecting freedom of establishment. Article 43 (ex art. 52) of the EC Treaty provides that:

---

[15] Case C-212/97 *Centros* v. *Erhvers- og Selskabsstyrelsen* [1999] ECR-I 1459.
[16] See below, 'European governance: the role of the social partners'.

restrictions on the freedom of establishment of nationals of a Member State in the territory of another Member State shall be prohibited. Such prohibition shall also apply to restrictions on the setting up of agencies, branches or subsidiaries by nationals of any Member State established in the territory of any Member State.

Freedom of establishment shall include the right to take up and pursue activities as self-employed persons and to set up and manage undertakings, in particular companies and firms within the meaning of the second paragraph of Article 48, under the conditions laid down for its own nationals by the law of the country where such establishment is effected...

For this purpose, Article 48 (ex art. 58) provides:

Companies or firms formed in accordance with the law of a Member State and having their registered office, central administration or principal place of business within the Community shall, for the purposes of [the chapter on freedom of establishment], be treated in the same way as natural persons who are nationals of Member States.

'Companies or firms' means companies or firms constituted under civil or commercial law, including cooperative societies, and other legal persons governed by public or private law, save for those which are non-profit-making.

The power to introduce harmonising measures in the field of company law is essentially ancillary to these rights of free movement for companies. Under Article 44(2)(g) (ex art. 54(3)(g)), the Council of Ministers can adopt directives aimed at 'coordinating to the necessary extent the safeguards which, for the protection of the interests of members and others, are required by Member States of companies and firms ... with a view to making such safeguards equivalent throughout the Community'. In other words, some degree of parity or equivalence in the laws protecting shareholders and 'others' – the latter term could include a range of stakeholder groups – was deemed by the Treaty's drafters to be necessary in order to remove disincentives to the movement of companies from one member state to another.[17]

During the early development of the Community's company law programme, the case for harmonisation echoed the claims made at around

---

[17] See C. Villiers, *European Company Law: Towards Democracy?* (Aldershot; 1998), 19.

the same time by the 'race to the bottom' school in the United States.[18] European commentators also thought that, without harmonisation, standards of shareholder and creditor protection within the EU would be eroded. In order to avoid a repeat of Delaware, harmonisation, in this view, should aim for the 'virtual unification of national company laws'.[19] This point of view could be reconciled with the principle of freedom of establishment, on the grounds that 'unharmonised national safeguards may make establishment too burdensome or even impossible'.[20] However, the same point of view also encompassed a substantive policy goal, namely the preservation of regulations conferring protections on various corporate constituencies, which, it was feared, a Delaware-style effect might otherwise undermine. It was partly this spirit of protective regulation which motivated the early company law directives, the so-called first generation directives which were heavily prescriptive in their approach.[21] The First Directive, adopted in 1968, laid down certain core minimum standards for both public and private companies and for limited partnerships relating to disclosure of basic information concerning the company's constitution and statutes. It also set standards for state laws concerning the validity of obligations entered into by the company with third parties, and the bases for the nullity of a company. The Second Directive, adopted in 1976, laid down a number of basic requirements for public companies, including the obligation to have a minimum paid-up share capital as well as rules relating to the maintenance of capital.

This early emphasis on uniformity and prescription soon gave way, however, to more flexible approaches which placed greater stress on member state autonomy. Charlotte Villiers describes the successive waves of measures as second-, third- and fourth-generation directives.[22] Characteristic second-generation measures were the so-called accounting directives, the Fourth (1978), Seventh (1983) and Eighth (1984).

---

[18] See W. Cary, 'Federalism and corporate law: reflections on Delaware' (1974) 83 Yale Law Journal 663.

[19] C. Schmitthoff, 'The future of the European company law scene', in C. Schmitthoff (ed.), *The Harmonisation of European Company Law* (London: 1973), 9.

[20] M. Wolff, 'The Commission's programme for European company law harmonisation: the winding road to a uniform European company law?' in M. Andenas and S. Kenyon-Slade (eds.), *EC Financial Market Regulation and Company Law* (London, 1993), 22.

[21] See generally Villiers, *European Company Law: Towards Democracy?*; V. Edwards, *European Company Law* (Oxford University Press, Oxford, 1999).

[22] *European Company Law: Towards Democracy?*

These laid down basic accounting and audit standards in the form of a set of options which essentially represented the predominant approaches which were then in operation in various member states.

The third-generation directives reflected the 'new approach' to harmonisation which the Commission instituted around the time of the passage of the Single European Act in 1986 and the initiation of the single market programme. The 'new approach' began in the context of product standard harmonisation, where it established a principle that Community intervention should be limited to the harmonisation of essential safety-related requirements. It also established the 'reference to standards' approach, under which it was presumed that a product which conformed to a standard set by a European-level body, or, failing that, to the relevant national standard, also complied with EC law.[23] Company law was one of the other areas in which this decentralising approach was applied. Hence the Twelfth Directive, on single-member private companies (1989), which was adopted in pursuance of the Community's goal of promoting the growth of small and medium-sized enterprises, explicitly left a range of regulatory issues concerning disclosure of information and creditor protection to be decided at member state level.

Fourth-generation measures took the process a stage further by adopting a 'framework' model for directives. This again favoured the articulation of general principles or standards rather than the promulgation of rigidly prescriptive rules. However, new techniques were also involved. The aim was to achieve policy goals by linking regulatory interventions to the activities and processes of autonomous rule-making bodies, such as industry-level associations and self-governing professional organisations in the financial sector. The draft Thirteenth Directive on takeover bids (notwithstanding the difficulties encountered in reaching agreement on its substantive content) exemplifies this approach, in particular in the scope it provides for its general principles to be implemented through local-level action by self-regulatory bodies (such as, in the UK context, the City Panel on Takeovers and Mergers, which is an entity formed by organisations and professional associations in the finance sector rather than a body emanating from the state).[24]

---

[23] K. Armstrong and S. Bulmer, *The Governance of the European Single Market* (Manchester, 1998), 152.

[24] Agreement on the text of the draft Thirteenth Directive has been held up on numerous occasions (most recently in the European Parliament) by failure to reach agreement on

This 'flexibilisation' of directives did not, however, make it any easier to reach agreement on some of the key proposals for company law harmonisation which were being discussed at this time. The draft Fifth Directive was first proposed in 1972; further versions appeared in 1982 and 1988 and amendments were most recently made in 1991. This draft Directive essentially laid out a model set of regulations for the governance of public companies. Large parts of the draft were relatively uncontentious. However, the proposal essentially foundered on the issues of board structure and employee representation, thereby suffering the same fate as the so-called Vredeling draft Directive of the mid-1970s, which would have introduced forms of employee participation in management decision-making into transnational companies. The original draft of the Fifth Directive provided for a two-tier board structure with employee representation on the supervisory board, more or less along the lines of the German codetermination system. This was later amended to allow for the possibility of a unitary board, but still with a basic requirement of employee representation either at board level or through a consultative council. But these provisions still proved unacceptable to a number of member states, including Britain.

The impasse on the issue of employee representation was first overcome by the adoption in 1994 of the Directive on European Works Councils (the 'EWC Directive'). In essence, this Directive adopts a labour law solution to the issue of information and consultation, by requiring transnational companies above a certain size to enter into negotiations with employee representatives for the establishment of a framework for information and consultation. In the event of the failure of negotiations, a default procedure is imposed by law.[25] The passage of the EWC Directive did not touch on the question of board structure and membership.

This issue has been addressed instead through proposals for a model European Company Statute. The idea of a model constitution for transnational European companies goes back to the earliest days of the Community and some versions even to pre-date the Treaty of Rome of 1957. The first concrete proposal was made by the Commission in 1970. More

the role (if any) of employee consultation during takeover bids. See S. Deakin, 'Regulatory competition versus harmonisation in European company law', in D. Esty and D. Geradin (eds.), *Regulatory Competition and Economic Integration: Comparative Perspectives* (Oxford, 2001), for an account of the background to this debate up to the late 1990s.

[25] On the EWC Directive, see generally C. Barnard, *EC Employment Law*, 2nd edn (Oxford, 2000), 526–38.

recent proposals essentially provide for a Regulation under which a European public company (a Societas Europea, or SE) may be established through a number of different mechanisms, most of which require the involvement of two or more companies which are governed by the laws of at least two member states. Significant features of the model constitution include the requirement for a minimum paid-up share capital; the identification of the company's registered office, which must be in the territory of the EU, with its central administration (an application of the *siège réel* principle[26]); and a range of options on board structure, including two-tier and unitary boards of various kinds. The Regulation is attached to a Directive which makes provision for employee representation. As with the draft Fifth Directive, a number of options are made available, ranging from employee membership of a supervisory or a unitary board to the establishment of a consultative council, and a collective agreement setting out the basis for employee participation. The Directive also lays down certain minimum requirements of information and consultation with regard to employees.[27]

Corporate governance and stakeholder voice in the systems of the member states

It can be seen from the preceding discussion that progress on harmonisation has faced most difficulty when it addressed the question of how to treat stakeholder groups, in particular employees. This failure is to some degree a reflection of the divide which exists, at the level of the laws of the member states, between 'insider' and 'outsider' systems of corporate governance.[28] Within 'insider' systems such as those of Germany and France, share ownership tends to be concentrated in the hands of family groups or held in large blocks by other corporations, thereby giving rise to cross-ownership of shares between companies. Hostile takeovers are extremely rare, with the result that there is only a minimal or embryonic market for corporate control. In some insider systems, although not all, these conditions are reflected in board structure. Germany has the most

[26] See further below, 'European governance: the role of the social partners'.
[27] See Villiers, *European Company Law: Towards Democracy?* 58–61, for an account of the history of this provision. It was finally adopted on 8 Oct. 2001; Regulation 2157/2001 and Directive 2001/86/EC are both due to come into force on 8 Oct. 2004.
[28] See C. Mayer, 'Corporate governance, competition, and performance' (1997) 24 Journal of Law and Society 152.

articulated and deeply embedded system of stakeholder participation in corporate decision-making. Two-tier boards of the kind which exist in Germany for public companies, in addition to providing for formal representation of the interests of a wide range of stakeholders, also offer continuity and a degree of entrenchment for managerial teams.

By contrast, in 'outsider' systems, the predominant mode of ownership in public companies is through the holdings of institutional investors, who strive to diversify their holdings in order to minimise risk. As a result, they frequently lack strong ties to particular companies. The interests of shareholders in an active market for corporate control are defended by takeover codes, which limit the scope for defensive actions by target managements. A number of other rules, in particular those relating to disclosure of investment information and the prohibition of insider dealing, aim to maintain a high degree of stock market liquidity. Employee representation operates (if at all) through collective bargaining and similar arrangements which lie strictly outside the framework of company law. This is broadly descriptive of the British system which, in most respects, more closely resembles that of the United States than it does those of its fellow EU member states.[29]

It is not surprising that, following the first enlargement of the EC in 1973 to include Britain, Denmark and Ireland, there was strong resistance to the attempt in the first version of the draft Fifth Directive to impose a system based on the German model of 'insider governance'. The emergence of more flexible regulatory techniques in subsequent drafts can be seen as indicating an acceptance of diversity. However, the long debate over the European Company Statute shows that it has been difficult to reach agreement on whether it is appropriate to address the issue of stakeholder representation through company law at all.

This, again, is a basic point of divergence in the company law systems of the member states. As just explained, the British system, with a very few exceptions, sees stakeholder rights as mainly lying outside

---

[29] See S. Deakin and G. Slinger, 'Hostile takeovers, corporate law and the theory of the firm' (1997) 24 Journal of Law and Society 124. The characterisation of the British and US systems in terms of dispersed shareholder ownership and an active market for corporate control is a central theme of recent seminal work claiming to demonstrate the existence of a link between forms of legal regulation and corporate governance forms and outcomes. See R. La Porta, F. Lopez de Silvanes, A. Shleifer and R. Vishny, 'Law and finance' (1998) 106 Journal of Political Economy 1113.

the framework of company law, which is predominantly concerned with the position of shareholders and, to a lesser extent, creditors. An important feature of some 'insider systems', of which Germany represents the best example, is not simply that they recognise certain claims of non-shareholder stakeholders which go unrecognised in outsider systems, but that they do so in such a way as to incorporate stakeholder voice directly into the processes of governance and control within companies. The most important illustration of this, as we have already seen, is the involvement of the representatives of employees and in some cases other stakeholders, such as local government and environmental interests, on the supervisory boards of public companies. Other features of stakeholder voice in Germany, such as the system of employee representation through works councils, do not operate at the level of company law as such; in the manner of the EWC Directive, they operate through the mechanisms of labour law. However, it is the close linkages between company law and labour law which are important here; in the German context, codetermination and the two-tier board are best viewed as closely interlocking elements of a single system of stakeholder representation.

In the context of directors' duties, the furthest English company law can go by way of recognition of the interests of non-shareholder stakeholders is the idea of 'enlightened shareholder value'.[30] In other words, directors may act out of concern for other stakeholder groups if, by so doing, they believe that they will maximise the value of the business and thereby meet shareholders' interests (which for this purpose may mean their longer term interests). This is quite different from the civil law idea that the company has an interest 'in itself'[31] which serves as a means of reconciling the different perspectives of a number of stakeholder groups, none of which is entitled to priority. In the words of the Viénot report (1995) on corporate governance in France,

> In Anglo-Saxon countries the emphasis is for the most part placed on the objective of maximising share values, whilst on the European continent and France in particular the emphasis is placed more on the human assets and resources of the company . . . Human resources

[30] See the document published by the Steering Group of the Department of Trade and Industry's Company Law Review, *Modern Company Law for a Competitive Economy: The Strategic Framework* (London, 1999), 37.

[31] See generally G. Teubner, 'Company interest. The public interest of the enterprise in itself', in R. Rogowski and T. Wilthagen (eds.), *Reflexive Labour Law* (Deventer, 1994).

can be defined as the overriding interest of the corporate body itself, in other words the company considered as an autonomous economic agent, pursuing its own aims as distinct from those of its shareholders, its employees, its creditors including the tax authorities, and of its suppliers and customers; rather, it corresponds to their general, common interest, which is that of ensuring the survival and prosperity of the company.[32]

Hence the French and other 'insider' systems of company law essentially see the business enterprise as having an *organisational* dimension which rests on the contributions made by a number of stakeholder groups, and not simply a *financial* dimension which describes the contribution of the shareholders. This divergence of approach operates at a fundamental conceptual level, so that even the terms used to define the business enterprise in legal terms are not precisely analogous. The English law concept of the 'company', for example, refers to the essentially financial relationship between managers and investors; there is no equivalent to those concepts which recognise the enterprise's organisational dimension, such as the French *entreprise* or German *unternehmen*.

The *siège réel* principle, which identifies the company's registered office with its central management or administration rather than with its chosen place of incorporation, is part of the same organisational orientation to the legal conceptualisation of the business enterprise. The recent challenge to the *siège réel* principle in the *Centros*[33] case is therefore also, unavoidably, a challenge to the stakeholder model of company law which has evolved in a number of EU member states. *Centros* has brought the debate full circle, back to the concerns of the early 1970s with the 'race to the bottom'. The Danish company registrar refused to register a branch of Centros Ltd, a company incorporated in the United Kingdom, so as to enable it to carry on business in Denmark. Centros Ltd was incorporated in English law by two Danish citizens, Mr and Mrs Bryde, solely for the purpose of avoiding the Danish law relating to minimum capital requirements for privately held companies. What was at stake was the access of Centros's founders to the low-cost regulatory regime

---

[32] See M. Viénot, 'Rapport sur le Conseil d'Administration des Sociétés cotées' (1995) 8 Revue de Droit des Affaires Internationales: 372, cited in A. Alcouffe and C. Alcouffe, 'Control, and executive compensation in large French companies' (1997) 24 Journal of Law and Society 85.

[33] Case C-212/97 *Centros* v. *Erhvers- og Selskabsstyrelsen* [1999] ECR I-1459.

of UK company law. The European Court of Justice ruled that the refusal to accede to the registration request was contrary to the right of freedom of establishment under Article 43 (ex art. 52) of the EC Treaty, read with Article 46 (ex art. 56) and 58 (ex art. 58). It held, first, that there was a potential infringement of freedom of establishment in any case where 'it is the practice of a member state, in certain circumstances, to refuse to register a branch of a company having its registered office in another member state'. This was because

> The provisions of the Treaty on freedom of establishment are intended specifically to enable companies formed in accordance with the law of a Member State and having their registered office, central administration or principal place of business within the Community to pursue activities in the Member States through an agency, branch or subsidiary.
>
> That being so, the fact that a national of a Member State who wishes to set up a company chooses to form it in the Member State whose rules of company law seem to him the least restrictive and to set up branches in other Member States cannot, by itself, constitute an abuse of the right of establishment. The right to form a company in accordance with the law of a Member State and to set up branches in other Member States is inherent in the exercise, in a single market, of the freedom of establishment guaranteed by the Treaty.[34]

The Court then went on to consider whether the Danish government could show that the refusal to register was justifiable in the circumstances. This involved a consideration of whether there was some countervailing policy objective behind the Danish practice and whether, in the particular circumstances of this case, the proportionality test could be said to be satisfied. The Danish government argued that the registrar's action was intended to maintain Danish law's minimum capital requirement for the formation of private companies. The purpose of this law was

> first, to reinforce the financial soundness of those companies in order to protect public creditors against the risk of seeing the public debts owing to them become irrecoverable since, unlike private creditors, they cannot secure these debts by means of guarantees and, second, and more generally, to protect all creditors, public and private, by

---

[34] *Centros*, Judgement, at paras. 26–7.

anticipating the risk of fraudulent bankruptcy due to the insolvency of companies whose initial capitalisation was inadequate.[35]

In many ways this was the crux of the case, and the most ambiguous and problematic aspect of the Court's judgement. The Court ruled that the justification offered was inadequate since, in the first place, 'the practice in question is not such as to attain the objective of protecting creditors which it purports to pursue since, if the company concerned had conducted business in the United Kingdom, its branch would have been registered in Denmark, even though Danish creditors might have been equally exposed to risk'.[36] In other words, the registrar's decision failed the proportionality test since it was inconsistent – the vital factor in his refusal was, it seems, the failure of the company to trade in the United Kingdom, but this was immaterial to the protection of creditors, since they would have been no better off if the company had previously traded and, as a result, had been able to get its branch registered in Denmark.

Forms of regulatory competition: competitive federalism and reflexive harmonisation

The *Centros* case illustrates the potential for judicial decisions on freedom of establishment and other aspects of single market law to undermine state-level regulation in the area of corporate governance. While we may be a long way still from a Delaware-like effect of 'competitive federalism' in EU law,[37] *Centros* clearly puts in peril laws imposing mandatory minimum capital requirements. Whatever the rights and wrongs of such laws, they represent a consensus, arrived at through the democratic process, on the balance to be struck between creditor protection and freedom of enterprise. If companies in future have the right to move between jurisdictions at will, they will be able to avoid otherwise mandatory state laws of this kind. In just the same way, then, they could choose whether to observe mandatory laws relating to employee participation or codetermination rights, in so far as the application of such laws was a function of the legal domicile of the company as opposed to its physical or economic presence on the territory of a particular jurisdiction. At present, thanks to decisions such as *Rush Portuguesa*,[38]

---

[35] Ibid., para. 32.   [36] Ibid., para. 35.   [37] See Deakin, 'Regulatory competition,' n. 24 above.
[38] Case C-113/89 *Rush Portuguesa Lda.* v. *Office Nationale d'Immigration* [1990] ECR 1417.

the principle of territoriality, rather than the company's legal domicile, tends to determine the application of most labour law rights.[39] However, some labour law rights may depend on the company's domicile rather than the place in which the employment is carried out. In particular, rules on stakeholder membership of supervisory boards in Germany and certain other member states relate to the corporate form or legal entity through which an organisation is constituted, and not just to its physical or business presence. *Centros* makes it more likely that such laws can be challenged.

More generally, who is to say that the Court's decision in *Rush Portuguesa*, endorsing the territoriality principle in labour law, will forever be immune from attack on the grounds that differential labour standards may form an obstacle to freedom of movement and/or establishment? While there is a case to be made against regarding differences in regulatory laws as barriers to trade,[40] the case law across the whole area of single market law is far from clear on this point.

The mere *possibility* that codetermination laws, for example, could be avoided through reincorporation, might induce states to repeal them. States could act in a self-interested way to remove mandatory laws if, by doing so, they thought they could attract more incorporations or retain those which they had: 'states competing to attract incorporations will have an incentive to focus on the interests of managers and shareholders and to ignore the interests of third parties not involved in incorporation decisions'.[41] It seems plausible, then, that a market for incorporations would lead to a reduction in mandatory laws of all kinds, and to an increase in permissive or 'default' rules which leave companies free to bargain around them. This could occur even if little or no movement of companies actually took place, as long as states could rationally take the view that companies would not submit to a mandatory regime which they did not perceive as being in their interests when they could choose between that system and a more permissive one elsewhere. This would have profound implications for corporate governance rules in the member states. One response, as we shall see below, would be to have social

---

[39] See P. Davies, 'Market integration and social policy in the Court of Justice' (1995) 24 Industrial Law Journal 49.

[40] See C. Barnard and S. Deakin, 'Market access and regulatory competition', in C. Barnard and J. Scott (eds.), *The Evolution of the Single Market* (Oxford, 2002).

[41] L. Bebchuk, 'The desirable limits of state competition in corporate law' (1992) 105 Harvard Law Review 1435, 1441.

rights which would steer the market towards legal rules. In the European context, the longevity and stability of systems which incorporate stakeholder voice into corporate governance processes suggests that, while such arrangements may not be ideal in all circumstances, they may possess a 'survival value' which is not reconcilable with the view that they are fundamentally inefficient. It is true that these systems have not been subjected to direct competition through the threat of corporate exit in the manner of the United States. However, they have been subject to less direct but, in the long term, highly significant constraints, in the form of product-market competition and other economic pressures on governments and law-makers to maintain effective conditions for business organisation. Moreover, given the degree of diversity which exists between systems, it is likely that there is some degree of matching of the rules and practices of company law to local conditions. Path dependence may also be expected to play a role, in the sense that increasing returns to particular institutional forms lead, if anything, to further divergence between systems over time rather than to convergence. These suggestions are reflected in research which compared corporate governance practices in large British and German companies. The study found that

> there is no 'one best' system of corporate governance. Rather, the two systems have different comparative advantages. The British corporate governance system better supports companies in sectors where there is a need to move quickly into and out of new markets and in which there is need for great flexibility in the use of employees. The German system, by contrast, better supports companies in sectors that require long-term commitments and investments by employees, suppliers and other 'stakeholders'.[42]

The crucial determinants of the respective 'comparative advantages' which companies enjoy are the differences in the organisation of capital markets, the rules of company law and the forms of employee participation in the two countries; these are reflected in the different ways in which corporate governance practice has evolved in response to issues of agency costs, delegation and stakeholder participation. For example, the German two-tier board system, with its emphasis on stakeholder involvement, enables large-scale restructurings to be handled on the basis

---

[42] S. Vitols, S. Casper, D. Soskice, and S. Woolcock, *Corporate Governance in Large British and German Companies* (London, 1997), 35.

of consensus. Moderate shareholder pressure, in contrast to the more intense scrutiny of British capital markets, enables strategic, long-term planning to be put in place and implemented. The British system, which concentrates managerial decision-making power in the hands of the board and the chief executive, possesses a 'major advantage' in terms of the speed with which decisions can be taken and implemented, but runs a greater risk of strategic mistakes being made by top management. On the basis of this analysis, the authors of this study argue that, even with the growing internationalisation of investment flows, the two systems are unlikely to converge: 'change can better be characterised as incremental adaptation rather than the wholesale adoption or replacement of corporate governance systems'.[43]

One reading of this study is that existing systems, since they are well matched to local conditions and hence 'efficient' in some sense, are unlikely to be destabilised by the introduction of greater regulatory competition. This, however, may be to underestimate the power of exit mechanisms of the kind which exist in the United States, where companies are virtually free to reincorporate at will in the jurisdiction of their choice, and which would come into play in the EU if the full logic of *Centros* was played out. At present, stakeholder-based systems such as the German one depend on the *siège réel* principle to make their laws governing employee voice effective. If the *siège réel* principle were to be found to be contrary to the rules of the single market, it is of course possible that stakeholder-orientated companies would not choose to reincorporate elsewhere, since to do so would threaten employee cooperation. However, in principle this is neither more nor less likely than the alternative, namely the initiation of a Delaware-type effect which would see companies reincorporating, en masse, in one particular jurisdiction. For the reasons explained above, it is unlikely that this jurisdiction would be stakeholder-friendly.[44]

In *Centros* the Court did not clearly address the implications of its decision for regulatory arbitrage. Although it evidently has deregulatory implications, *Centros* can also be seen as an encouragement to the member states to legislate, through directives, as part of the process of

---

[43] Ibid., 36.

[44] For further discussion of this point, see S. Deakin, 'Two types of regulatory competition': competitive federalism versus reflexive harmonisation. A law and economics perspective on *Centros*' (1999) 2 Cambridge Yearbook of European Legal Studies 231.

promoting market integration. The form such regulation takes therefore becomes a crucial issue. Most labour law directives set basic or minimum standards as a 'floor of rights' from which member states must not derogate, but upon which they may improve by setting superior standards.[45] These directives, then, implicitly encourage a 'race to the top', while ruling out less socially desirable aspects of regulatory competition.[46]

The form of harmonisation which has been termed 'reflexive harmonisation'[47] makes explicit the idea that the aim of Community-level intervention is not an end to regulatory competition as such. Rather, the aim of harmonisation is to preserve a space for local-level experimentation and adaptation, contrary to the 'levelling-down' agenda of negative harmonisation, but also in contrast to the idea that harmonisation in the form of a 'European labour code' must occupy the field at the expense of local autonomy. Reflexive harmonisation may also offer a way forward in the formulation of European corporate governance rules.

The essence of reflexive law is the acknowledgement that regulatory interventions are most likely to be successful when they seek to achieve their ends not by direct prescription, but by inducing 'second-order effects' on the part of social actors. In other words, this approach aims to 'couple' external regulation with self-regulatory processes. Reflexive law therefore has a *procedural orientation*. What this means, in the context of economic regulation, is that the preferred mode of intervention is for the law to underpin and encourage autonomous processes of adjustment, in particular by supporting mechanisms of group representation and participation, rather than to intervene by imposing particular distributive outcomes. This type of approach finds a concrete manifestation in legislation which seeks, in various ways, to devolve or confer rule-making powers on self-regulatory processes. Examples are laws which allow collective bargaining by trade unions and employers to fill out the substance of individual employment rights. This is very much the approach adopted by the more recent EC social directives and which now features heavily in the debates surrounding the political governance of the EU.

[45] S. Deakin and F. Wilkinson, 'Rights versus efficiency? The economic case for transnational labour standards' (1994) 23 Industrial Law Journal 289.

[46] C. Barnard, 'Social dumping revisited: lessons from Delaware' (1997) 25 European Law Review 57.

[47] S. Deakin, 'Regulatory competition', n. 24 above; see also idem, 'Two types of regulatory competition', 231.

III. European governance: the role of the social partners

The involvement of the social partners in law- and policy-making,[48] with penetration at all levels in the chain from the EU to enterprise level, is central to the new EU governance agenda.[49] Thus, at EU level the interprofessional social partners (ETUC, UNICE and CEEP) do not just have the right to be consulted on the possible direction of Community action and on the content of the envisaged proposal,[50] but may also negotiate collective agreements[51] which can be given *erga omnes* effects by a Council 'decision'.[52] This process, initiated at Maastricht in 1992, has led to the enactment of three intersectoral directives – on Parental Leave,[53] Part-time Work[54] and Fixed-term Work[55] – and two sectoral directives – on the organisation of working time of seafarers[56] and those working in the civil aviation industry.[57] This process is reflexive harmonisation writ large. The striking feature of these directives is that not only do they result from a process of transnational negotiation, but they also envisage local-level implementation through collective bargaining or similar methods of joint regulation at industry or plant level. In other words, they provide space for the member states and/or social partners to flesh out their content. For example, the Parental Leave Directive envisages two main rights: men and women workers are

---

[48] This chapter will focus primarily on the law-making aspect.

[49] COM(2001) 428, 2, 13 and 14 and the Commission's Social Agenda COM(2000) 379, 14. See further C. Barnard, 'Governance and the social partners' (2002) 8 European Law Journal.

[50] Art. 138(1) and (2) (ex art. 3(2) and (3) SPA).

[51] Art. 139(1) (ex art. 4(1) SPA). See generally B. Bercusson, 'Maastricht – a fundamental change in European Labour Law' (1992) 23 Industrial Relations Journal 177; and 'The dynamic of European Labour Law after Maastricht' (1994) 23 Industrial Law Journal 1. These provisions were included as the direct result of the 'Val Duchesse' social dialogue between the intersectoral (cross-industry) Social Partners (UNICE and CEEP on the employers' side and ETUC on the workers') which started in 1985. On 31 Oct. 1991 they reached an agreement which formed the basis of Arts. 3 and 4 SPA (new arts. 138 and 139).

[52] Art. 4(2) (new art. 139(2)). The term 'decision' is not used in the sense of Art. 249 (old art. 189), but has been interpreted to mean any legally binding act, in particular, directives. See further A. Adinolfi, 'Admissibility of action for annulment by social partners and "sufficient representativity" of European agreements' (2000) 25 European Law Review 165.

[53] Council Directive 96/34/EC of 3 June 1996 on the framework agreement on parental leave concluded by UNICE, CEEP and the ETUC (OJ [1996] L145/4).

[54] Council Directive 97/81/EC (OJ [1998] L14/9).

[55] Council Directive 97/81/EC (OJ [1998] L14/9 as amended by Council Directive 98/23/EC (OJ [1998] L131/10 and Council Directive 99/70/EC (OJ [1999] L175/43), respectively.

[56] Council Directive 99/63/EC (OJ [1999] L167/33).

[57] Council Directive 2000/79/EC (OJ [2000] L302/57).

entitled to parental leave for at least three months on the birth or adoption of a child, and workers are entitled to time off on the grounds of force majeure for urgent family reasons.[58] The agreement then provides, inter alia, that member states and/or management and labour may specify 'the conditions of access and modalities of application of this clause'.[59] In the United Kingdom, legislation implementing this Directive, the Employment Relations Act 1999 and relevant delegated legislation, has made self-regulation the preferred means of implementation, by allowing the relevant standards to be given effect through a collective agreement or workforce agreement. It is only in the absence of either a collective or a workforce agreement that a set of 'default' rules comes into play, prescribing basic standards.[60] Whether this is a fully appropriate implementation of the directives may be questioned. A 'workforce agreement' need not imply independent representation, that is, representation through an independent trade union, in the same way that a collective agreement does. This could be seen, then, as a means of watering down the relevant labour standards.

The more recent directives adopted via the conventional legislative route also make provision for a space for local experimentation and adaptation by enterprise-level social partners. At the intersection of labour law and company law, the European Works Councils Directive[61] provides a good illustration of this. As previously explained, the Directive does not set out directly to impose any particular model of employee representation, in marked contrast to the techniques tried out unsuccessfully in the context of the Vredeling proposals and the draft Fifth Directive. Instead the Directive provides the transnational companies coming under its scope[62] with an incentive to enter into negotiations with employee representatives for the establishment of a works council

---

[58] Cl. 3(1).

[59] Other key matters left to the member states and/or management and labour can be found in Arts. 2(3)(a)–(f), and 2(7).

[60] See SI 1999/3312.

[61] Council Directive 94/95/EC (OJ [1994] L254/64), as amended by Council Directive 97/74/EC (OJ [1998] L10/22; consolidated legislation (OJ [1998] L10/20).

[62] The Directive applies to 'Community-scale undertakings' which are undertakings with at least 1,000 employees in the EU as a whole and 150 employees in at least two member states; a similar definition applies to group undertakings operating at Community level. For a valuable discussion of the Directive in the context of a wider argument in favour of using EU-level interventions to maintain national and sub-national diversity, see W. Streeck, 'Competitive solidarity: rethinking the "European social model"', MPIfG Working Paper 99/8, Max Planck Institut für Gesellschaftsforschung, Cologne.

or a similar mechanism for information and consultation. The incentive is provided in the form of a default procedure which applies in the event of the failure of negotiations. However, employers have a number of opportunities to avoid this outcome. First, employers who agreed an information and consultation procedure of their own with their employees and implemented it before the Directive came into force are effectively exempted from the provisions of the Directive (or of the national-level law implementing it). Second, employers who fail to do this may nevertheless escape the default procedure by arriving at an agreement with a 'special negotiating body' of employees within three years of negotiations beginning.

The Directive operates, then, through a 'penalty default' rule,[63] in other words, a fallback provision which induces a more powerfully placed or better informed party (here, the employer) to enter into a bargaining process when it otherwise would lack an incentive to do so. The justification for the Directive derives from the failure on the part of the member states to put in place similar mechanisms to deal with the particular issue of information and consultation in transnational companies. The Directive can therefore be seen as a response to a co-ordination failure at the level of the states. However, it takes effect not by imposing a uniform solution but by encouraging *both* member states, through their laws, *and* companies themselves, through negotiations with employee representatives, to develop local-level solutions.

Directive 2002/14/EC on information and consultation procedures at national level provides another example of a measure which creates space for local diversity and experimentation. According to Article 5,[64]

> Member States may entrust management and labour at the appropriate level, including at undertaking or establishment level, with defining freely and at any time through negotiated agreement the practical arrangements for informing and consulting employees. These agreements, and agreements existing on the date laid down in Article 11, as well as any subsequent renewals of such agreements, may establish,

---

[63] I. Ayres and R. Gertner, 'Filling gaps in incomplete contracts: a theory of default rules' (1989) 99 Yale Law Journal 87.

[64] Directive 2002/14/EC of the European Parliament and Council establishing a general framework for informing and consulting employees in the European Community (OJ [2002] L80/29).

while respecting the principles set out in Article 1 [object and prin-
ciples] and subject to conditions and limitations laid down by the
Member States, provisions which are different from those referred to
in Article 4 [practical arrangements for information and consultation].

The social partners can also implement directives[65] and, in the case
of the Working Time Directive 93/104, 'collective agreements or agreements between the two sides of industry' can be used to set certain
standards, such as the duration and terms on which a rest break can be
taken,[66] and to derogate from those standards.[67] In the Working Time
Regulations,[68] the British government has allowed for such agreements
not only at national and enterprise level but also at the level of the individual, permitting three types of agreement. The Regulations make
provision for collective agreements as defined in section 178 of the Trade
Union and Labour Relations (Consolidation) Act 1992 where the trade
unions are independent within the meaning of section 5 of that Act;
'workforce agreements', which are designed to provide a mechanism for
employers to agree working time arrangements with workers who do
not have any terms and conditions set by collective agreement;[69] and
'relevant agreements', which are defined as any provision of a collective
agreement which forms part of a contract between the worker and the
employer, a workforce agreement, or any other agreement in writing
which is legally enforceable as between the worker and the employer.

The striking feature of all of these developments is the emphasis they
place on deliberation and involvement of the social partners at all levels,
almost to the exclusion of any consideration of the quality of the end
result. Thus, the fact that the Directive on Parental Leave was concluded was more important than a qualitative consideration of whether
the content of the Directive was satisfactory. Using the jargon, there is
'input-oriented legitimacy' rather than 'output-oriented legitimacy'.[70]
Of course, judging the quality of output is a highly subjective matter, and

---

[65] Article 137(4) (ex Article 2(4)) EC. See also Directive 91/353 (OJ L 288/32) on conditions
applicable to the contract of employment and Directive 98/59/EC on collective redundancies
(OJ [1998] L 225/6) and the Working Time Directive 93/104/EC (OJ L 307/18).
[66] Art. 4.
[67] Art. 17. This is most unusual: collective agreements usually improve upon statutory
protection.
[68] SI 1998/1833.   [69] Ibid., Sch. 1, para. 2.
[70] F. Scharpf, *Governing in Europe – Effective and Democratic* (Oxford, 1999), 6.

so it may be easier to assess the benefits of the social dialogue in terms of the space it creates for continued learning and experimentation. This space for learning is not, however, confined to the technical area of reflexive harmonisation. As Teague observes, active engagement with EU-level policy deliberations not only introduces national actors to new ideas, routines and practices, but also encourages them to pursue regulatory or collaborative solutions to integration problems that are more ambitious than was first considered necessary.[71] He cites the example of how the European social dialogue pushed organised labour to rethink the role of the ETUC which in turn spurred deeper reflection about what objectives the trade unions should pursue in EU-level discussions on industrial relations. He terms this process 'deliberative supranationalism',[72] drawing on the literature of deliberative democracy.[73] This would suggest that one way of addressing the perceived democracy deficit in the EU is to consider democracy in the EU less in terms of representative democracy and more in terms of participation[74] and deliberation.[75] As Eriksen and Fossum explain, deliberative democracy 'places the emphasis on obtaining a shared sense of meaning and common will,[76] both of which are the product of the communicative process'; it is based on arguing, reason giving and learning leading to the transformation, rather than simply the aggregation, of preferences. In its discussion paper on NGOs, the Commission says:

> The decision making process in the EU is first and foremost legitimised by the elected representatives of the European people. However, NGOs

---

[71] P. Teague, 'Macroeconomic constraints, social learning and pay bargaining in Europe' (2000) 38 British Journal of Industrial Relations 429.

[72] See also E. Eriksen, 'The Question of Deliberative Supranationalism in the EU' ARENA Working Paper 99/4; B. Kohler-Koch, 'The evolution and transformation of European Governance', in R. Eising and B. Kohler-Koch(eds.), The Transformation of Governance in the European Union (London, 1999).

[73] See generally J. Elster, Deliberative Democracy (Cambridge, 1998).

[74] P. Craig, 'Democracy and Rule-making Within the EC: An Empirical and Normative Assessment' (1997) 3 ELJ 3, 121.

[75] For an overview of the historical development of 'deliberative democracy' see 'Introduction' in J. Bohman and W. Rehg (eds.), Deliberative Democracy: Essays on Reason and Politics (Cambridge, MA, 1997) and J. Elster, 'Introduction' in Elster (ed.), Deliberative Democracy (Cambridge, 1998).

[76] See the challenges to the possibility of obtaining a 'common will' in the literature on social choice theory and David Miller's response to this in David Miller, Citizenship and National Identity (Cambridge, 2000), ch. 1.

can make a contribution in fostering a more participatory democracy both within the European Union and beyond.[77]

Similar ideas underpin the Green Paper on *Promoting Corporate Social Responsibility*. The Commission says:

> implementing corporate social responsibility needs commitment from top management, but also innovative thinking and, thus, new skills and closer involvement of the employees and their representatives in a two-way dialogue that can structure permanent feedback and adjustment. Social dialogue with workers' representatives, which is the main mechanism of definition of the relationship between a company and its workers therefore plays a crucial part in the wider adoption of socially responsible practices.[78]

The open method of coordination (OMC), especially in its more decentralised form, has much in common with this deliberative perspective on dialogue. OMC, which emerged from the proceedings of the Lisbon European Council in 2000, involves 'fixing guidelines for the Union, establishing quantitative and qualitative indicators and benchmarks as a means of comparing best practice, translating these European guidelines into national and regional policies by setting specific targets, and periodic monitoring, evaluation and peer review organised as "mutual learning processes" '.[79] This technique was initiated in the context of EMU and then spilled over into the Employment Strategy, where guidelines are set which are then reflected in national action plans. As we saw above, OMC has since been emphasised in the context of the emerging agenda for EU corporate governance and corporate social responsibility.[80] The success of OMC has been stated to depend on the successful integration of a variety of actors, including 'the Union, the Member States, the regional and local levels *as well as the social partners and civil society... using variable forms of partnership*.'[81] Yet behind this rhetoric

---

[77] *Commission and non-governmental organisations: Building a stronger partnership* COM(2000) 11. This builds on the Commission's Communication *Promoting the Role of Voluntary Organisations and Foundations in Europe* COM(97) 241 final.

[78] COM(2001) 366, 18.

[79] Presidency Conclusions, Lisbon European Council, 23 and 24 March 2000, para. 37.

[80] See note 3, above; Presidency Conclusions, Lisbon European Council, 23 and 24 March 2000, at para. 39.

[81] Presidency Conclusions, Lisbon European Council, 23 and 24 March 2000, para. 38 and COM(2000) 379, p. 8 (emphasis in original).

lies a further challenge to the role of the social partners: OMC can allow national and subnational actors to be sidelined or even bypassed. Although the Commission claims otherwise,[82] it seems that OMC is now preferred to legislation as the means of giving effect to policy.[83]

Nevertheless, there are risks attached to this emphasis on proceduralisation and deliberation. First, it requires careful examination of the identity of those carrying out the relevant negotiations.[84] In the context of the social dialogue, this raises the thorny question of representativity (and accountability) of the social partners. This eventually came to a head in the *UEAPME* case[85] where UEAPME, representing small and medium-sized employers, made an unsuccessful challenge to the hegemony of the ETUC, CEEP and UNICE in negotiating the parental leave agreement.[86] In that case the court of first instance (CFI) raised the stakes of the importance of the social dialogue to democracy in the EU. Referring to measures, such as the Parental Leave Directive, adopted under the Maastricht social dialogue where there is no official involvement by the European Parliament, it said:

> the principle of democracy on which the Union is founded requires . . .
> that the participation of the people be otherwise ensured, in this instance through the parties representative of management and labour who concluded the agreement which is endowed by the Council . . . with a legislative foundation at Community level.[87]

The second risk in conceptualising democracy too far in terms of process lies in the fact that, from the perspective of the individual citizen, whom the governance reforms are primarily intended to benefit, the process seems remote and alienating. The feeling is that the

---

[82] 'The means to achieving these objectives [modernising the European Social Model] include OMC, legislation, the social dialogue and the structural funds' COM(2000)379, 14 and 20–2.

[83] See the Communication on an open method of coordination for the Community immigration policy COM(2001) 387.

[84] L. Betten, 'The democratic deficit of participatory democracy in Community social policy' (1998) 23 European Law Review 20.

[85] Case T-135/96 *UEAPME* [1998] ECR II-2335. See further Adinolfi, 'Admissibility of action', and B. Bercusson, 'Democratic legitimacy and European labour law' (1999) 28 Industrial Law Journal 153.

[86] Case T-135/96 *UEAPME* [1998] ECR II-2335. UEAPME also challenged the agreement on part-time workers T-55/98 *Union européenne de l'artisanat et des petites et moyennes entreprises (UEAPME)* v. *Council*, but this action was removed from the Court's register on 14 Jan. 1999.

[87] Para. 89.

discussion takes place between elites for elites. It does not furnish the citizen with detailed, legally enforceable rights. Furthermore, there is a risk that reflexive labour law brings with it increased transaction costs and the unlikelihood of it occurring in all but the largest workplaces. For these very reasons, there is still a need for a core of protection based on fundamental rights.

IV. Governance and social rights

The importance of the Community having its own catalogue of fundamental rights has long been advocated.[88] The Amsterdam Treaty took one small step in this direction: Article 136 (ex art. 117) requires the Community and the member states to have 'in mind fundamental social rights' as defined in the European Social Charter 1961 and the 1989 Community Charter of Fundamental Social Rights of Workers. Subsequently, the Simitis Committee[89] argued that 'Clearly ascertainable fundamental rights stimulate the readiness to accept the European Union and to identify with its growing intensification and expanding remits.'[90] This led to the European Council, meeting in Cologne in June 1999, putting in motion the drafting process of a charter of rights. It said that 'Protection of fundamental rights is a founding principle of the Union and

---

[88] See, for example, *For a Europe of Civic and Social Rights*, Report by the Comité des Sages chaired by Maria de Lourdes Pintasilgo, Brussels, Oct. 1995–Feb. 1996, Commission, DGV. The responses of the European Parliament, ECOSOC and the ETUC to the Commission's Green Paper on Social Policy also called for 'the establishment of the fundamental social rights of citizens as a constitutional element of the European Union' COM (94) 333, 69. The *Molitor Report* (COM(95) 288 final/2, 39) on legislative and administrative simplification called for the adoption of a Bill of Rights. See also J. Kenner, 'Citizenship and fundamental rights: reshaping the social model', in J. Kenner (ed.), *Trends in European Social Policy: Essays in Memory of Malcolm Mead* (Aldershot, 1995); R. Blanpain, B. Hepple, S. Sciarra and M. Weiss, *Fundamental Social Rights: Proposals for the European Union* (Leuven, 1996); B. Bercusson, S. Deakin, P. Koistinen, Y. Kravaritou, U. Mückenberger, A. Supiot and B. Veneziani, 'A manifesto for a social Europe' (1997) 3 European Law Journal 189; A. Lo Faro, *Regulating Social Europe. Reality and Myth of Collective Bargaining in the EC Legal Order* (Oxford, 2000); A. Supiot (ed.), *Au-delà de l'emploi: Transformations du travail et l'avenir du droit du travail en Europe. Rapport pour la Commission Européenne* (Paris, 1999); P. Alston, *Human Rights Agenda for the European Union for the Year 2000* (Oxford, 1999).

[89] *Affirming Fundamental Rights in the European Union: Time to Act*, Report of the Expert Group on Fundamental Rights, Brussels, February 1999. The EU heads of government meeting at Tampere, Finland, in October 1999 set up a committee to begin drafting an EU charter of fundamental rights.

[90] See, for example, P. Cappelletti, *The Judicial Process in Comparative Perspective* (Oxford, 1989).

an indispensable prerequisite for her legitimacy ... There appears to be a need, at the present stage of the Union's development, to establish a Charter of fundamental rights in order to make their overriding importance and relevance more visible to the Union's citizens.' The resulting Charter of Fundamental Rights,[91] itself achieved through a (largely) transparent and deliberative process,[92] led to the identification of fifty rights, including a wide range of social rights. The rights include a rather guarded provision on information and consultation[93] and a carefully circumscribed provision on collective bargaining and collective action. It raises the profile of rights and, for our purposes, it places social rights (although rather narrow in scope) on the same footing as traditional civil and political rights. It offers a rights-based backbone to the constitutionalisation process. However, at present these rights are not directly enforceable before the courts.[94] This means that most workers still need to rely on traditional legislative methods producing substantive rights.[95]

However, the particular juridical form of social rights is difficult to define precisely. Lo Faro helpfully suggests that 'the notion of social rights can refer to a series of predominantly, but not exclusively, financial benefits bestowed by the public machinery within the context of social policies of the redistributive type'.[96] The problem with this idea, as he notes, is that many of the 'rights' in question depend, for their realisation, on certain economic and political conditions which are independent of the legal form of the benefits or claims in question. The

---

[91] OJ [2000] C 364/1. See generally K. Lenaerts and E. de Smijter, 'A Bill of Rights' for the European Union' (2001) 38 Common Market Law Review 273 and the special issue of the Maatricht Journal of European and Comparative Law (2001) 8 MJECL 3-112.

[92] See G. de Burca, 'The drafting of the European Union Charter of Fundamental Rights' (2001) 26 European Law Review 126. The Convention received more than one thousand documents from more than two hundred different agents. Less than half of these documents came from the secretariat or the presidium of the Convention (http://db.consilium.eu.int/df/default.asp?lang=en).

[93] Art. 27: 'Workers or their representatives must, at the appropriate levels, be guaranteed information and consultation in good time in the cases and under the conditions provided for by Community law and national laws and practices.'

[94] There is already some evidence that the Charter will come to attain legal force by case law. See, for example, AG Tizzano's Opinion in Case C-173/99 *BECTU* v. *Secretary of State for Trade and Industry*, Opinion delivered on 8 Feb. 2001. Members of the European Parliament expressed this view in November 2000. http://www.europa.eu.int/comm/justice-home/unit/charte/en/charter03.html. See also L. Betten, 'The EU Charter on Fundamental Rights: a Trojan horse or a mouse?' (2001) 12 International Journal of Comparative Labour Law and Industrial Relations 151.

[95] Betten, 'The EU Charter on Fundamental Rights', at p. 152.

[96] *Regulating Social Europe*, 152; see also Ch. 6 below, by Ivan Hare.

idea of the 'right to work' can be cited as one example of this problem; its effective realisation appears to depend upon external economic conditions or, according to taste, on various kinds of government action, which the legal system is more or less powerless to affect. The 'substantive' version of social rights may be contrasted, Lo Faro suggests, with a 'procedural' version based upon constitutional guarantees of freedom of association and collective representation. This, he suggests, would have the twofold merit of avoiding the straightforward association of social rights with economic 'costs', and stressing the links between social rights and participative democracy.

As we have seen, the merits of the procedural approach must be carefully weighed against the costs in terms of uncertainty over the meaning and application of legal rights. Nevertheless, there is a close link, in practice, between procedural rights and substantive outcomes. At the micro level of collective bargaining (or its equivalent) over working time, then, the thrust of 'reflexive' harmonising measures such as the Working Time Directive is that general principles (such as the principle of the humanisation of work) become reference points capable of 'steering' or 'channelling' the process of negotiation between the social partners. Thus social dialogue at all levels is framed by the existence of fundamental social rights. Very much the same process may be observed at the macro level of regulatory competition between different legal orders within the parameters of the single market. Here, too, the role of social rights is to set the parameters within which procedural solutions are sought. This can be seen from a consideration of decisions in which the European Court of Justice has attempted to resolve potential conflicts between the social policy provisions of the EC Treaty, and those parts of the Treaty which are concerned with free movement of economic resources and the removal of restrictions and distortions of competition. In *United Kingdom v. Council (Working Time)*,[97] the Court gave a broad reading to the term 'working environment' in Article 137 (ex art. 118a) EC, holding that 'a broad interpretation of the powers which Article 118a confers upon the Council for the protection of the health and safety of workers' was appropriate.[98] In *Albany International*,[99] the Court's decision that

---

[97] Case C-84/94 [1996] ECR-I 5755.
[98] See C. Barnard and S. Deakin, 'A year of living dangerously? EC social rights, employment policy, and EMU' (1999) 30 Industrial Relations Journal 355.
[99] Case C-67/96 *Albany International* v. *Stichting Bedrijfspensioenfonds Textielindustrie* [1999] ECR I-5751 considered by R. Van den Bergh and P. Camesasca, 'Irreconcilable Principles?

collective agreements were not, as such, subject to review under the competition policy provisions of the Treaty, was based on an analysis which recognised the strong encouragement given by the Treaty itself to collective bargaining, in the form of Article 138 (ex art. 118) and the provisions of the Maastricht Agreement on Social Policy (now part of art. 137).[100] What the Court was doing, in each case, was to use the social policy provisions of the EC Treaty to guide the process of rule formation; in the one case, the Council itself and, in the other, the social partners could legitimately act to regulate terms and conditions of employment, without, in the Court's view, infringing the economic freedoms which the Treaty also guarantees.

V. Conclusion

In the sphere of social dialogue, social rights frame the interaction between the social partners and steer the processes of benchmarking, bargaining and regulatory learning. A similar approach should, in our view, be adopted in the emerging field of EU-level corporate governance and corporate social responsibility. At present, judicial intervention, through decisions such as *Centros*, is creating an environment conducive to the emergence of US-style competitive federalism as the main driver of legal change. By contrast, social dialogue and the OMC point towards a framework for devolved law-making which recognises the role played by institutions of civil society, including the social partners, in promoting regulatory learning, rather than one in which regulatory arbitrage and capital flight set the agenda for company law. From this perspective, European governance and corporate governance are two sides of the same coin. The direction taken by the debate on political and institutional governance will therefore be of pivotal importance for the development of a distinctive European approach to corporate governance and responsibility.

The Court of Justice Exempts Collective Labour Agreements from the Wrath of Antitrust' (2000) 25 ELRev 492. See also Joined Cases C-180/98 to C-184/98 *Pavel Pavlov. v. Stichting Pensioenfonds Medische_Specialisten*, [2000] ECR I-6451, Case C-222/98 *van der Woude* v. *Stichting Beatrixoord*, [2000] ECR I-7111. See S. Evju, 'Collective agreements and Competition Law: the *Albany* Puzzle, and *Van der Woude*' (2000) 16 IJCLLIR 165.

[100] See Barnard and Deakin, 'Market access and regulatory competition', n. 40 above.

III

Constitutionalisation and enforcement
of social rights: some comparisons

III

6

Social rights as fundamental human rights

IVAN HARE

For there is no man so indigent or wretched, but he may demand a
supply sufficient for all the necessities of life from the more opulent
members of the community.

Blackstone's *Commentaries on the Laws of England* (1778)[1]

The purpose of this chapter is to consider whether social rights should
be protected as constitutional rights, that is, rights enforceable through
substantive judicial review and protected from amendment by the ordinary legislative process. To this end, I shall address a range of rights which
is in one sense broader and in another narrower than most other contributors to this collection. My concerns are broader in that the rights I
discuss have the potential to be genuinely universal and are not confined
to those members of the community who are economically active.[2] They
are narrower in that they are limited to four basic rights: to education,
housing, health care and a minimum income.[3] Such rights are frequently
described as second generational: the offspring of the first generation of
civil and political liberties and the forebears of third-generation rights

---

[1] W. Blackstone, *Commentaries on the Laws of England*, 8th edn (Oxford, 1778), I, 131.

[2] Entitlements limited to the economically active would include rights to just and favourable
conditions of work and to form and join trade unions (arts. 7 and 8 of the International
Covenant on Economic, Social and Cultural Rights (ICESCR), 1966). B. A. Hepple, 'The
Right to Work' (1981) 10 CLJ 65.

[3] C. Fabre defines social rights as 'rights to the meeting of needs – standardly rights to
adequate income, education, housing, and healthcare' in *Social Rights Under the Constitution –
Government and the Decent Life* (Oxford, 2000), 1; P. Hunt eschews a definition of social
rights but includes 'an adequate standard of living, food, shelter, health and education'
in *Reclaiming Social Rights: International and Comparative Perspectives* (Aldershot, 1996),
2. See T. H. Marshall, *Sociology at the Crossroads and Other Essays* (London, 1963) and
H. Shue, *Basic Rights: Subsistence, Affluence, and US Foreign Policy* (Princeton, NJ, 1980),
38–46.

to, for example, self-determination and a clean environment.[4] Social rights are also often characterised as group-based, as claim rights and as positive rights to distinguish them from the more familiar Western canon of individual and generally negative liberties.

The basic thesis of this chapter is that although many of the traditional objections to the constitutional protection of social rights are either simplistic or overstated, nevertheless there remain substantial principled and pragmatic obstacles to granting the ultimate decision-making power over the extent of such rights to the judicial branch of government. The structure of the chapter is as follows. In Part I, I attempt to sketch some of the historical background to the protection of social rights. Part II revisits some of the traditional objections to the judicial enforcement of social rights. In Part III, I discuss these objections in the light of recent legal developments in three principal contexts: the United Kingdom, the European Convention for the Protection of Human Rights and Fundamental Freedoms (ECHR) and South Africa.

I. Historical context

Social rights have undoubtedly been the poor cousins of the rights movement since its inception. Some of the reasons for this are historical. Although the Universal Declaration on Human Rights contains both civil and political and social rights, it reads like two distinct documents which have been rather inelegantly stuck together (with the join still visible somewhere between arts. 21 and 22). The ideological divisions between East and West after the Second World War also explain why a separate international document containing civil and political rights and another including economic, social and cultural rights were produced.[5]

---

[4] The generational approach to rights is criticised by A. Eide and A. Rosas, 'Economic, Social and Cultural Rights: A Universal Challenge' in A. Eide, C. Krause and A. Rosas (eds.), *Economic, Social and Cultural Rights – A Textbook* (Dordrecht, 1995), 16; and F. Klug, *Values for a Godless Age: The Story of the United Kingdom's New Bill of Rights* (London, 2000), 9–12. See further C. Scott, 'Reaching Beyond (Without Abandoning) the Category of "Economic, Social and Cultural Rights"' (1999) 21 HRQ 633.

[5] M. C. R. Craven, *The ICESCR – A Perspective on its Development* (Oxford, 1995); H. J. Steiner and P. Alston, *International Human Rights in Context – Law, Politics, Morals* (Oxford, 2000), Ch. 4; and S. Morphet, 'Economic, Social and Cultural Rights: The Development of

The differences are not all of form. For example, the enforcement mech-anisms provided in the social rights Covenant are also more limited. A similar contrast is discernible between the familiar and relatively strong enforcement machinery of the ECHR (which is overwhelmingly con-cerned with civil and political rights) and that of the European Social Charter which is based on biennial reports and does not provide for individual standing.[6]

At the domestic and comparative level, the great rights documents of the Western canon from Magna Carta to the Declaration of the Rights of Man and of the Citizen and the United States Bill of Rights are concerned almost exclusively with a view of freedom which regarded the absence of state control and limits on the powers of government as the indicia of liberty. This emphasis on civil and political rights was considered entirely consistent with societies which manifested radical inequalities in social and economic status. Where social rights are mentioned in the text of modern constitutions, they tend to appear as so-called Direc-tive Principles of State or Social Policy. In the Irish (1937) and Indian (1949) constitutions, the Directive Principles are contained in separate sections from those which deal with fundamental rights and the Princi-ples are expressly stated to be 'not cognizable by any Court' and 'not to be enforceable in any court' respectively.[7]

It is, however, misleading to suggest that previous generations did not regard the alleviation of indigence and the provision of social welfare as proper functions of the state – as the quotation from Blackstone at the head of this paper reveals. Indeed, Thomas Paine devoted a significant part of *The Rights of Man* to proposing a programme of social support (which included provisions for pensions and child benefit) to be funded

Governments' Views, 1941–88', in R. Beddard and D. M. Hill (eds.), *Economic, Social and Cultural Rights: Progress and Achievement* (London, 1992). It has been suggested that the reason for having separate Covenants was to ensure that state parties were not deterred from ratifying the International Covenant on Civil and Political Rights (ICCPR) by the inclusion of social rights in it. If true, this fear has proved to be unfounded since, of the two Covenants, more states have now ratified the ICESCR.

[6] D. Harris, 'Lessons from the reporting system of the European Social Charter', in P. Alston and J. Crawford (eds.), *The Future of UN Human Rights Treaty Monitoring* (Cambridge, 2000).

[7] Art. 45 of the Constitution of Ireland and art. 37 of the Constitution of India. It should be said that the Irish Constitution does contain a right to education in its section on Funda-mental Rights (art. 42) and that this right explicitly imposes on the state the obligation to provide free primary education.

by progressive taxation. In summary, Paine said:

> Civil government does not consist in executions; but in making that
> provision for the instruction of youth, and the support of age, as to
> exclude, as much as possible, profligacy from the one, and despair from
> the other.[8]

The law reports even reveal rare examples of common law intervention
to protect the rights of those without visible means of support. The
leading example is *R* v. *Eastbourne (Inhabitants)*,[9] in which it was argued
that a parish owed no duty of support to foreigners who could not
demonstrate a sufficient connection with the area. In response to this
argument, Lord Ellenborough CJ stated:

> As to there being no obligation for maintaining poor foreigners before
> the statutes ascertaining the different methods of acquiring settle-
> ments, the law of humanity, which is anterior to all positive laws,
> obliges us to afford them relief, to save them from starving; and those
> laws were only passed to fix the obligation more certainly, and point
> out distinctly in what manner it should be borne.[10]

However, such expressions were exceptional and the provision of assistance to alleviate the conditions of the poor and infirm was generally
regarded more as an example of largesse and an act of charity than as a
matter of the state's duty.[11] In particular, there was no suggestion that
social provision should be elevated to the level of a fundamental legal
right as opposed to being at the discretion of the distributors of the poor

---

[8] T. Paine, *The Rights of Man* (1791–2), Part II, ch. 5 in M. Foot (ed.), *The Thomas Paine Reader* (Harmondsworth, 1987), 314. 'Paine, in this chapter, set a course towards the social legislation of the twentieth century' (E. P Thompson, *The Making of the English Working Class* (Harmondsworth, 1980), 102). '[M]aternity benefits, free education, prison reform, full employment; much of the future later offered by the British Labour Party was previously on offer, in better English, from Thomas Paine' (M. Foot, 'Introduction' in *The Thomas Paine Reader*, 34). See also Paine's *Agrarian Justice* (1795) in the same volume. Paul O'Higgins traces some of the possible origins of Paine's thought in his introduction to L. Heffernan (ed.), *Human Rights – A European Perspective* (Dublin, 1994), 245–9.

[9] (1803) 4 East 103. The case was cited with approval by the Court of Appeal in *R* v. *Secretary of State for Social Security, ex parte Joint Council for the Welfare of Immigrants* [1997] 1 WLR 275. See also *R* v. *Wandsworth London Borough Council, ex parte O* [2000] 4 All ER 590.

[10] *R* v. *Eastbourne*, 107.

[11] For example, John Locke's chapter 'Of Property' in J. W. Gough (ed.), *The Second Treatise of Civil Government* (Oxford, 1946). In contrast, Paine said of his proposals for payments to those over 50 years of age: 'This support . . . is not of the nature of a charity, but of a right' (*The Thomas Paine Reader*, 337).

law. Even today, there is a discernible judicial reluctance to classify the relationship between welfare provider and recipient as one of private legal right rather than public law discretion. For example, a claimant for breach of statutory duty under English law must show that the relevant Act was intended to confer a benefit on specific individuals or a group of individuals and not upon society in general. In *O'Rourke* v. *Camden London Borough Council*[12] the claimant sought to argue that the public authority was liable in damages for breach of its statutory duty to house him. The House of Lords held that the claim should be struck out and that any challenge to the decisions of the authority would have to proceed by way of judicial review. For the House, Lord Hoffmann stated:

> the Act is a scheme of social welfare, intended to confer benefits at the public expense on grounds of public policy. Public money is spent on housing the homeless not merely for the private benefit of people who find themselves homeless but on grounds of general public interest: because, for example, proper housing means that people will be less likely to suffer illness, turn to crime or require the attention of other social services. The expenditure interacts with expenditure on other public services such as education, the National Health Service and even the police. It is not simply a private matter between the claimant and the housing authority.[13]

Throughout the nineteenth century, concerns about the conditions of the poor (and especially those living in the expanding urban centres) continued to grow. However, it was not until the last century that they were formulated in terms of rights, perhaps most famously in F. D. Roosevelt's State of the Union Address in 1941.[14] There, Roosevelt

---

[12] [1998] AC 188. See M. Partington, 'Citizenship and Housing' in R. Blackburn (ed.), *Rights of Citizenship* (London, 1993).

[13] *O'Rourke*, 193C–E. This judicial tendency has also emerged in other fields of welfare provision (such as education – *Phelps* v. *Hillingdon London Borough Council* [1999] 1 All ER 421). In the light of the decision in *Osman* v. *United Kingdom* (1999) 29 EHRR 245, the House has proved less willing to resolve these cases at the stage of striking out (*Barrett* v. *Enfield London Borough Council* [1999] 3 WLR 79). See now *Z and Others* v. *United Kingdom* [2001] 2 FLR 612. On judicial attitudes towards the interpretation of social legislation, see H. Dean, *Welfare, Law and Citizenship* (London, 1996), 167–190 and the classic: W. I. Jennings, 'Courts and Administrative Law – The Experience of English Housing Legislation' (1936) 49 Harv LR 426.

[14] An early example was the Constitution of the German Reich (1919) which included a duty on the state and municipalities to maintain the purity, health and social welfare of the family (H. L. McBain and L. Rogers, *The New Constitutions of Europe* (New York, 1923)).

included 'freedom from want' as one of his 'Four Freedoms' along with the freedoms of speech and of religion and freedom from fear.[15] Nor can one identify a linear and progressive acceptance of the idea of social rights since then. Indeed, social rights are considered inconsistent with the vision of freedom and society advanced in a number of strands of modern political philosophy including those labelled communitarian and neo-libertarian.[16] If not hostile, many of the major figures of contemporary political philosophy (including Rawls, Nagel, Raz and Dworkin) have either neglected the question of constitutionalising social rights or have marginalised their significance.[17] Therefore, despite the official view of the United Nations and a number of human rights organisations that civil, political, social and economic rights are 'universal, indivisible and interdependent and interrelated',[18] this view is not broadly accepted. It is noticeable that, at the level of positive law, Canada, New Zealand and the United Kingdom have all sought to reinvigorate the protection of fundamental rights in their jurisdictions in the past twenty years and all have focused almost exclusively on civil and political rights.[19]

The fact that social rights have a shorter legal pedigree and that they form a less significant part of the Western philosophical tradition does not mean, of course, that they should not be given constitutional protection if the arguments in favour of so doing are compelling. In addition, there have been developments in the past decade which suggest

[15] M. R. Ishay, *The Human Rights Reader* (New York, 1997), 403–6.
[16] Fabre, *Social Rights*, 23–26 and D. Beetham, 'What Future for Economic and Social Rights?' (1995) 63 Pol Studies 41.
[17] Fabre, *Social Rights*, 4.
[18] For example, Vienna Declaration and Programme of Action, para 5 (United Nations Second World Conference on Human Rights, 14–25 June 1993) reported in [1993] 14 HRLJ 352. For a perspective based on the experiences of a number of developing countries, see M. B. Oliviero: 'Human needs and human rights: Which are more fundamental?' 1991 Emory LJ 911.
[19] Although there was a proposal to include non-judicially enforceable social rights in the debate preceding the New Zealand Bill of Rights Act (*Final Report of the Justice and Law Reform Committee on a White Paper on a Bill of Rights for New Zealand* (1988)). See P. A. Joseph, 'The New Zealand Bill of Rights Experience' in P. Alston (ed.), *Promoting Human Rights Through Bills of Rights* (Oxford, 1999) 283, 289. Some commentators did advocate incorporation of social rights in the UK Human Rights Act: K. D. Ewing, 'Democratic Socialism and Labour Law' (1995) 24 ILJ 103; (with C. A. Gearty), 'Rocky Foundations of Labour's New Rights' (1997) 2 EHRLR 146 and 'Social Rights and Constitutional Law' [1999] PL 104. A further example of the rejection of social rights is described in A. Byrnes, 'And Some Have Bills of Rights Thrust Upon Them: Hong Kong's Bill of Rights Experience', in Alston, *Promoting Human Rights*, 323–3.

that the traditional view of social rights may be changing. First, there has been a tangible growth in the apparent willingness of courts in a number of jurisdictions to address questions which have a significant impact on welfare provision. This has been matched by an increase in the quantity of academic writing on the subject.[20] Second, there are now the concrete examples of the Indian Supreme Court's social rights jurisprudence and South Africa's constitutional commitment to the protection of social rights.[21] Third, we now have the European Union's Charter of Fundamental Rights which includes, among many others, rights to social security and health care.[22] These developments suggest that now may be a good time to reflect further on some of the objections which have been raised to the constitutional protection of social rights.

II. The traditional objections to social rights revisited

Positive and negative rights

One of the most frequent objections to social rights is based on the supposed distinction between negative and positive rights. Negative rights are generally thought to be the traditional civil and political rights to be left alone by government. Positive rights are defined as those that require government action (frequently in the form of expenditure) to ensure their protection. However, this objection is not very persuasive since a number of traditional civil and political rights, such as the right to a fair trial, may require very substantial government expenditure.[23] A useful illustration of this is provided by the Canadian decision in *R* v. *Askov*.[24]

---

[20] In addition to the works already cited, see C. Sampford and D. J. Galligan (eds.), *Law, Rights and the Welfare State* (London, 1986) and K. Arambulo, *Strengthening the Supervision of the International Covenant on Economic, Social and Cultural Rights: Theoretical and Procedural Aspects* (Antwerp, 1999).

[21] A number of former members of the Soviet Union and Warsaw Pact included social rights in their post-communist constitutions. For example, Constitution of the Russian Federation (1993, arts. 37–43); Constitution of the Republic of Hungary (1989, Chapter XII); Constitutional Act of Poland (1992, Chapter 8); Constitution of the Slovak Republic (1992, Chapter Two, Part Five); and Constitution of Romania (1991, Title II, Chapter II). See further R. R. Ludwikowski, *Constitution-Making in the Region of Former Soviet Dominance* (Durham, NC, and London, 1996).

[22] Arts. 34 and 35.

[23] S. Holmes and C. R. Sunstein, *The Cost of Rights: Why Liberty Depends on Taxes* (New York, 1999).

[24] [1990] 2 SCR 1199.

The Canadian Charter of Rights and Freedoms includes the provision: 'Any person charged with an offence has the right... to be tried within a reasonable time.'[25] In the present case, the Supreme Court held that a delay of thirty-four months between the defendant's first appearance to the dismissal of the case against him violated this right. The result of the decision was that 50,000 criminal charges were set aside in Ontario alone and the provincial government there spent the equivalent of over US$28 million on improving court resources and recruiting more personnel to reduce delays in the criminal process.

The European Convention on Human Rights contains several provisions which necessarily require expenditure by the state, such as the right to free legal assistance when charged with a criminal offence (art. 6(3)(c)), the right to education (art. 2, Protocol 1) and the state's duty to hold free and periodic elections (art. 3, Protocol 1). Decisions of the European Court of Human Rights (ECtHR) have gone some way beyond this and provide further examples of the positive obligations which may flow from a commitment to respecting ostensibly negative civil and political rights. A celebrated early example was the decision in *Airey* v. *Ireland* in which the applicant claimed that the absence of legal aid for divorce proceedings violated her right to family life under Article 8 and to a fair hearing in the determination of her civil rights under Article 6. In upholding Airey's complaint, the Court stated:

> The Convention is intended to guarantee not rights that are theoretical or illusory but rights that are practical and effective.... It must therefore be ascertained whether [the applicant's] appearance before the High Court without the assistance of a lawyer would be effective, in the sense of whether she would be able to present her case properly and satisfactorily.[26]

More recently and more controversially, the Court has held that the state's duty to protect the right to life (art. 2) includes the obligation to install 'effective criminal law provisions to deter the commission of offences against the person backed up by law-enforcement machinery for the prevention, suppression and sanctioning of breaches of such provisions'.[27] In certain circumstances, this duty would include the affirmative obligation to take operational measures to protect individuals

---

[25] Section 11(b).   [26] (1979–80) 2 EHRR 305, para. 24.
[27] *Osman* v. *United Kingdom*, para. 115.

whose lives were placed in jeopardy by the activities of others. Such obligations plainly have significant resource implications for the state. The Court has also applied the concept of positive duties to a number of Convention rights other than the right to life.[28] It is not therefore accurate to describe civil and political rights as only imposing the negative obligation on the state to leave the individual alone.

Economic rights of a different kind from those which are the focus of this paper provide another illustration. Under the law of the European Union, quantitative restrictions on imports and all measures having equivalent effect are prohibited between the member states.[29] The European Court of Justice has held that this provision may impose affirmative duties on the member states when read in conjunction with a state's responsibility to ensure the fulfilment of its obligations under Article 10 (ex art. 5) of the EC Treaty. Thus the European Commission brought proceedings against France for its passivity in the face of sometimes violent protests by French farmers which impeded the entry of agricultural produce from a number of other member states. The Court concluded that:

> Article 30 therefore does not prohibit solely measures emanating from the State which, in themselves, create restrictions on trade between Member States. It also applies where a Member State abstains from adopting the measures required in order to deal with obstacles to the free movement of goods which are not caused by the State.[30]

These examples should be sufficient to demonstrate that rights other than social rights may impose positive obligations on the state.

Conversely, it is possible for certain rights frequently defined as social rights to contain negative elements which require no more than that the state should not interfere with their exercise. The right to join a trade union and not to be penalised for doing so is often given as an example. The conceptual similarity between this social right and the right to freedom of association (which is usually regarded as a civil and political right) robs this illustration of some of its force. However, there

---

[28] For example, the right to respect for private and family life (*X and Y* v. *The Netherlands* (1985) 8 EHRR 235 and *Glaser* v. *United Kingdom* [2000] 3 FCR 193) and freedom of assembly (*Plattform 'Aertze fur das Leben'* v. *Austria* (1991) 13 EHRR 204). See K. Starmer, *European Human Rights Law* (Legal Action Group, 1999), Ch. 5.

[29] Art. 28 (formerly art. 30) of the EC Treaty.

[30] Case C-265/95 *Commission* v. *France* [1997] ECR-I 6959, para. 30.

are other examples including the right not to be evicted unlawfully from one's dwelling which has been held to be an actionable part of the right to housing in the South African Constitution.[31]

There is little which is original in the above description, but I hope that it establishes that the traditional tendency to categorise all civil and political rights as negative and all social rights as positive is unduly simplistic. However, to demonstrate that an orthodox dichotomy is not watertight is very far from proving the case for the constitutional protection of social rights. The point about the areas in which domestic and international courts have accepted that positive duties may flow from a constitutional commitment to civil and political rights is that, in almost all such cases, the obligations result from one of two characteristics of the litigation. They are either examples of the state pursuing the individual through the legal process and of the court imposing obligations to ensure equality of arms between state and citizen (as in *Askov*); or they involve the situation where expenditure is essential instrumentally to ensure the protection of an existing civil and political right (as in *Airey*). It is noticeable that the majority of cases about the right to a fair trial concern criminal proceedings instituted by the state where the imbalance of resources between the parties is at its most extreme and where the potential for prejudice to the fundamental rights of the citizen (through a miscarriage of justice leading to a loss of liberty) is acute.

A further characteristic of cases in which positive obligations have been imposed through constitutional litigation is evident where the state has either created or exacerbated a situation of dependency on the part of the claimants. The most obvious example of this is where the individual is incarcerated in a state-funded prison. Decisions concerning prison conditions have clear cost implications. In *Hamilton* v. *Love*, the Arkansas Supreme Court announced the following principle:

> Inadequate resources can never be an adequate justification for the state's depriving any person of his constitutional rights. If the state cannot obtain the resources to detain persons awaiting trial in accordance with minimum constitutional standards, then the state simply will not be permitted to detain such persons.[32]

A similar principle was applied post-conviction by the Privy Council in its recent change of heart concerning the conditions in which death

---

[31] *Government of South Africa & Ors* v. *Grootboom*, 2001(1) SA 46.
[32] 328 F Supp 1182, 1194 (ED Ark 1971).

row inmates are kept in some of the Caribbean countries of the Commonwealth. In earlier decisions,[33] the Privy Council had made it clear that even detention in conditions which were unlawful would not render the subsequent execution unconstitutional unless the conditions objectively aggravated the death sentence and were different from the treatment endured by other prisoners. Moreover, earlier Boards had held that there were more suitable remedies than commutation of sentence to deal with the often appalling conditions in Caribbean prisons. However, the majority of the Board in *Lewis & Others v. Attorney General of Jamaica*[34] rejected this line and stated themselves to be disturbed that the applicants' challenges based on the conditions of their incarceration had not been adequately investigated by the lower courts. The majority appeared to favour the view that the state can forfeit its right to carry out the death sentence if it treats its death row prisoners contrary to a constitutional prohibition on inhuman and degrading treatment. These decisions have clear resource implications for developing and developed states, but again, do not provide general support for the imposition of positive obligations through judicial review. They are plain illustrations of cases where public authorities are responsible for the violation of civil and political rights because the state has directly and intentionally reduced the citizen to a situation of dependency.

Even the recent decisions of the Constitutional Court in South Africa in interpreting their constitutional protections for health and housing have an element of this factor.[35] When addressing the right not to be refused emergency medical treatment in *Soobramoney*, the Court emphasised that South Africa had only recently emerged from a system in which the provision of health services depended upon race and in which seriously injured people were refused access to ambulance services or denied entrance to the nearest or best-equipped hospital on explicitly racial grounds.[36] Likewise, in *Grootboom*, the Court expressly stated that the 'cause of the acute housing shortage lies in apartheid'[37] and then proceeded to explain that the Western Cape had previously imposed strict controls on the influx of Africans in pursuit of its policy of encouraging coloured workers into the area. As a result, the provision

[33] *Thomas v. Baptiste* [2000] 2 AC 1, and *Higgs v. Minister of National Security* [2000] 2 AC 228.
[34] [2001] 2 AC 50.
[35] See below, nn. 97–107 and accompanying text, for the facts of these cases.
[36] *Soobramoney v. Minister of Health, Kwazulu-Natal* 1998 (1) SA, 665, 774, fn. 10, *per* Chaskalson P.
[37] *Government of South Africa & Ors v. Grootboom*, para. 6, *per* Yacoob J.

of family housing for African families was frozen in 1962. At the same time, colonial dispossession of farmland and the racial distribution of land in rural areas made large-scale influxes of Africans to urban areas inevitable, with the result that vast squatter settlements grew around urban centres associated with persistent harassment by officials and periodic forced removals.[38]

This tendency to impose positive obligations only in response to, or as a qualification of, the exercise of state power is also visible in the jurisdiction most frequently cited as an example of high levels of judicial protection for social rights: India. As is well known, the Indian Supreme Court has used the Directive Principles of State Policy in Part IV of the Constitution (which deal, among other things, with social interests in work, welfare and education) to interpret the scope of the enforceable civil and political rights in the Constitution.[39] For example, the Court has held that the right not to be deprived of life or liberty except in accordance with a procedure established by law (art. 21) includes the right to consultation with legal counsel.[40] In that case, the Court went on to state that Article 21

> includes the right to live with human dignity and all that goes along with it, namely, the bare necessities of life such as adequate nutrition, clothing and shelter... Every act which offends against or impairs human dignity would constitute deprivation *pro tanto* of this right to live.[41]

The same expansive interpretation of this provision was advanced in a case concerning the Bombay pavement dwellers who claimed that their right to life would be violated if they were evicted from their shelters without the provision of alternative accommodation.[42] Yet even these were cases in which the state had pursued the individual or group in some way: either by arresting and detaining them in *Mullin* or by proposing to carry out the eviction in *Tellis*. In any event, the right to consult a lawyer is very frequently found among the canon of civil and political rights, and the pavement dwellers' interests in *Tellis* were held to be adequately protected by the hearing they had before the Supreme Court.

[38] Ibid.

[39] It has been suggested that the Supreme Court's willingness to protect social rights is part of an attempt by the Court to recapture some of the public support it lost through its role in the 1975 Emergency (U. Baxi, *The Supreme Court and Politics* (Lucknow, 1980)).

[40] *Frances Mullin v. Union Territory of Delhi* [1981] 2 SCR 516.   [41] Ibid., 529.

[42] *Olga Tellis v. Bombay Municipal Corporation* [1985] 2 Supp SCR 51.

The Bombay Corporation was permitted to proceed with the evictions after the hearing and the end of the monsoon season.

Thus, although it is not plausible rigidly to categorise civil and political rights as negative and social rights as positive, the distinction retains force in the majority of cases. What emerges, then, is a general judicial reluctance to impose positive obligations on the state in the fields of civil and political *and* social rights.[43] This reticence is usually only overcome where the state has itself created or exacerbated the situation in which the rights violation has occurred. Although this approach is common to both areas of rights protection, it is most likely to be relevant in the field of social rights, which will almost invariably impose substantial affirmative obligations on the state which are difficult to quantify and balance within the confines of the judicial process.

Resource implications

A related, but in some circumstances distinct, objection to the judicial enforcement of constitutional social rights arises from the fact that there are frequently resource implications to their fulfilment. The resource implications of a decision need not constitute an absolute bar to the judicial enforcement of social rights as the South African Constitutional Court has decided in the *Certification* judgement. There, the Court held that social rights in the Constitution

> are, at least to some extent, justiciable. As we have stated . . . , many of the civil and political rights entrenched in the . . . [Constitution] will give rise to similar budgetary implications without compromising their justiciability. The fact that socio-economic rights inevitably give rise to such implications does not seem to us to be a bar to their justiciability. At the very minimum, socio-economic rights can be protected from improper invasion.[44]

Nevertheless, judges are thought to be (and perceive themselves to be) particularly ill-suited to substitute their view for that of elected

---

[43] An example of the judicial reluctance to question resource allocation decisions in the field of economic rights under EU law is *R* v. *Chief Constable of Sussex, ex parte International Trader's Ferry Ltd* [1999] 2 AC 418 (discussed in C. Barnard and I. Hare, 'The Right to Protest and the Right to Export: Police Discretion and the Free Movement of Goods' (1997) 60 MLR 394, 397–402).

[44] *Ex parte Chairperson of the Constitutional Assembly: In Re Certification of the Constitution of the Republic of South Africa, 1996* 1996 (4) SA 744, para. 78.

politicians and professional civil servants on how spending on social programmes and other legitimate areas of governmental expenditure (or between different social programmes) should be balanced. This explains why a number of domestic and international protections for social rights are expressly subject to resource considerations.

An obvious illustration is provided by the respective provisions in the ICCPR and ICESCR concerning the responsibilities of states who ratify the Covenants. The ICCPR requires all state parties to undertake 'to respect and to ensure to all individuals . . . the rights recognized in the present Covenant'.[45] By contrast, state parties to the ICESCR undertake 'to take steps, individually and through international assistance and co-operation, especially economic and technical, to the maximum of its available resources, with a view to achieving progressively the full realization of the rights recognized in the present Covenant'.[46]

One of the few genuine social rights contained in the ECHR provides a further illustration of this point. The original wording of Article 2, Protocol 1 stated that 'every person has the right to education'. During the *travaux préparatoires*, this was changed to the present formulation: 'No person shall be denied the right to education.'[47] The change of wording was held to be significant in one of the few cases to reach the ECtHR on its interpretation. In the *Belgian Linguistic Case (No 2)*, the Court held that

> The negative formulation indicates . . . that the Contracting Parties do not recognise such a right to education as would require them to establish at their expense, or to subsidise, education of any particular type or at any particular level.[48]

---

[45] Art. 2(1).

[46] Art. 2(1). The Committee on Economic, Social and Cultural Rights did not find a violation of the Covenant until 1990 (S. Leckie, 'The Committee on Economic, Social and Cultural Rights: Catalyst for change in a system needing reform', in Alston and Crawford, *Treaty Monitoring*). See further M. C. R. Craven, 'The Domestic Application of the International Covenant on Economic, Social and Cultural Rights' (1993) 40 NILR 367. Some commentators have sought to give substance to this provision by emphasising the minimum or core content of social rights: A. Eide, 'Realization of Social and Economic Rights and the Minimum Threshold Approach' (1989) 10 HRLJ 35 and UN Committee on Economic, Social and Cultural Rights: 'The Nature of State Parties' Obligations (art. 2, para. 1 of the Covenant)', General Comment No 3, UN Doc E/1991/23, Annex III (adopted in Dec. 1990).

[47] A. H. Robertson, 'The European Convention on Human Rights – Recent Developments' (1951) BYIL 359, 362–4.

[48] (1968) 1 EHRR 252, para. 3.

In other words, the right is only that of equal access to existing facilities and imposes no obligation to provide further educational resources.[49]

A further characteristic of this article is the number of contracting states which has appended reservations.[50] In relation to the duty to respect the religious and philosophical convictions of parents, the United Kingdom's reservation is typical: the obligation is accepted 'only so far as it is compatible with the provision of efficient instruction and training and the avoidance of unreasonable public expenditure'.[51] Several domestic social rights provisions make explicit reference to the resource implications of their full realisation. For example, the state's general duties to provide access to health care and housing under the South African Constitution (which were in issue in *Soobramoney* and *Grootboom*) are expressly to 'take reasonable legislative and other measures, *within its available resources*'.[52]

III. Recent developments

In this section I consider legal developments in a number of jurisdictions which have been used by some commentators to suggest that social rights are now protected through the same mechanisms of judicial enforcement as civil and political rights. The argument of this section is that this is an overstatement and that the level of protection afforded to social rights is limited to that provided by administrative law standards based on rationality and fair procedures rather than more intrusive scrutiny which is traditionally applied to constitutional norms.[53] The distinction can be illustrated by two comparative examples.

---

[49] The Court went on to hold that the state could take account of the resource implications of educational provision. The United Kingdom has successfully defended the limited availability of schools for children with special educational needs on cost grounds (*Simpson* v. *United Kingdom* (1989) 64 DR 188). See further, *O'Connor* v. *Chief Adjudication Officer and Secretary of State for Social Security* [1999] 1 FLR 1200, 1215 (*per* Auld LJ).

[50] Including Germany, Ireland, Malta, the Netherlands, Portugal and Sweden.

[51] The reservation is incorporated in the Human Rights Act 1998 by section 15(1)(a) and is included in Schedule 3, Part II. This formula is also included in the Education Act 1996, on which see *B* v. *Harrow London Borough Council* [2000] 1 WLR 223. It should be noted that the European Commission of Human Rights has questioned the validity of the UK reservation (*SP* v. *United Kingdom* (1997) 23 EHRR CD 139).

[52] Sections 27(2) and 26(2) (emphasis added).

[53] This distinction is discussed in D. M. Beatty, 'The Last Generation: When Rights Lose Their Meaning' in D. M. Beatty (ed.), *Human Rights and Judicial Review: A Comparative Perspective* (Dordrecht, 1994) and J. Waldron, *Law and Disagreement* (Oxford, 1999), 218 (criticised in C. Fabre, 'The Dignity of Rights' (2000) 20 OJLS 271).

The first is that of the United States. As noted above,[54] the US Constitution makes no reference to social provision and it has been said that
'Rights in the United States remain in essence eighteenth-century freedoms.'[55] When considering state action which violates a fundamental
constitutional right, the US Supreme Court applies a concept of strict
scrutiny which requires a compelling state justification for the proposed
action. However, in the field of social rights, the Court has repeatedly
held that government programmes are lawful if they cross the much
lower threshold of possessing a rational basis. State programmes which
imposed an upper limit on the amount of welfare payable to families
irrespective of their size, which produced marked disparities in funding by linking education expenditure to property values in the school
district or which charged a fee for a school bus service have all been
upheld through applying this deferential standard of review.[56] This is
not to say that the Supreme Court has provided no protection for social
rights. However, where it has done so the protections have been purely
procedural or limited to those provisions which affect a fundamental
civil or political right.[57]

Perhaps more illustrative is the example of Hungary. As has already
been mentioned,[58] the Hungarian Constitution expressly protects certain social interests, including the right to social security.[59] When the
government sought to enact an austerity package which contained

[54] P. 155, above.

[55] L. Henkin, 'Economic Rights Under the United States Constitution', 32 Colum J Transnat'l
L 97, 128 (1994).

[56] *Dandridge* v. *Williams*, 397 US 471 (1970); *San Antonio Independent School District* v.
Rodriguez, 411 US 1 (1973) and *Kadrmas* v. *Dickinson Public Schools*, 487 US 450 (1988)
respectively. The Court has also held that there is no constitutional right to housing
(*Lindsey* v. *Normet*, 405 US 56 (1972)) or to medical services (*Harris* v. *McRae*, 448 US
279 (1980)). It has been suggested that the rational basis standard of review should not
be applied by state Supreme Courts when interpreting the welfare provisions of state constitutions (H. Hershkoff, 'Positive Rights in State Constitutions: The Limits of Federal
Rationality Review', 112 Harv L Rev 1131 (1999)).

[57] *Goldberg* v. *Kelly*, 397 US 254 (1970) (XIV Amendment requires an evidentiary hearing
before the termination of certain welfare benefits) and *Shapiro* v. *Thompson*, 394 US 618
(1969) (one year residency requirement for welfare assistance violated the Equal Protection
Clause since it impinges upon the fundamental right of inter-state travel). Even the classic
article by C. A. Reich, 'The New Property' 73 Yale LJ 733 (1963–1964), which greatly influenced the Court in *Goldberg*, 262, fn 8, *per* Brennan J.) is principally concerned with securing
rights of due process for welfare recipients and others. The Court recently affirmed *Shapiro*
in *Saenz* v. *Roe*, 526 US 489 (1999).

[58] N. 21, above.   [59] Art. 70/E.

substantial reductions in some social benefits in 1995, a challenge was brought before the Constitutional Court. In a controversial ruling, the Court accepted that the constitutional right to social security 'means neither a guaranteed income, nor that the achieved living standard of citizens could not deteriorate as a result of the unfavourable development of economic conditions'.[60] However, while acknowledging the state's legal power to alter the benefit system from one based on citizen's rights to one based on need, the Court imposed certain limitations. First, a minimum level of protection must be maintained. Second, the state must implement the changes in a manner consistent with the Constitution's commitment to the rule of law and the protection of property rights. Thus drastic changes could not be introduced overnight and the acquired rights and legitimate expectations of current claimants must be respected.[61] Once again, these principles are in essence procedural and are thus distinct from the judicial approach to the vindication of substantive civil and political rights.

It should be acknowledged at this stage that the more intensive form of judicial scrutiny which is associated with the adjudication of disputes over civil and political rights is not a monolithic standard. The ECtHR defines a margin of appreciation when applying the Convention to situations where national authorities are better placed than the Court to assess the necessity of a disputed restriction because of 'their direct and continuous contact with the vital forces of their countries'.[62] Although the doctrine has correctly been confined to supranational legal bodies by English courts applying the Human Rights Act, an analogous domestic principle has emerged. For example, in the context of legislation which reversed the onus of proof for certain terrorist offences, Lord Hope of Craighead referred to

> questions of balance between competing interests and issues of pro-
> portionality ... where ... difficult choices may have to be made by the
> executive or the legislature between the rights of the individual and
> the needs of society. In some circumstances it will be appropriate for

---

[60] Dec 772/B/1990 AB ABH 1991, 519, 520.
[61] Decision 43/1995 (30 June 1995) extracted and translated in L. Solyom and G. Brunner (eds.), *Constitutional Judiciary in a New Democracy: The Hungarian Constitutional Court* (Ann Arbor, 2000), 323–32.
[62] *Handyside v. United Kingdom* (1979) 1 EHRR 737, para. 48.

the courts to recognise that there is an area of judgement within which the judiciary will defer, on democratic grounds, to the considered opinion of the elected body or person whose act or decision is said to be incompatible with the Convention.[63]

However, the crucial point in disputes over civil and political rights is that the 'discretionary area of judgement' is only applicable to the exceptional case where the public authority is able to advance specific policy considerations which are relevant to its resolution. On the other hand, such considerations in the forms of limited resources and revenue-raising priorities are always likely to be present in social rights cases.

Developments in the United Kingdom

Recent cases in the United Kingdom might appear to provide some support for the view that social rights are already enforced through the judicial review procedure. The argument of this section is that, although there is some truth in this contention, the decisions are all explicable on traditional administrative law grounds and do not support the argument for providing constitutional, as opposed to statutory, protection for social rights.

One group of recent cases suggests that, in some areas of welfare provision, the courts will not permit public authorities to rely upon limited resources to defeat claims against them. The leading decision is *R v. East Sussex County Council, ex parte Tandy.*[64] Beth Tandy had suffered from myalgic encephalomyelitis since the age of seven which made it impossible for her to attend school regularly. The local authority therefore made arrangements for her to receive five hours per week of home tuition.[65] In October 1996 the authority informed Tandy's parents that budgetary constraints required them to reduce this home

---

[63] *R* v. *Director of Public Prosecutions, ex parte Kebilene* [2000] 2 AC 326, 380–1 (*per* Lord Hope of Craighead). See further, *Brown* v. *Stott* [2001] 2 WLR 817, 834–5 (*per* Lord Bingham of Cornhill) and 842–3 (*per* Lord Steyn) and A. Lester and D. Pannick, *Human Rights Law and Practice* (London, 1999), 73–6.

[64] [1998] AC 714.

[65] At the time at which the dispute arose, this was provided under the authority's duty to make arrangements for children of compulsory school age who by reason of illness might not otherwise receive suitable education (section 298, Education Act 1993 – now re-enacted in section 19, Education Act 1996).

tuition from five to three hours. The House of Lords held that financial resources were irrelevant to a proper assessment of what would constitute 'suitable education' under the Education Act and that the authority had to arrive at its determination by reference to pertinent factors such as the child's age, ability and any special needs. In response to the authority's argument that a lack of resources could prevent the statutory duty to provide suitable education from arising, Lord Browne-Wilkinson stated:

> the county council has as a matter of strict legality the resources necessary to perform its statutory duty under section 298. Very understandably it does not wish to bleed its other functions of resources so as to enable it to perform the statutory duty under section 298. But it can, if it wishes, divert money from other educational, or other, applications which are merely discretionary so as to apply such diverted moneys to discharge the statutory duty laid down by section 298. The argument is not one of insufficient resources to discharge the duty but of a preference for using the money for other purposes. To permit a local authority to avoid performing a statutory duty on the grounds that it prefers to spend the money in other ways is to downgrade a statutory duty to a discretionary power.[66]

The House emphasised that each such case will turn on the construction of the particular statutory language,[67] but the reasoning in *Tandy* has not been confined to the educational context. For example, in *R* v. *Sefton Metropolitan Borough Council, ex parte Help the Aged*[68] the Court of Appeal had to determine the relevance of resources to the discharge of a council's duty to make arrangements for the provision of accommodation for those who by reason of age, illness, disability or any other circumstances are in need of care and attention.[69] The Court held that once the council decided that the applicant was in need, they were under

---

[66] [1998] AC 714, 749A–D.

[67] The House had to distinguish its own recent decision in *R* v. *Gloucestershire County Council, ex parte Barry* [1997] AC 584 in which it had held (by a narrow majority) that the authority was entitled to take account of its limited resources when considering the needs of a disabled person under section 2(1) of the Chronically Sick and Disabled Persons Act 1970. See E. Palmer and M. Sunkin, 'Needs, Resources and Abhorrent Choices' (1998) 61 MLR 401 and B. Schwehr, 'The legal relevance of resources – or a lack of resources – in community care' (1995) 17 Journal of Social Welfare and Family Law 179.

[68] [1997] 4 All ER 532.

[69] The duty arises under section 21(1)(a), National Assistance Act 1948.

a duty, regardless of resource implications, to provide accommodation.[70] Later courts have gone so far as to issue mandatory orders requiring the authority to identify suitable housing within three months of the court's order and to make the accommodation available to the claimant within a further three months.[71]

Once again, however, it is possible to overstate the significance of these cases for the debate on social rights. First, in a number of areas of welfare provision, the court has held that the question of entitlement is one of discretion for the authority and not of right for the applicant.[72] This is, of course, inevitable if the answer always depends on the construction of the particular statute. Second, and most significantly, in those cases where resources were held to be irrelevant, the existence of the public authority's duty was always held to be conditional on a prior finding *by the authority itself* that the claimant was in need.[73] In arriving at its discretionary determination of need, all the cases establish that an authority's limited resources are relevant and may be taken into account. The determination of need thus becomes the crucial stage of the decision-making process and here the court will only interfere with the authority's determination on traditional administrative law grounds. Thus all the court is really saying is that the authority cannot consistently with its statutory duties hold that the individual is in need, but then plead its limited resources to avoid fulfilling its statutory duty to cater for that need.

The other principal area in which the resource implications of welfare decisions have been litigated is in the field of clinical decision-making.[74] Here again, there are examples of successful challenges. In

---

[70] To similar effect, see *R* v. *Wigan Metropolitan District Council, ex parte Tammadge* [1998] 1 CCLR 581; *R* v. *Royal Borough of Kensington and Chelsea, ex parte Kutjim* [1999] 2 CCLR 340 and *R (on the application of Mukoko Batantu)* v. *London Borough of Islington* [2001] 4 CCLR 445.

[71] *Ex parte Tammadge* and *Mukoko Batantu*, above.

[72] *Ex parte Barry*. A recent example is *R (on the application of A)* v. *Lambeth London Borough Council* [2001] EWCA Civ 1624.

[73] In relation to cases such as *Tandy* where the crucial determination was not of need, the House held that where there was more than one way of providing 'suitable education', the authority was entitled to have regard to its limited resources in deciding which to provide.

[74] Fabre accepts that 'healthcare is probably the most problematic of all the kinds of welfare provision mentioned in this book' (*Social Rights*, 37). See J. Montgomery, 'Recognising a Right to Health' in Beddard and Hill, *Progress and Achievement*; M. Brazier, 'Rights and Health Care' in Blackburn, *Citizenship*; B. Toebes, 'Towards an Improved Understanding of the International Right to Healthcare' (1999) 21 Human Rights Quarterly 661, and C. Witting, 'National Health Service Rationing: Implications for the Standard of Care in Negligence' (2001) 21 OJLS 443.

the first judicial review of a medical decision to refuse treatment, the court indicated that it would be prepared to declare illegal a policy which barred care on racial or religious grounds.[75] Subsequently, a successful challenge was mounted by three transsexuals who sought gender re-assignment surgery, but were refused pursuant to a policy which accorded low priority to procedures regarded by the authority as clinically ineffective in terms of health gain. On judicial review, the Court of Appeal held that the authority had not genuinely exercised its discretion at all because the policy amounted to a blanket ban on such surgery.[76] The refusal was therefore quashed and the matter remitted to the authority. *R v. North Derbyshire Health Authority, ex parte Fisher*[77] concerned arrangements for the introduction of a new drug for multiple sclerosis called beta-interferon. Wien J. decided that the authority's decision not to allocate funds for the purchase of the drug constituted a failure to take into account the national policy of gradual introduction.

As should be clear, these cases did not involve the court in asserting that the treatment should be available as a matter of right, but merely that the relevant public authority had conducted itself in a manner which offended the principles of legality which constrain all exercises of public power.[78] Indeed, it is noticeable that even though the judge in *Fisher* concluded that the decision was unlawful, the claimant's entitlement to treatment was expressly 'subject to clinical judgement and availability of resources'.[79] Indeed, the courts' general reluctance to review medical decisions is amply illustrated by a number of cases.

In *R v. Cambridge Health Authority, ex parte B*[80] the court was confronted with a challenge brought by the father of a terminally ill child to the authority's decision not to fund further treatment. The applicant

---

[75] *R* v. *Ethical Committee of St Mary's Hospital (Manchester), ex parte H* [1988] 1 FLR 512. However, the court held that there could be no complaint where, as on the present facts, the decision was based on clinical judgment.

[76] *North West Lancashire Health Authority* v. *A, D and G* [1999] Lloyd's Rep Med 399.

[77] [1997] 8 Med LR 327.

[78] Lenaghan rejects a substantive right to health care in favour of procedural rights for patients and a national code of practice on the rationing of health care resources (J. Lenaghan, *Rationing and Rights in Healthcare* (London, 1996)). See generally, D. Galligan, 'Procedural Rights in Social Welfare' in A. Coote (ed.), *The Welfare of Citizens* (London, 1992).

[79] [1997] Med LR 327, 338, *per* Wien J. On the general relevance of resource limitations in clinical decision-making, see J. K. Mason and R. A. McCall-Smith, *Law and Medical Ethics*, 5th edn (London, 1999), Ch. 11.

[80] [1995] 1 WLR 898. See R. James and D. Longley, 'Judicial review and tragic choices: *Ex Parte B*' [1995] PL 367 and D. O'Sullivan, 'The Allocation of Scarce Resources and the Right to Life under the European Convention on Human Rights' [1998] PL 389.

succeeded at first instance substantially on the procedural grounds that
the authority had failed both to explain its spending priorities adequately
and to take into account the wishes of the patient.[81] Laws J. stated that
it was not sufficient for the public body to 'toll the bell of tight resources'.[82] Nevertheless, the judge refused to order that the treatment
should proceed and instead merely asked the authority to reconsider
its previous decision. The Court of Appeal regarded even this form of
intervention as too intrusive and allowed the authority's appeal. The
authority could not be required to explain its spending priorities and
the other grounds of challenge were held to be unfounded. In particular,
Sir Thomas Bingham MR stated:

> Difficult and agonising judgements have to be made as to how a limi-
> ted budget is best allocated to the maximum advantage of the maxi-
> mum number of patients. That is not a judgement which the court can
> make.[83]

All of these decisions are informed by a judicial awareness of the fact
that requiring expenditure on one patient will mean that others (who are
not represented before the court) will go untreated and a recognition
that the decision about the best interests of the patient and patients
generally is (within the obvious constraints of legality) one better left
to clinical judgement. The concern was articulated by Hoffmann LJ in
the Court of Appeal case of Anthony Bland, who was left in a persistent
vegetative state for over three years after the Hillsborough disaster:

> one is bound to observe that the cost of keeping a patient like Anthony
> Bland alive is very considerable and that in another case the health
> authority might conclude that its resources were better devoted to
> other patients.[84]

My final example comes from the field of residential care.[85] As a result of a car accident in which she was rendered severely disabled, Miss

---

[81] (1995) 25 BMLR 5. Laws J. also held that the authority had misrepresented the proposed
treatment as experimental and had incorrectly calculated its cost.

[82] Ibid., 17.

[83] [1995] 1 WLR 898, 906E–F. See also *R* v. *Secretary of State for Health, ex parte Hincks* (1979)
123 Sol Jo 436. For a similar case in which the court was not even prepared to grant leave,
see *R* v. *Central Birmingham Health Authority, ex parte Walker* (1987) 3 BMLR 32.

[84] *Airedale NHS Trust* v. *Bland* [1993] AC 789, 833B–C. To similar effect, see *In re J (A Minor)
(Child in Care: Medical Treatment)* [1993] Fam 15, 28C (*per* Lord Donaldson of Lymington
MR). *NHS Trust A* v. *M, NHS Trust B* v. *H* [2001] 2 WLR 942 consider the compatibility of
Bland with the Human Rights Act.

[85] *R* v. *North and East Devon Health Authority, ex parte Coughlan* [2001] QB 213.

Coughlan was in accommodation provided by the predecessor of the health authority. In 1993 and on the basis of an assurance that she would be able to live there for the rest of her life, Miss Coughlan agreed to be moved to a purpose-built facility at Mardon House. Five years later, the authority decided to close Mardon House and to transfer responsibility for her care to the local authority. Miss Coughlan sought judicial review of this decision and succeeded in the Court of Appeal. For present purposes, the most important ground was that based on the legitimate expectation to which the promise of a home for life at Mardon House had given rise. The significance of the case for present purposes is clear: the court's decision required the health authority to maintain a residential facility indefinitely and this had obvious resource implications for the discharge of its other responsibilities.

Again, though, the case is consistent with orthodox administrative law principles and many of the fears which generally deter judicial intervention in welfare cases were not present. For example, the decision would only affect a small number of identifiable individuals and the applicant's right to respect for her home as protected by Article 8 of the ECHR was implicated. Most importantly, the court was not placed in the position of having to identify for itself what the appropriate level of care for Miss Coughlan was because it could rely on the undertaking given by the authority that she could remain in Mardon House for the rest of her life. Since the authority had regarded this as an appropriate way to discharge its responsibilities in the past, the court could legitimately require a powerful justification for a change of practice. This decision also illustrates one of the reasons for the persistence and success of claims based on legitimate expectations or on equality. In such cases, the court does not have to determine what the appropriate level of social provision is. Instead the court merely requires the previous balance struck by the public authority to be maintained or insists on the removal of a distinction between two classes of claimant which cannot be objectively justified.[86]

All of the above cases are intended to illustrate the point that although English courts will not regard administrative determinations which have resource implications as non-justiciable for that reason alone, there is a very clear distinction between the task which they are performing in requiring compliance with traditional principles of judicial review and the

[86] J. Jowell, 'Is Equality a Constitutional Principle?' (1994) 47 CLP 1 and B. A. Hepple, 'Social Values in European Law' (1995) 48 CLP 39.

task which they would perform if they were given primary jurisdiction to determine the extent of social rights.

Social rights under the ECHR

Turning to international influences, some have argued that the ECHR already acknowledges the importance of protecting social rights in at least three respects: the right to education (art. 2, protocol 1), through the definition of 'civil rights' under Article 6(1) and as a legitimate object of policy which may restrict the exercise of other rights.[87] I have already discussed the right to education and the limited protection for social rights it has been held to provide.[88] The argument based on Article 6(1) requires further analysis.

The ECtHR applies an autonomous meaning to the term 'civil rights' and so is not bound by their classification in domestic law.[89] Beginning with the case of *Feldbrugge* v. *Netherlands*[90] the Court has expanded its definition of civil rights to include statutory sickness benefit (as in *Feldbrugge*) and a statutory widow's pension.[91] These decisions were originally justified by analogy with private law contributory benefits, but in *Salesi* v. *Italy* the Court held that Article 6(1) applied equally to a monthly disability payment which was based on need and not contributions.[92]

However, two points should be made about the significance of these cases for the general protection of social rights under the ECHR. The first is that the advantages of falling within the definition of civil rights are purely procedural (entitling the applicant to a fair and impartial tribunal, disclosure, an adversarial hearing, a decision within a reasonable time and reasons), but confer no entitlement to the substance of any benefit. Secondly, even these procedural protections will only apply to cases where the applicant has a *right* to the benefit in question and Article 6(1) is irrelevant to the distribution of discretionary welfare payments which constitute the vast majority of such provision.[93]

That leaves the recognition of social rights as legitimate objects of state policy which has occurred principally in relation to the right to

---

[87] M. Scheinin, 'Economic and Social Rights as Legal Rights' in Eide et al., *Economic, Social and Cultural Rights – A Textbook.*

[88] See nn. 47–51 above and accompanying text.   [89] *Konig* v. *Germany* (1978) 2 EHRR 170.

[90] (1986) 8 EHRR 425.   [91] *Deumeland* v. *Germany* (1986) 8 EHRR 448.

[92] (1993) 26 EHRR 187 and *Schuler-Zraggen* v. *Switzerland* (1993) 16 EHRR 405.

[93] *Machatova* v. *Slovak Republic* (1997) 24 EHRR CD 44.

property under Article 1, Protocol 1. The outstanding example is the case of *James and Others* v. *United Kingdom*[94] in which trustees for the freeholders of large parts of central London challenged the validity of legislation which permitted tenants to enfranchise their leases in certain circumstances. The ECtHR held that the loss of the reversion involved no violation of the right to property:

> Eliminating what are judged to be social injustices is an example of the functions of a democratic legislature. More specifically, modern societies consider housing of the population to be a prime social need, the regulation of which cannot entirely be left to the play of market forces. The margin of appreciation is wide enough to cover legislation aimed at securing greater social justice in the sphere of people's homes, even where such legislation interferes with existing contractual relations between private parties and confers no direct benefit on the State or the community at large. In principle, therefore, the aim pursued by the leasehold reform legislation is a legitimate one.[95]

The limitations of this principle should be obvious. The Court was here acknowledging that it was compatible with the ECHR for the *legislature* to qualify the right to property in pursuit of social objectives as part of the exceptions to a Convention right. The result would have been very different if the Court had been asked to uphold the *right* to leasehold enfranchisement. Article 1 of Protocol 1 protects a right to retain property and confers no entitlement on those without property.[96] Thus it is an overstatement to suggest that the ECHR provides meaningful protection for substantive social rights.

South Africa

Much attention in the recent past has focused on the constitutional protections for social rights in the South African Constitution.[97] The two

---

[94] (1986) 8 EHRR 123. For a similar result in the context of rent reductions, see *Mellacher and Others* v. *Austria* (1989) 12 EHRR 391.

[95] (1986) 8 EHRR 123, at para. 47.

[96] See further *Burton* v. *United Kingdom* (1996) 22 EHRR CD 135 and *D* v. *United Kingdom* (1997) 24 EHRR 423. Cf. K. J. Gray, 'Equitable Property' (1994) 47 CLP 157 and K. Gray and S. F. Gray, 'Civil Rights, Civil Wrongs and Quasi-Public Space' [1999] EHRLR 46.

[97] D. M. Davis, 'The Case Against the Inclusion of Socio-Economic Demands in a Bill of Rights Except as Directive Principles' (1992) 8 SAJHR 475 and South African Law Commission, *Final Report on Group and Human Rights* (Project 58, 1994). Cf. G. van Bueren, 'Alleviating Poverty through the Constitutional Court' (1999) 15 SAJHR 52.

most significant cases to emerge from the Constitutional Court concerned health care and housing.[98] In the first case,[99] Soobramoney was
a 41-year-old unemployed man who had diabetes and was suffering from
ischaemic heart disease and cerebro-vascular disease. In 1996 he suffered
kidney failure. His condition was chronic, but his life could be pro-
longed by regular renal dialysis. He sought treatment at the Addington
State Hospital in Durban, which had twenty kidney dialysis machines,
but was refused on the ground of limited resources. The hospital had,
in fact, formulated a policy whereby those suffering acute renal failure
which can be treated and remedied were given treatment automatically;
those with a chronic treatment might qualify if they were eligible for
kidney transplant. To qualify for a transplant, the patient must be free
of other relevant disease which Soobramoney was not.

The constitutional claim was based on two rights: that 'no one may
be refused emergency medical treatment' and that 'everyone has the
right to life'.[100] The Court began by rejecting Soobramoney's argument
that the right to emergency medical treatment extended to cover the
ongoing treatment of chronic illnesses. Instead, the claimant's case was
held to fall within the general right of access to health care services
which is explicitly subject to the availability of resources. The Court
then accepted that the policy of the hospital was designed to ensure that
more patients would benefit in the long term from the available dialysis
machines. Rejecting Soobramoney's challenge, Chaskalson P. stated:

> It has not been suggested that these guidelines are unreasonable or
> that they were not applied fairly and rationally when the decision was
> taken.[101]

He concluded that:

> A court will be slow to interfere with rational decisions taken in good
> faith by the political organs and medical authorities whose responsi-
> bility it is to deal with such matters.[102]

The second case is *Government of South Africa & Ors v. Grootboom*,[103]
in which the claimant represented a group of over 500 people. The

---

[98] C. Scott and P. Alston, 'Adjudicating Constitutional Priorities in a Transnational Context:
A Comment on *Soobramoney's* Legacy and *Grootboom's* Promise' (2000) 16 SAJHR 206.
[99] *Soobramoney v. Minister of Health, Kwazulu-Natal* 1998 (1) SA 765.
[100] These rights are contained in sections 27(3) and 11 of the Constitution.
[101] *Soobramoney*, para. 25.   [102] Ibid., para. 29.   [103] (2001)(1) SA 46.

claimants had previously lived in a squatter settlement in Wallacedene in the Eastern Cape without water, sewage or refuse removal services in small shacks, 95 per cent of which lacked electricity. Many of those in the settlement had been on the waiting list for public housing for as long as seven years. A group of the residents of Wallacedene decided to move on to some privately owned vacant land nearby. The landowner responded by issuing eviction proceedings which resulted in the claimants being forcibly removed and their shelters bulldozed. Unable to return to their original dwellings in the squatter camps, which had been occupied by other families, many of the claimants sheltered on the Wallacedene sports field and, from there, launched the present legal action. They claimed a violation of their constitutional right of access to adequate housing and of the children's right to shelter.[104]

The Court again began by emphasising that the duty to provide access to housing is explicitly subject to the availability of resources. Moreover, although the children's right to shelter was not expressly subject to such a limitation, the Court felt that the two provisions had to be read together and that the duty to provide children with shelter would only be imposed on the state (as opposed to the child's parents) where, for example, the child had been removed from her family. Ultimately, the Court felt that the question became whether the state had adopted measures for the realisation of the right which were reasonable: the same standard as in *Soobramoney*. Yacoob J. delivered the judgement of the court:

> A court considering reasonableness will not enquire whether other more desirable or favourable measures could have been adopted, or whether public money could have been better spent.... It is necessary to recognise that a wide range of possible measures could be adopted by the state to meet its obligations. Many of these would meet the requirement of reasonableness. Once it is shown that the measures do so, this requirement is met.[105]

Applying this method to the present case, the Court noted that the respondent's programme for dealing with the housing shortage contained only medium- and long-term objectives and made absolutely no

---

[104] Sections 26 and 28(1)(c). Interestingly, it is in relation to the right to housing and protection from eviction that the UN Committee on the ICESCR has been most active (S. Leckie, 'Catalyst for change', 135–44).

[105] *Grootboom*, para. 41.

provision for those in acute need of emergency housing. The Court held that this was unreasonable, although it emphasised that the precise allocation of funding between short- and longer-term projects was for the state to determine. The municipality's misconduct was exacerbated by the fact that it funded the forced evictions which occurred in a style which the Court held to be reminiscent of the apartheid era. The Court therefore awarded mandatory relief requiring the state 'to devise and implement within its available resources a comprehensive and coordinated programme progressively to realise the right of access to adequate housing'.[106]

The much-vaunted South African example thus turns out to involve the application of the familiar standards of administrative law based on reasonableness, rather than an intense form of constitutional scrutiny appropriate to the vindication of an inviolable right.[107]

IV. Conclusion

The normative argument in favour of the protection of social rights is a powerful one. It must be true that those who live in wretchedly deprived conditions cannot lead full and rewarding lives. It is also probably correct to argue that indigence and dire living conditions reduce the extent to which many individuals will exercise their civil and political rights and participate fully in society. However, the question remains: what is the most appropriate means of providing protection for social welfare interests? It is not sufficient to discount the legal protection of social rights simply because they have resource implications. On the other hand, it is important not to exaggerate the significance of legal developments across the range of jurisdictions which have been considered above. Any convincing account of the most appropriate means for protecting social rights must include and justify not only what would lead to the highest level of their protection, but also the impact such protection may have on the structure and character of the state and the relations

---

[106] Ibid., para. 99.

[107] Some commentators, while accepting the case for the inclusion of social rights in the interim South African Constitution, argued in favour of protecting them through review for 'sincerity and rationality' on the ground that 'the procedural benefits would be immense' (E. Mureinik, 'Beyond a Charter of Luxuries: Economic Rights in the Constitution' (1992) 8 SAJHR 464, 474, 472).

between its governing organs. If the legal protection of social rights is confined to administrative law principles, the question of legitimacy is less acute.[108] However, the separate question is then raised as to whether it devalues the nature of fundamental rights in general to include social rights in a constitutional document. If social rights are to be fully constitutionalised, its proponents will have to justify the shift in power from the political to the judicial branch on questions of competing public interests and state expenditure: questions which remain at the core of political debate in most democracies.[109]

---

[108] It may still be necessary to introduce procedural reforms to liberalise further the rules on standing or those which govern the admissibility of evidence. Scott has suggested that a relaxation in the doctrine of precedent would also be required (C. Scott, 'The Judicial Role in Relation to Constitutional Social Rights' (1999) 1(4) Economic and Social Rights Review 4).

[109] J. Tweedy and A. Hunt, 'The Future of the Welfare State and Social Rights: Reflections on Habermas' (1994) 21 Journal of Law and Society 288.

7

The legal efficacy and significance of fundamental social rights: lessons from the European experience

ANTOINE LYON-CAEN

I. Introduction

The EU Charter of Fundamental Rights opens a new phase of discussion in Europe on the legal efficacy and significance of social rights.

This is not the primary controversy that the Charter raises. The most important and difficult issue is: to what legal form does the Charter correspond? Is it simply a new declaration of rights of regional ambit? Or is it a major element of a constitutional framework in the process of construction? The aim of this chapter is not to elaborate on this debate, which has vast dimensions. But there is an immediate connection between this complex theme and the question of the recognition, legal efficacy and significance of fundamental social rights. As time goes by, certain political circles will undoubtedly seek to limit the Charter to a mere political declaration by the Heads of States and Governments of the European Union. They will wish to undervalue its possible legal force. This they may be able to do, because the Charter uses phrases that irresistibly evoke fundamental social rights in language that is full of incongruities and less than useful or dangerous pomposity, appropriate only in the context of political discourse.

The Charter, as the fruit of skilful compromise, carefully avoids the usual terminology of social rights. However, it revives the notion and its history. Although, in several articles, it entitles workers to certain fundamental rights – stating[1] and apparently embracing the idea that

---

[1] See for example, arts. 27, 28 and 31 devoted, respectively, to the right to information and consultation, to the right of collective bargaining and action, and to fair and just working conditions.

social rights are workers' rights or, at least, rights relating to work – the Charter displays its originality in a different way. It frequently focuses on the obligations to allocate goods, to provide a service, and to create a guarantee. Respect for human dignity, with which the Charter begins (art. 1), constitutes one of the terms that illustrate the relativity of the distinction between *droits-libertés* and social rights (see below). The right to life (art. 2), the right to the integrity of the person (art. 3), or the right to private and family life (art. 7) also cannot easily be inserted in a rigid classification. Other provisions of the Charter use the usual formulation of social rights, such as the right to education (art. 14), the right of children to protection and care as is necessary for their wellbeing (art. 24), the worker's right to information and consultation within the undertaking (art. 27), the right of access to placement services (art. 29), the right to protection against unjustified dismissal (art. 30), and the right to fair and just working conditions (art. 31). Articles 34 and 35, relating to access to social security and health care, are also firm in their formulation. In these respects, the provisions merit, with more certainty than with regard to workers' rights, the designation of social rights.

The focus on obtaining a good, a service or a guarantee, in short the fact of giving prominence to a deontic mode that traditional fundamental rights seem to ignore, constitutes the cornerstone, the heart of the historical problem of social rights. A long analysis cannot be developed here; a few guidelines are sufficient. Despite forms that have varied, the distinction that has long been used as a guide is that which separates *droits-libertés* and *droits-créances*, or, following the famous classification of Jellinek, rights of negative status and rights of positive status. At first sight, *droits-libertés* constitute defences against the state, whereas *droits-créances* require its action. Their opposition would thus be radical, in that the first tend to prevent the intervention of the state, whereas the second tend to provoke it. As a matter of fact, their opposition would not only be one of logic; it would also be one of structure. *Droits-libertés* would require no mediation to be opposed to the state, contrary to *droits-créances*, which are incapable without mediation of efficacy in the legal order. Following these observations, it is tempting not only to denounce the threats that hang over *droits-libertés* because of *droits-créances*, but, above all, to refuse all legal value to *droits-créances*: they would be mere political statements and would promote state ideologies.

Other less caricatural perspectives are possible. These question the commonplace legal and political analysis which distinguishes *droits-créances* and *droits-libertés*. In the French literature, it is certainly L. Duguit who deserves the credit for demonstrating that *droits-libertés* and 'social rights'[2] both require public interventions, in the form of public services. According to him, public services aim at providing services to individuals of necessity, both in order to protect freedoms and also to ensure the concrete exercise of social rights.[3] Thus, the two categories of fundamental rights are in opposition neither as to their logic nor as to their structure. After all, some rights, clearly qualified as social rights, contain the same primary features as *droits-libertés*: such is the case of the right to strike or the right to freedom of association. This analysis echoes the current efforts of the European Court of Human Rights to bring out positive obligations of the state to ensure the efficacy of fundamental rights, even though the rights which the Court seeks to protect are conceived as *droits-libertés*. Indeed, these efforts address a perception which is widely shared: even the 'police state' (*état-gendarme*) and the so-called 'night-watchman state' (*veilleur de nuit*) must organise an efficient system of police or night-watchmen. A pure abstention would constitute an infringement of freedom by the state. Should one follow this path and condemn the distinction for being both unjustified and of no use? Holding that it is a construction without justification and scope would not be easily accepted, but this is not the main point. First, it would prevent us from understanding the necessary complementarity of freedoms and social rights. Do not the latter provide individuals with the conditions that enable them to make the choices protected by freedoms? Second, it would eliminate the need to take account of the variety of forms that the actions of the beneficiaries of fundamental rights and the bearers of the corresponding obligations may take.[4] In fact, it is precisely this variety that should be taken seriously.

Rich lessons may be drawn from the unique European experience as to the legal efficacy and significance of social rights that, at first sight, appear to require action by the state. This richness is provided by the diversity of constitutional formulations. In some, social rights – or

---

[2] L. Duguit was one of the first to propose this wording, to which G. Gurvitch then gave full recognition: see G. Gurvitch, *La déclaration des droits sociaux* (Paris, 1946).

[3] L. Duguit, *Traité de droit constitutionnel*, 2nd edn (Paris, 1923), III, 563.

[4] See O. Pfersmann, *Droits des libertés fondamentales* (Paris, 2001).

droits-créances – are not part of constitutional statements: this is the case for Austria and Belgium, despite the assertion, since 1988, of a right to education. In others, the constitution recognises social rights: such is the case for France, Greece, Italy, Portugal and Spain. The Federal Republic of Germany seems to belong to the first group, considering that its Basic Law does not recognise, apart from one nuance, any social right. Nevertheless, the Basic Law constitutes the Federal Republic as a social state and the principle of the social state *implies*, according to the Constitutional Court, concrete consequences.

This last example by itself shows that the very presence of a statement however far from the usual formulation of *droits-libertés* is likely to produce effects in the legal field. Other examples confirm this hypothesis. Indeed, the Italian Constitution recognises the right of the worker to fair wages 'at least sufficient to provide for him and his family a free and dignified existence'.[5] Despite this formulation as a right to obtain a guarantee, Italian judges have conferred direct legal efficacy on this provision. It is the basis, for example, on which the worker not covered by a collective agreement, can require from his employer wages equivalent to those provided by the most closely connected collective agreement. These examples strengthen the hypothesis: the modes of legal efficacy of social rights, or, if you like, their legal means of action, are various. These modes of action are discussed in the next part of the chapter.

But it would be inappropriate to content oneself with following what the legal discourse and its enrichment owe to social rights. These rights also contribute to an understanding of the development of the law. In this respect, it is their legal significance rather than their efficacy that will be described in the final part of the chapter.

II. The legal modes of action of social rights

The legal modes of action of social rights are distorted by a naïve representation of legal rules. It is indeed usual, where they confer on their beneficiaries a permission to act and impose on the bearers of the corresponding obligations an interdiction not to act, to believe that the very fact that they are enunciated is sufficient to provide the expected legal effects. However, experience proves that legal rules do not act in this

---

[5] Art. 38 of the Italian Constitution.

way. They require, in order to produce effects in the legal field, to be invoked or, to use a more suggestive expression, to be mobilised and thus to be included in an exchange of arguments.[6]

At the expense of a more accurate vision of the legal modes of action of rules, social rights reveal their strength, or at least, their potential. One of their modes of action has long been identified: social rights are capable of *orienting the interpretation of other rules*. The examples are numerous. Indeed, in a dispute concerning a dismissal or an accident, it is possible to invoke or mobilise such-and-such a social right to orient the interpretation of such-and-such an applicable rule. The right to work, where it is recognised, can, in this way, inflect the meaning and scope of provisions limiting the exercise of the employer's prerogatives. For example, the requirement of a reason for dismissal, following the reorganisation of a business, can be interpreted as requiring from the employer the demonstration that he made all possible efforts to avoid the dismissal, notably the investigation of alternative employment, the creation of new activities or adjustments to the organisation of work, and all these in the benevolent light of the right to work.

This form of action, the orientation of the interpretation of other rules, requires, in order to be elucidated, that judges be familiar with the reasoning that favours or tolerates an increased level of generality. In such a context, it is indeed easier for protagonists to claim and for judges to accept that such-and-such an applicable rule should draw its reasonable meaning from a fundamental right. Indeed, this context exists in European Community law: the European Court of Justice willingly adopts an increased level of generality, under cover of what is usually called a teleological interpretation. It is thus not far-fetched to foresee that the Charter of Fundamental Rights will have its first legal effect as a guide for the interpretation of European Community law. This mode of action of fundamental rights is, by definition, not specific to social rights. If it deserves to be mentioned, it is because social rights do not present any particular feature that justifies its non-application.

The second mode of action of social rights conceals an unsuspected strength: it consists of the *justification of rules, mechanisms or institutions*. What is the potential significance of this means of action? It is

---

[6] See A. Jeammaud and M. Le Friant, 'L'emploi est-il un droit?' (1999) 2 Travail Genre et Sociétés 29.

difficult, sometimes even impossible, for public authorities to content themselves with the procedural legitimacy that the political mechanisms of election confer. Legitimacy of action comes as much, if not more, from adherence to values, principles or rights on the basis of which consensus is formed. This requirement is paramount for the authorities of the European Union. Lacking full sovereignty they need to prove that, within their competence, they act in accordance with the appropriate aim. Let us nevertheless limit ourselves to public authorities other than those of the European Union. The values, principles and rights that they must invoke, and the adherence that the one and the other manage to create, reinforce the efficacy of rules and legal mechanisms. We shall return to this point.

At present, it is common in a number of member states of the European Union to state that social rights confer a basis for social policies, such as employment policy, policy against exclusion, housing policy and health policy. Nevertheless, a further step is necessary for a better understanding of the legal efficacy of social rights. The justification of public action that these values, principles and rights constitute are not a matter of pure political discourse; they provide a resource to restrict or contest the influence of 'market' mechanisms, in other words the dynamic of competition law, in its broadest sense. In other words, in systems where the market is a mode of coordination protected and promoted by the law, social rights offer legal justifications to circumscribe its limits, to enable public education to exist against the market of training, social protection to resist the extension of the market of private insurance, and public security not to be diluted by an extensive market of private surveillance. The immunity of certain institutions against competition law in its broadest sense has its source in social rights.

Alongside the limitation of the legal model of the market appears a third mode of action of social rights: they constitute a *means of controlling the generation of norms* in ways that can offer a protection against the excesses of legislative opportunism. Social rights can, indeed, be invoked to contest such-and-such a regulation established in the name of other imperatives, should they be principles or values having similar authority. Procedures and structures to test legality undoubtedly possess specific characteristics in various countries, depending whether there exists an established means by which the conformity of legislative rules with the Constitution can be tested, whether a monopoly is conferred on a specific body for the control of constitutionality, and whether or not a criterion of proportionality has been developed as a test of legality. Within these procedures and structures, the way is open for a possible challenge to the rules laid down by public authorities, on the basis of their non-compliance with social rights. For example, the validity of a regulation on immigration can be contested if it has violated – without sufficient justification or lack of moderation of its material provisions – the right to respect for family life. It has been suggested that this legal mode of action of social rights should be designated normative efficacy. An original illustration of this normative efficacy is offered by the impeding effect (*effet d'obstacle*) that social rights can create. This impeding effect was first underscored in the field of *droits-libertés*. The law can, in principle, only regulate their exercise so as to make them more effective. As a consequence, it cannot abrogate the provisions that ensure fundamental freedoms without replacing them by others of equivalent efficacy. There is no reason why this reasoning should not be extended to social rights, as happens in practice.

This impeding effect, known in France as the jurisprudence of the *cliquet*, deserves at least two comments. First, it almost corresponds to ordinary legislative action. It is not characteristic of a more daring control of constitutionality, the control of legislative abstention. The EU member states that apply this technique of unconstitutionality by omission are very few indeed. Portugal provides one example. In its more ordinary form, the impeding effect can be one of the most important means of legal resistance to opportunist movements of deregulation.

Social rights are not only able to control the generation of legal norms but also can *control the organisation of public services* or, to adopt a more European formulation, general interest public services. One of the limitations generally attributed to *droits-créances* lies in their incapacity to generate true subjective rights for individuals, capable of being enforced against anyone. In fact, where social rights are accepted, they are able to give rise to subjective rights. Nevertheless, their objective is not that of the right proclaimed (employment, social protection, housing and so on), but that of *access* to institutional mechanisms that enable or promise sooner or later the fulfilment of the right proclaimed.[7] A fourth mode

---

[7] See R. Lafore, 'Les nouveaux modes de régulation juridique', in P. Auvergnon (ed.), *L'Etat à l'épreuve du social* (Paris, 1998).

of action of social rights can thus be identified: they open the way to the control of their mechanisms of implementation. In this way, gradations can be conceived. At first, it is equality which is the most fundamental right determining access to the guarantees of enjoyment of other rights. Yet the concept of equality at stake is one that has been enriched and, as a consequence, it has moved away from the notion of formal equality to cope more effectively with social differentiation. The enrichment of the notion of equality has an influence on the means of control that are correlatively enriched. From time to time, one can see the emergence of claims, in the name of the fundamental right which justifies them, that concern the very quality of the services or benefits provided. Contrary to widespread belief, social rights can be mobilised to combat bureaucratic rigidities. Their implementation can certainly generate some; but their vitality can contribute to reducing them. This mode of action of social rights has a close connection with the question of their significance.

III. The legal significance of fundamental rights

Social rights are intimately linked to change. They are promises for change. They also change the state and the law itself. It is the latter perspective that must be pursued for a moment, without pretending to offer an exhaustive analysis, but rather setting out a few hypotheses relative to the transformations both of the law and of the social state or welfare state.

The right to work, right to education, right to fair and just working conditions, right to the minimum means for living, right to respect for private and family life and so on and so on: it is not necessary to expand this enumeration in order to underline a legal feature of social rights. Looked at in terms of the modes of action of those to whom they are addressed – as we will see, unduly limited to the state – they do not generate obligations to achieve results. Such an observation is imperfect, however. What should be emphasised, rather, is that they do not consist of material norms, from which one could immediately deduce derived norms, or norms of application. Where the language enables one to differentiate, one should, to be exact, speak of the implementation of social rights rather than their application. The concept of application suggests a predetermined intellectual act, according to which the model – the rule applied – pre-exists, precisely defined, before its application. On the other hand, implementation suggests the conception, translation and interpretation of mechanisms of mediation.

Social rights constitute, above all, principles of action and evaluation whose purpose, in pluralist societies, is to create a convergence of the diverse social representations and to integrate them.[8] It is at this stage that an hypothesis takes shape. The movement of convergence and integration that social rights provoke or should provoke can less and less be seen as a linear, one-way movement, from the top (central political authorities or supreme judges) to the bottom (the various local bodies of regulation). Rather, it covers complex exchanges between a plurality of actors. If the hypothesis is confirmed, then social rights participate less in the organisation of a hierarchy of norms than they contribute to the development of an axiological system whose function is to organise differing social representations and logics and integrate them around a common purpose. The movement described and studied by some contemporary analysts[9] under the expression of *proceduralisation* of the law would thus be closely linked with social rights. Moreover, it is almost certain that these transformations of the law accompany the evolution of the social state or welfare state.

Social rights have enabled the market economy to be structured in a more just and equitable fashion. They have allowed the insertion of regulations, institutions and redistributive and corrective mechanisms, and thus the creation and development of guarantees constituting a real status for workers. Nevertheless, just as important were the conception and development of public services; these are likely to ensure a benefit or provide a facility or a service. Their beneficiary is neither the consumer nor the market, not even the worker, but the user of the service or the party eligible for a facility or a service. The user or the eligible party have guaranteed access, on the basis of social rights, to durable and centralised mechanisms in their management, or, at least, in their delivery.

It is this historical architecture that seems to have been the subject of a fundamental evolution, one that can be detected in the institutions

---

[8] Ibid., 44.

[9] See among the more recent publications, Ph. Coppens et J. Lenoble (dir.), *Démocratie et procéduralisation du droit, Travaux des XVIe Journées* (J. Dabin, Bruxelles, Bruylant, 2000); O. de Schutter, N. Lebessis et J. Paterson, *La gouvernance dans l'Union européenne*, Luxembourg (Office des publications officielles des E.E. 2001).

and mechanisms on which social rights are founded. Not only do they lose their uniformity but they also associate multiple actors in what is a far from traditional representation of the state. In this way, it is a greater sensitivity to the conditions of fulfilment of social rights that seems to be pursued. Lying within institutional transformations, it is a reinterpretation of social rights that is under way. These fundamental rights would aim not so much at creating a relation of debtor and creditor between the state and those entitled to social rights but more to ensure the participation of the latter in the whole collective life. This rereading of social rights provides the framework for the reflection that the difficult quest for a wider citizenship requires. One may also note that it tends to recreate a link between two categories of fundamental rights that Jellinek had differentiated: the rights of positive status (or *droits-créances*) and the rights of active status (those that confer on citizens the means to take part in the very definition of the conditions of collective life).

This discussion of the significance of social rights, albeit brief, may disturb those who seek simplicity. It enables the discovery or rediscovery that fundamental rights do not consist of material norms from which one may mechanically draw intangible models for action. On the contrary, does it not underscore the fundamental quality of the *dynamism* of social rights, rights whose contents require continual updating? This dynamism of social rights makes the analysis of their legal efficacy all the more useful. The European experience demonstrates, we believe, their valuable diversity, far removed from an excessively synthetic and crude vision of their justiciability.

8

An American perspective on
fundamental labour rights

CYNTHIA L. ESTLUND

As a general matter, the American perspective on labour market issues can hardly be said to get too little attention these days. That perspective is closely identified with the ascendancy of the market and a receding role for state regulation in an increasingly global economy. It is hailed by some as a stimulant to economic growth and expanding employment, and it is decried by others as a licence for increasing economic inequality and insecurity. So on the question of fundamental labour rights – which I take to mean rights grounded in some legal source such as a constitution that is not changeable through ordinary national legislation – the American perspective might seem predictably and numbingly negative. I hope to convince you that, quite to the contrary, the American perspective on fundamental labour rights is interestingly and complicatedly negative.

I will mostly forego what may be the expected comparison between a market-centred and a rights-centred approach to employment, though I will return to it briefly at the conclusion of this chapter. And I will mostly resist any imagined invitation to offer an American view of British or European developments. Instead I will focus primarily on the American experience with workplace rights and some institutional questions about their location and degree of entrenchment: just how fundamental are American labour rights, and how did they get that way?

I. The lie of the land

Let me begin by recalling some very basic and familiar principles of American constitutional law that are usefully kept in mind. Simply stated, these principles of federalism, constitutionalism, and separation of powers provide as follows. First, federal power, as opposed to the plenary power of the several states, is limited to constitutionally enumerated areas, such as the regulation of interstate commerce, but it is supreme within those areas. Second, constitutions, federal and state, constrain what legislatures can do, and this constraint is enforced chiefly by the courts exercising the power of judicial review or the power to invalidate unconstitutional legislation. Third, when operating within those constitutional constraints, the legislature is supreme, and can override common law decisions and statutory interpretation by the courts.

When we speak of rights being 'fundamental', I take that to mean that those rights are beyond the reach and revision of ordinary legislation and shifting democratic majorities. Most clearly, in the American context, it refers to constitutional rights. Federal constitutional rights are the most 'fundamental'; they are nationwide in scope and, given the unwieldiness of the amendment process, highly resistant to political revision, though they may expand and contract with judicial interpretation. State constitutional rights, provided they do not conflict with federal law, may be similarly resistant to change, depending on the particular state's constitutional amendment process. I have not incorporated international law into this account, and I will not take up the status of international labour rights here; that would require another whole essay.[1]

With that background in mind, we can divide labour rights into four categories: *Collective labour rights*, such as the right to representation in the workplace; *equal status rights*, such as the right not to be subject to discrimination or harassment on the basis of race or sex; *individual employee rights*, such as rights of privacy or the right not to be fired for bad or arbitrary reasons; and *minimum terms of employment*, such as minimum wages, maximum hours, job safety and mandated vacation or parental leave. I will have rather little to say about the last of these categories, though it will make an appearance in our historical tour.

Putting aside the public sector, where the federal Constitution plays an important role (for reasons I will come to), none of these categories of

---

[1] For an illuminating discussion of this topic, see James A. Gross, 'A Human Rights Perspective on United States Labor Relations Law: A Violation of the Right of Freedom of Association' (1999) 3 Employee Rights and Employment Policy Journal 65.

rights has a solid footing in anything more fundamental than ordinary legislation:

Collective labour rights, or the domain of unions and collective bargaining, are almost exclusively the province of federal legislation; state and local regulation of unions and collective bargaining among private sector workers is preempted by the federal scheme.

Equal status rights, which ban discrimination on the basis of race, ethnicity, religion, sex, age and disability, are grounded primarily in federal legislation; state and local legislation supplements the federal scheme and sometimes covers additional protected traits, such as sexual orientation.

Individual employee rights to privacy, liberty and job security stem largely from state common law (subject to legislative revision) and state legislation, though state constitutions have played some role in this area.

Minimum terms of employment, which are notoriously minimalist as compared with the European scene, are entirely the product of state and federal legislation.

I want to begin by asking how it is that federal constitutional rights play essentially no role in these areas, while they play such a large role in such diverse matters as reproductive rights, voting rights, electronic communications and campaign finance.

II. The role of the state action requirement

One possible answer lies in the simple fact that ours is an old constitution that lacks provisions designed to deal with the modern employment relationship. We cannot lay claim, especially in comparison with Europe, to much that is old. But as constitutions go, ours is old. And the formal amendment process is arduous. Does that explain the virtual absence of constitutionally grounded labour rights, which are comparatively recent developments? Not exactly.

The federal Constitution has often proven to be remarkably adaptive in the interpretive hands of the federal courts, as suggested by the foregoing examples of reproductive freedom, electronic communication and campaign finance. In the magisterial language of the Fourteenth Amendment, one of the three constitutional amendments enacted in the wake of the Civil War, one might have found room for the development of workplace rights. The Fourteenth Amendment provides that 'No State shall make or enforce any law which shall abridge the privileges or immunities of citizens of the United States; nor shall any State deprive any person of life, liberty, or property, without due process of law; nor deny to any person within its jurisdiction the equal protection of the laws.' And the Fourteenth Amendment has long been held to incorporate the equally magisterial and open-textured provisions of the First Amendment, with its freedoms of expression, association, and assembly, and much of the rest of the Bill of Rights. If those old phrases can be read to grant the right to an abortion, one might think they leave room for at least some workplace rights.

But those phrases do contain clues to the puzzling absence of constitutional labour rights: the rights they secure, as well as nearly all of the other individual rights secured by the federal constitution, operate only against the government. Except for the Thirteenth Amendment's ban on involuntary servitude, the federal Constitution gives citizens no rights against non-governmental action. This is the state action requirement. And the courts have resisted the siren song of Legal Realism, which sees the state everywhere in the construction of nominally private relationships. The Constitution does not normally come into play in the mere enforcement of private property and contract rights, and gives no positive entitlement to government protection from private oppression.[2]

The Constitution has been an important source of employee protections in the public sector, where the employer is the state and discipline or discharge of employees is undeniably state action. The First Amendment thus protects certain free speech rights of public employees against employer reprisals,[3] and the Due Process Clause requires fair procedures for the termination of employment where the public employer has made a promise of job security.[4] The Equal Protection Clause effectively bans most discrimination on the basis of race, national origin, religion and sex, though statutes, state and federal, have largely overtaken this field of public employee rights.

But the state action requirement means that, in the private sector employment relationship, constitutional rights enter the picture only when

---

[2] Note the famously exceptional case of *Shelley* v. *Kramer*, 334 US 1 (1948), which struck down on equal protection grounds a state court's enforcement of a private racially 'restrictive covenant' – an agreement between buyer and seller of land, binding on successors, not to sell to non-whites.

[3] See, e.g., *Rankin* v. *McPherson*, 483 US 378 (1987).

[4] See, e.g., *Loudermill* v. *Cleveland Bd. of Educ.*, 470 US 532 (1985).

the government intervenes, and only as a shield against such intervention. And the government rarely intervenes in the private employment relationship against employees.[5] The government's role in the private sector workplace has generally been to seek to protect employees against employer abuse and opportunism. Employers derive their power over employees from the baseline rights of property and contract, the enforcement of which does not generally count as state action; beyond those baseline entitlements, what employers usually want from the government is to be left alone – alone with the formidable state-backed economic power of their property rights and their right to make and enforce contracts.

So the state action requirement largely neutralises the federal Constitution as a source of employee rights in the private sector. But the right of employers to be left alone itself enjoyed a dramatic constitutional existence that still shapes American consciousness about the role of the law in labour and employment relations. So let me briefly recount that pivotal history. I take as my text the work of my colleague Professor William Forbath, a leading chronicler of the history of labour and the American Constitution.[6]

III. Free labour and liberty of contract: the American history of fundamental (anti-)labour rights

Many of the American founders held that wise governance in a democratic republic must be in the hands of economically independent citizens. The ideal citizen was a land-owning head of household, while economically dependent members of the household, including servants, slaves and apprentices, were disqualified from citizenship by their dependency on the master. As the class of dependent wage-earners grew, their claim to citizenship became politically and ideologically irresistible.

---

[5] An interesting exception arises in the law of discriminatory harassment, which effectively requires employers to censor and punish employee speech. See Cynthia L. Estlund, 'Freedom of Expression in the Workplace and the Problem of Discriminatory Harassment' (1997) 75 Texas Law Review 687.

[6] In what follows, I draw primarily upon the following works: William E. Forbath, 'The Ambiguities of Free Labor: Labor and the Law in the Gilded Age' 1985 Wisconsin Law Review 767; William E. Forbath, *Law and the Shaping of the American Labor Movement* (Cambridge, MA, 1991); and William E. Forbath, 'Caste, Class, and Equal Citizenship' (1999) 98 Mich. L. Rev. 1.

Property qualifications for the franchise were largely eliminated within a few decades of the founding of the republic, long before this movement took hold in Europe. The expansion of the franchise left unresolved, however, the question of civic virtue and its economic foundation. And the question became more pressing as the burgeoning factory system increasingly swallowed up independent artisans, relegating both them and their apprentices to a dependent position in the labour market.

For republican-minded Americans, the growing class of dependent wage labourers posed a grave threat to American democracy, one that was intertwined with the even greater threat posed by slavery. Wage labour was likened to 'wage slavery', and both the factory system and slavery were at odds with the republican ideal of 'free labour'. But the proponents of the cause of Northern workers and the anti-slavery activists divided over the meaning and thickness of the free labour ideal. For the abolitionists, free labour consisted essentially of self-ownership and the right to make contracts to sell one's labour. For the nascent labour movement, self-ownership was insufficient. The man who owned only himself had no choice but to sell his labour – to sell himself, in essence – in order to subsist. Without ownership of productive property, labour was not free.

Strains of this thicker notion of 'free labour' were heard after the Civil War in the debates leading to the adoption of the Fourteenth Amendment. But once slavery was vanquished, the thin version of 'free labour' as self-ownership acquired a new and more ambiguous pedigree in the ideology of laissez-faire capitalism. And it acquired a new champion in the federal judiciary.

The ideal of free labour became 'liberty of contract' – the right to sell one's labour, and to buy the labour of others, on such terms as the market permitted, free from interference by the state (or, for that matter, by organised labour). And 'liberty of contract' found a constitutional home in the 'due process' clauses of the Fifth and Fourteenth Amendments (the former running against the federal government and the latter against the states). Interference with liberty of contract was held to deprive employers and employees of liberty without due process unless it was found to be a 'reasonable' exercise of the police power; and that power was limited to protecting the public health and safety, narrowly construed.

During what has become known as the *Lochner* era,[7] liberty of contract became the constitutional basis for judicial invalidation of virtually every kind of legislation, state and federal, sought by organised labour and its supporters in the first few decades of the twentieth century. Minimum wage and maximum hours laws, laws legitimising organised labour activity, even laws prohibiting the discharge of union activists were struck down by federal courts as unlawful interference with the right of employers *and of workers* to buy and sell labour on such terms as they saw fit.[8] This was the unique American version of constitutional labour rights: the right to be free from the shackles of protective labour legislation.

The *Lochner* era ended in 1937, in the famous confrontation over Roosevelt's New Deal. A new majority of the Supreme Court largely repudiated the constitutional liberty of contract and ushered in a new era of deference to the legislature in economic matters, particularly with regard to the workplace.[9] At the same time, the Court abandoned its narrow view of 'interstate commerce' which, under the Constitution of enumerated federal powers, sharply limited the power of the federal government, as opposed to the states, to regulate the economy.[10] It upheld, among other laws, the National Labor Relations Act (NLRA),[11] which prohibited discrimination against union activists and established the framework for union representation and collective bargaining, and the Fair Labor Standards Act,[12] which established minimum wages and maximum hours in much of the private labour market.

But the *Lochner* era left an indelible mark on the American conception of labour rights. Professor Forbath argues, for example, that the frustration of labour's political programme at the hands of the judiciary, together with the even more direct confrontation with the courts' use of the labour injunction to stifle solidaristic labour activity, were crucial factors in the retreat of the main currents of organised labour

---

[7] So-named after *Lochner* v. *New York*, 148 US 45 (1905), which struck down as violative of the liberty of contract a state law establishing maximum hours for bakers.

[8] In addition to *Lochner*, see, e.g., *Adkins* v. *Children's Hospital of Dist. of Columbia*, 261 US 525 (1923) (invalidating minimum wage law); *Adair* v. *U.S.*, 208 US 161 (1908) (invalidating a law banning discharge of union activists); Truax v. Corrigan, 527 US 312 (1921) (invalidating a law restricting use of injunctions in labour disputes).

[9] See *West Coast Hotel Co.* v. *Parrish*, 300 US 379 (1937).

[10] See, e.g., *NLRB* v. *Jones & Laughlin Steel Corp.*, 301 US 1 (1937).

[11] 29 USC §151 et seq.   [12] 29 USC §201 et seq.

from politics and towards narrow trade unionism.[13] Even after the successes of the New Deal, the experience with substantive due process shaped labour's view of law and politics. The most 'fundamental' rights of American workers were won in a battle for legislative supremacy and against the courts and their constitutional power of judicial review.

IV. A fleeting nod towards fundamental (pro-)labour rights

Yet the Supreme Court in 1937 did not simply give up its extraordinary power of judicial review in favour of judicial deference; it redirected its scrutiny away from the economic sphere towards issues of political liberty and equality. The Supreme Court's new constitutional project, foreshadowed in the famous Footnote Four of its 1937 *Carolene Products* decision, was to safeguard individual liberties of free expression and association, especially as they contributed to democratic politics, and to protect 'discrete and insular minorities' and groups, especially black citizens, whose access to the political process was impaired.[14] Under the decisions that followed, the First Amendment became a significant constraint on governmental interference with free expression, and the Equal Protection Clause became a real threat to the system of racial apartheid in the South.

Initially there was some ambivalence about where labour activism would fit in this sharply dichotomised universe: was organised labour a social movement that sought to participate in and redefine politics and to advance the cause of social equality? In that case, it deserved energetic constitutional protection against hostile legislation, which was still widespread in the South. Or was labour simply a market actor struggling for its share in the division of the economic surplus? In that case, its activities lay in the constitutional domain of deference, and the legislature could regulate more or less as it saw fit. Of course, labour could present either face at different times. But what about labour's everyday forms of protest – strikes, pickets, boycotts – in support of representation rights and collective bargaining gains? Were those to be viewed as more like social and political protest or more like the competitive tactics of one economic actor against another?

[13] Forbath, *Law and the Shaping.*
[14] See *United States* v. *Carolene Products Co.*, 304 US 144, 152 n.4 (1938).

For a short time after the enactment of the National Labor Relations Act, the Supreme Court espoused the former vision of labour as a politically important social movement deserving of constitutional protection. A breakthrough 1939 decision establishing the First Amendment freedom of expression in public streets and gathering places involved labour organising activity.[15] And in 1940 the Court struck down a state ban on peaceful labour picketing under the First Amendment, proclaiming the facts of a labour dispute to be an undeniable 'matter of public concern'.[16]

But in hindsight, this brief experiment with constitutional pro-labour rights may have represented less a substantive conception of labour rights than an expedient transitional device in the transfer of authority over labour relations from states to the federal government. For the experiment largely fizzled out once Congress was deemed to have fully occupied the field of labour–management relations. There was little talk of the constitutional rights of labour protesters after the enactment of the 1947 Taft–Hartley amendments to the NLRA, which banned certain labour activities as a matter of federal law. Beginning in the late 1950s, state and local legislation hostile to organised labour was struck down on the basis of federal preemption, not the constitutional rights of labour.[17] Labour activity and labour rights were relegated largely to the domain of economic activity, where deference to Congress ruled the day. Deference ruled even when Congress itself moved to restrict peaceful labour expression, as it did in several provisions of the Taft–Hartley amendments. Faced with clear state action infringing labour's signature forms of expression, the Court found no First Amendment violation: Congress had struck an elaborate balance, and the Court was loathe to disturb it.[18]

So in the years following the New Deal, collective labour rights were firmly grounded in the domain of ordinary economic legislation, where the searching light of constitutional scrutiny would rarely shine. This has not in fact made those legal rights much more subject to revision than

---

[15] *Hague* v. *Congress of Industrial Organizations*, 307 US 496 (1939).

[16] *Thornhill* v. *Alabama*, 310 US 88 (1940).

[17] See generally Archibald Cox, Derek Bok, Robert Gorman and Matthew Finkin, *Labor Law: Cases and Materials*, 12th edn (Westbury, NY, 1996) 915–43 (on federal labour preemption doctrine).

[18] See *NLRB* v. *Retail Store Employees Union, Local 1001*, 447 US 607 (1980); *International Brotherhood of Electrical Workers*. v. *NLRB*, 341 US 694 (1951). Both decisions upheld NLRA prohibitions of certain forms of peaceful labour picketing.

if they had been embedded in the Constitution. Even with large shifts in the political make-up of Congress, both organised labour and employers have commanded enough support to block any reform that they strongly opposed.[19] As a result, there has been no major labour law reform – that is, reform of collective labour rights and labour–management relations – since 1947, when the Taft–Hartley amendments added a rash of anti-labour provisions to the original National Labor Relations Act.[20] At the same time, the increasingly broad scope of federal labour law preemption has foreclosed any significant reform or experimentation at the state and local level. The net result has been a system of collective labour relations that has been almost entirely insulated from ordinary democratic politics, yet equally insulated from the potentially progressive influence of constitutional commitments to liberty and equality.

V. The civil rights transformation

After 1960, rising opposition to racial segregation and discrimination ushered in a new era of employment law. Because of the state action requirement, the Fourteenth Amendment's Equal Protection Clause did not bring racial equality into the private sector workplace. Indeed, under the old *Civil Rights Cases* of 1883, there was substantial doubt whether Congress even had the power under the Fourteenth Amendment to prohibit discrimination in private sector workplaces.[21] So it was primarily under the Commerce Clause power that Congress enacted the Civil Rights Act of 1964, including the employment discrimination provisions of Title VII.[22] Title VII targeted discrimination on the basis of race, sex, ethnicity and religion in hiring, firing, promotions, and other terms and conditions of employment.

The importance of Title VII and the principle of equal employment opportunity is hard to overstate. Especially for African-American

---

[19] This is partly due to some unusual institutional restraints on purely majoritarian legislative action, such as the ability of a minority of senators to 'filibuster' subject to the ability of a supermajority of 60 out of 100 senators to end debate.

[20] Labor–Management Relations Act of 1947, 61 Stat. 136 (1947) ('Taft–Hartley Act').

[21] *In re Civil Rights Cases*, 109 US 3 (1883).

[22] Congress invoked both the Commerce Clause and Section 5 of the Fourteenth Amendment in support of the Civil Rights Act, see S. Rep. No. 88-872, at 12 (1964). The Supreme Court relied only on the Commerce Clause in upholding the Act in *Heart of Atlanta Motel* v. *United States*, 379 US 241, 250 (1964).

workers, it helped to advance economic status and welfare; it accelerated the breakdown of patterns of occupational segregation that were especially pronounced in the South; and it began to bring about a degree of racial integration in American workplaces. Women, too, advanced dramatically in the labour market in the years following Title VII.

Just as important as the consequences for the particular groups identified by Title VII was the establishment of the principle that individuals' prospects in the labour market should not be based on immutable traits such as race or sex but on individual abilities and experience. This principle proved to be a powerful rallying cry for other groups that suffered discrimination and disadvantage in employment. Title VII was followed by federal laws banning discrimination on the basis of pregnancy, age and disability.[23] Each of these new forms of discrimination required some tinkering with the meaning of discrimination. In the case of discrimination on the basis of disability, it required a major innovation in the form of a requirement of 'reasonable accommodation', whose consistency with the basic principles of anti-discrimination is a matter of current scholarly debate.[24]

The anti-discrimination principle has expanded in other ways, too. By judicial interpretation, later ratified by Congress, the anti-discrimination laws have been held to entail a ban on harassment based on the enumerated traits.[25] Even harassment by non-supervisory co-workers can sometimes constitute employment discrimination by the employer. Harassment law represents an ambitious attempt to change the culture of the workplace, and to reconstruct social relations in this central domain of life. In my own view, the harassment laws have sometimes pushed employers too far in the direction of censoring expression and squelching informal interaction in the workplace.[26] Even so, sexual harassment law in particular has had an extraordinary and largely healthy impact on the economic prospects and wellbeing of women in their work lives.

---

[23] See Age Discrimination in Employment Act of 1967, 29 USC §§621–634; Pregnancy Discrimination Act of 1978, 42 USC §2000e(k); Americans with Disabilities Act of 1990, 29 USC. §706.

[24] Compare Samuel Issacharoff and Justin Nelson, 'Discrimination with a Difference: Can Employment Discrimination Law Accommodate the Americans with Disabilities Act?' (2001) 79 North Carolina Law Review 307, with Christine Jolls, 'Accommodation Mandates' (2000) 53 Stanford Law Review 223.

[25] See, e.g., *Meritor Savings Bank* v. *Vinson*, 477 US 57 (1986).

[26] Cynthia L. Estlund, 'Freedom of Expression in the Workplace and the Problem of Discriminatory Harassment' (1997) 75 Texas Law Review 687.

While employment discrimination law originated at the federal level, and federal law continues to dominate the field, this is not an area of exclusive federal control. Every state has its own anti-discrimination statute. The provisions are typically parallel to those of Title VII, but they sometimes afford a more employee-friendly forum, remedies and procedures. Moreover, these state laws sometimes extend the reach of the anti-discrimination principle to protect additional groups. Most notably, several states have banned discrimination on the basis of sexual orientation, while a national consensus for such a law has yet to coalesce.

There has been significant controversy and legal reform around the margins of these laws – with regard to details of the doctrine, remedies and procedures. But the core of anti-discrimination law can be described as 'fundamental' in all but the formal sense. It is fundamental in the sense that it draws moral and doctrinal inspiration and cultural support from the constitutional ideal of equality and the Equal Protection Clause. And it is fundamental in the sense that it appears to be politically sacrosanct. It is not simply that the civil rights community has the power to block significant legislative cutbacks in these laws, which it does; or that it can secure legislative reversal of restrictive Supreme Court interpretations of these laws, which it has done.[27] It is also fundamental in the sense that the basic animating principle of equal employment opportunity commands a powerful moral consensus that has fuelled the expansion of this branch of employment law even during politically conservative times. In this one area at least, the formal absence of fundamental labour rights appears to be largely unimportant.

But I want to suggest two significant caveats to this claim. The first stems from the steps taken by the current Supreme Court majority to limit congressional power as against the states. One is tempted to conclude that, with the end of the Warren and Burger Court era of expanding individual rights of liberty and equality, the Court's conservative majority had to find a new project – a new arena in which to flex its most powerful muscles and command the national stage through the extraordinary power of judicial review. The current majority seems set on carrying out, under the banner of federalism, a limited form of 'devolution' to the states.

---

[27] Civil Rights Act of 1991 (substantially reversing five restrictive Supreme Court decisions on employment discrimination law during the 1989–90 term).

These moves have come through several constitutional avenues: The Eleventh Amendment's guarantee of the states' 'sovereign immunity' has been held to limit the power of Congress to subject the states to suits for damages, hence the demise of private lawsuits by public employees under the Fair Labor Standards Act, the Age Discrimination in Employment Act, and the Americans with Disabilities Act.[28] The Court has also begun to demand that Congress justify with extensive factfinding the exercise of its enumerated powers, especially the Commerce Clause power and the enforcement powers under the Fourteenth Amendment, particularly but not only when it acts directly against the states.[29] As yet, these federalism decisions have not cut into the power of Congress to regulate private sector employment, which seems still to be understood as part of the core domain of Congress under the Commerce Clause. But it is hard to say where the Court is headed.

The second caveat to my claim that the formally non-constitutional nature of anti-discrimination law is unimportant lies in another more extreme form of 'devolution': the privatisation of employment discrimination law. I refer here to the increasing use of arbitration as a substitute for judicial resolution of employment claims, including federal employment discrimination claims. The Court's recent decision in *Circuit City* removed all doubt about the ability of employers to demand as a condition of employment that employees waive their right to bring a discrimination claim (or any other employment claim) to court, and agree instead to submit those claims to private arbitration.[30] The arbitration process must meet some rather undemanding standards of fairness, the precise contours of which do remain in doubt; moreover, arbitrators must be empowered to grant all the same remedies available under the statute. But in its current form, arbitration is believed by many observers to tilt in favour of employers; at the very least it threatens to dilute both the power and the public nature of the anti-discrimination laws. In particular, the very limited opportunity for judicial review of arbitration awards threatens to undermine the quality and uniformity

---

[28] See *Alden* v. *Maine*, 527 US 706 (1999); *Kimel* v. *Florida Bd. of Regents*, 528 US 62 (2000); *Board of Trustees* v. *Garrett*, — S.Ct. —, No. 99-1240 (Feb. 21, 2001). All were 5–4 decisions.

[29] See *United States* v. *Lopez*, 514 US 549 (1995); *City of Boerne* v. *Flores*, 521 US 507 (1997); *United States* v. *Morrison*, 120 S.Ct. 1740 (2000). Except for *City of Boerne*, which was decided by a 6–3 vote, all these decision, too, were decided 5–4.

[30] Circuit City Stores, Inc. v. Adams, S Ct, No. 99-1379 (21 Mar. 2001). See Hepple, ch. 10 below.

of employment discrimination law, and to rob this area of employment law of its distinctly public (and 'fundamental') character.

In approving mandatory arbitration of employment discrimination claims, the Court treated those claims as essentially like any other statutory claims. We might speculate that the approval of mandatory arbitration and the resulting privatisation of employment discrimination law would have triggered more searching scrutiny if that law were formally more 'fundamental' than ordinary legislation. That need not mean the blanket disapproval of arbitration, which in some forms might be a fair and more accessible alternative to costly litigation. But a more 'fundamental' conception of anti-discrimination rights might have helped to bring forth the necessary improvements in the arbitration process.

VI. The rise of individual employment rights

Perhaps the most interesting recent development in American employment law is the proliferation of individual employee rights, especially privacy rights and protections against discharge. This area is interesting in part because it has been one of virtually unconstrained state-by-state experimentation and variation. The complete lack of national uniformity and universality suggests the antithesis of 'fundamental' rights. I address it here for two reasons. First, the absence of any general protection against unjust discharge, and the hodgepodge of law that has grown up in the absence of such protection, stands in striking contrast to the arguably fundamental right against unjust discharge that prevails throughout Europe. Second, it is in this area of employment law that formally fundamental constitutional provisions – state constitutional provisions, that is – play the greatest role.

The enormous variations in the law of individual employee rights make it impossible to convey anything but a highly schematic picture here. But those variations all begin from a uniform starting point: the peculiarly American rule of 'employment at will'. In the absence of the parties' agreement to employment for a term or to limitations on the power of discharge, an employer may fire an employee at any time 'for good reason, bad reason, or no reason at all'. That is the common law rule in every American jurisdiction except for Montana.[31] Employment at will

---

[31] See Wrongful Discharge from Employment Act, Montana Code §§39-2-902 et seq.

has been softened by developments in the law of employment contracts that make it easier for employees to show an express or an implied promise of job security. And it has become riddled with exceptions, beginning with the National Labor Relations Act, the Civil Rights Act, and many other state and federal prohibitions on discharge for designated 'bad reasons'. But it remains the case that most private sector employees can lawfully be fired with no explanation and no demonstrable cause.

Not all individual employee rights take the form of protections against discharge. Privacy rights, for example, may be invoked by employees against their current employer. I focus here on employment at will and wrongful discharge law because employers' power to fire employees gives them enormous power to dictate employee conduct and to control their work lives as long as they are on the job. Moreover, as most individual employee rights are enforceable in court through civil litigation, they are rarely invoked until the employee is fired. That is when the stakes might be great enough to justify litigation.

Let us begin with the basic distinction between contractual and noncontractual rights. I will have little to say about the law of express and implied employment contracts, except to note that this law has sought to hold employers to their own assurances about job security. Again, states vary in how much and what kind of evidence it takes to show an enforceable expectation of job security. And the pattern is not necessarily what one might expect. New York is, for example, among the most rigid adherents to the default rule of employment at will.[32] Courts in New Jersey and California have been more willing to find implicit assurances of job security.[33] To the extent that employers find it in their interest to foster employees' expectations of job security – and that may be in doubt in some of the most fluid sectors of the labour market – the law of employment contracts in many states now affords some remedy to employees who believe they have been fired without justification. That

---

[32] See, e.g., *Murphy* v. *American Home Products Corp.*, 448 NE 2d 86 (NY 1983) (reaffirming employment at will, rejecting implied covenant of good faith and fair dealing as a limitation on power to discharge at-will employee); *Weiner* v. *McGraw-Hill, Inc.*, 443 NE 2d 441 (NY 1982) (enforcing express employee handbook promises on which employee relied).

[33] See, e.g., *Woolley* v. *Hoffman-LaRoche, Inc.*, 491 A 2d 1257, modified, 499 A 2d 515 (NJ 1985); *Pugh* v. *See's Candies, Inc.*, 171 Cal. Rptr. 917 (1981). Even California has regressed somewhat towards the mean in recent cases. See *Guz* v. *Bechtel Nat'l, Inc.*, 24 Cal. 4th 317, 8 P 3d 1089 (2000).

remedy is immediately useful only to those employees who get such a promise, and more importantly to those employees who have the where-withal to hire an attorney and bring a lawsuit. Few low- and middle-income employees fit that description.

Notwithstanding some doctrinal movement in recent decades to-wards the recognition of employees' right to job security, the issue is still deemed to be a matter of contract. There is still nothing like a fundamental right to job security or freedom from arbitrary discharge. Without any security against arbitrary discharge, there is reason to doubt the efficacy of many other employment rights, the existence of which does not depend on contract, but the enforcement of which depends on employees' willingness to speak out and resist violations.[34]

The non-contractual doctrines take many forms. I will focus on one large category: the doctrine of wrongful discharge in violation of public policy. With the usual caveat about state-by-state variation, state courts have given a remedy for employees fired for the fulfillment of certain public duties (such as jury service);[35] for the exercise of certain legal rights (such as the filing of a worker's compensation claim);[36] for the refusal to engage in illegal and especially criminal conduct (such as the refusal to engage in perjury in support of the employer);[37] and for the disclosure of illegal conduct under some circumstances (such as reporting violation of criminal laws to enforcement agencies).[38] In effect these wrongful discharge doctrines recognise employee rights grounded in public policy, which may be found in state and sometimes federal statutes and regulatory schemes as well as, in some states, common law and state constitutions.[39]

Some state statutes codify these protections. But most of this law is judge-made common law. That means that it tends to develop slowly

---

[34] See Cynthia Estlund, 'Wrongful Discharge Protections in an At-Will World' (1996) 74 Texas Law Review 1655.

[35] See, e.g., *Nees* v. *Hocks*, 536 P 2d 512 (Ore. 1975) (en banc).

[36] See, e.g., *Frampton* v. *Central Indiana Gas Co.*, 297 NE 2d 425 (Ind. 1973).

[37] See, e.g., *Petermann* v. *International Bhd. of Teamsters*, 344 P 2d 25 (Californian Court of Appeal 1959).

[38] See, e.g., *Palmateer* v. *International Harvester Co.*, 421 NE 2d 876 (Ill. 1981).

[39] In one case, even federal constitutional rights. See *Novosel* v. *Nationwide Ins. Co.*, 721 F 2d 894 (1983) (finding, under Pennsylvania law, that discharge for refusing to lobby for legislation favoured by employer would violate public policy underlying First Amendment). The potential implications of the *Novosel* theory were vast, but, perhaps for that reason, the decision has generated little following.

and incrementally, and that the legislature can always step in and over-rule the courts. The Arizona legislature did so, for example, when the Arizona Supreme Court, in the very entertaining *Wagenseller* decision, upheld the tort claim of a woman whose discharge allegedly stemmed from her refusal to bare her buttocks at a raucous musical performance in which several co-workers and her supervisor participated during an off-duty camping trip.[40] That discharge was found to violate the public policy underlying Arizona's law against indecent exposure. The legisla-ture responded with a hysterical diatribe against judicial activism and a reaffirmation of employment at will, coupled with a partial overrul-ing of *Wagenseller* and a moderate statutory codification of the law of wrongful discharge.[41] The *Wagenseller* decision and its aftermath may illustrate the decidedly non-fundamental nature of the employee rights in these public policy cases. Yet it is interesting that even the aggravated and conservative Arizona legislature could not bring itself to abolish the tort of discharge in violation of public policy, which exists in some form in almost all states, or even to disapprove of the specific result in *Wagenseller*.

Not all of these decisions are equally susceptible to legislative revi-sion. In the *Luedtke* decision, the Alaska Supreme Court entertained the wrongful discharge claim of two brothers fired for failing a drug test.[42] Noting its prior recognition of a fundamental state constitutional right to smoke marijuana in one's own home, the Court found the employer's power to test for and punish marijuana use to be strictly limited. The legislature's power to modify this kind of decision through ordinary leg-islation is less clear because of the constitutional source of the public policy on which it is based.

Luedtke, in its vindication of privacy rights, exemplifies one of the most dynamic areas of individual employee rights, and the one in which state constitutions have played a particularly important role as a source of public policy and employee rights. As in *Luedtke*, some state courts have interpreted state constitutions, or some of their provisions, as con-taining no state action requirement; the result is a rich source of potential constitutional constraints on the power of private sector employers over their employees. California courts, for example, have invoked state

---

[40] *Wagenseller v. Scottsdale Memorial Hosp.*, 710 P 2d 1025 (Ariz. 1985).
[41] See Employment Protection Act, Ariz. Rev. Stats. § 23-1501 et seq.
[42] *Luedtke v. Nabors Alaska Drilling, Inc.*, 768 P 2d 1123 (Alaska 1989).

constitutional rights of privacy in upholding the claim of an employee fired for dating the employee of a competitor, as well as a tort claim by employment applicants who were required, as a condition of employment, to submit to a written test that included intrusive questions about religious beliefs and sexual orientation.[43] Privacy rights appear to be a growth area in employment law, and are likely to become increasingly important as the technology of surveillance and information-gathering becomes ever more sophisticated. The legislatures are entering the fray. But in the meantime some courts, faced with what they regard as oppressive employer conduct, are turning to the broad affirmations of human dignity and integrity that are found in many state constitutions as a basis for relief.

This partial snapshot of the law of individual employment rights may suggest a bit of a paradox: sometimes leaving the development of employee rights to lower and more local sources of legal authority yields rather ambitious and durable employee rights. Perhaps there is some trade-off between the aspiration to universality and the creativity and scope of legal rights – some tension between these two dimensions of 'fundamentality' in the nature of employee rights. That observation brings me to some final reflections.

VII. Reflections on European labour rights from an American perspective

I have largely resisted the impulse to offer an 'American view' of the very exciting developments on the eastern side of the Atlantic, about which I am still learning. But I will briefly give in to temptation.

I did not recount the peculiar American history of 'liberty of contract' as a cautionary tale but as an explanation for the virtual absence in the United States of political momentum towards the recognition or addition of judicially enforceable federal constitutional rights in the workplace. The perils seen in that history – a recalcitrant judiciary steeped in the ideology of laissez-faire capitalism, armed with old and open-textured constitutional provisions, and seeking to hold the line

---

[43] See *Rulon-Miller* v. *IBM Corp.*, 208 Cal. Rptr. 524 (Ct. App. 1984) (recognising state constitutional privacy right in dating relationship); *Soroka* v. *Dayton Hudson Corp.*, 1 Cal. Rptr. 2d 77 (Ct. App. 1991) (upholding state constitutional right against intrusive 'honesty testing').

against organised labour and a majoritarian tide of workplace regulation – seem remote in present-day Europe. Or perhaps not so remote. To American ears, there is a familiar ring to the contemporary conflict between European principles of competition – part of the founding and seemingly fundamental principles of the federation – and national legislation regulating labour markets. There are distinct echoes in that conflict of the *Lochner*-era battles between free market ideas, dressed up in the language of constitutional rights and wielded by judges with the power of judicial review, and labour's efforts to tame the market through legislation.

The current move to balance the European constitution through the introduction of fundamental labour and social rights seems to be a straightforward remedy to the problem. Of course, at any time when majorities make law that is beyond the ready reach of future majorities, care must be taken to anticipate changing times and ideas, and to leave room for future developments, without leaving too much room for invidious interpretations of the law. That is a commonplace observation about constitution-making, and it is one that may seem to be of little concern here. The 'founding generation' for the current European version of fundamental labour rights is the present generation. Working people and their representatives, sensitive to the realities of the modern workplace, are at the table and make up the constitutive political majorities that are formulating this law.

But the American drama of the *Lochner* era may hint at some deeper tension between the interests of working people and the language of rights. Even labour rights can come into conflict with labour's interests; it was, after all, workers' 'liberty of contract' as much as that of employers that was invoked against labour activity and labour legislation in the *Lochner* era. There is something in the language of rights, at least in judicial hands, that tilts in a highly individualistic direction. And there is something, too, in the judicial mindset that does not love collective action and collective institutions. Those traditional vehicles of working-class progress are often loud and unruly and at odds with legalistic conceptions of how rights are secured and conflicts resolved. I leave it to European readers to consider whether or not the fundamental social and labour rights that are on the books or under consideration could come back to haunt working people, and especially their ability to assert their own interests through collective action.

I will be more brief with the rest of my reflections. If there is any lesson to be taken from the American attachment to a 'state action' limitation on the scope of federal constitutional rights, it is a complex one that cannot be treated adequately in this chapter. I will offer only these tentative observations. It is clear that the state action requirement in American constitutional law has operated as a shield for private power, insulating private sector employers, among others, from constitutional norms in their 'governance' of less powerful individuals. But the state action requirement shields a range of private associations and private decision-making from constitutionally inspired legal scrutiny. There may be some value in that delineation of a private sphere in which even widely shared constitutional norms are suspended and private liberty reigns (though there may also be more sensible ways of drawing the line than the doctrine of state action).

The American experience with employment discrimination legislation – fundamental in all but form – already appears to have offered some useful lessons to British and European lawmakers. But it also stands as a negative lesson – indeed, two negative lessons – on how to enforce labour rights. On the one hand, it would be a mistake to go too far down the distinctly American path of dependence on individual litigation for the enforcement of most workplace rights. That path has proven fruitful in many ways for employees. Most importantly, the fear of litigation has induced many employers to provide internal mechanisms of due process that are designed in part to avoid wrongful discharges and wrongful discharge claims. But litigation is very slow and costly, and is effectively out of reach for many employees. On the other hand, it would also be a mistake to go too far down the new American path of compelling private arbitration of these claims – or rather, of allowing employers to demand agreements to arbitrate. If the cost of employment claims mounts in Europe, it would not be surprising to see employers looking for cheaper forms of adjudication.

Arbitration might prove to be eminently resistible here. First, the role of private contract – which has been the vehicle for the imposition of mandatory arbitration – is neither so pervasive nor so presumptively determinative in most of Europe as it in the United States. Second, the malady to which arbitration is thought to provide a remedy – the explosion of costly employment litigation – has not reached the epidemic proportions or aroused the alarm that it has in the United States. That may be a function of the role of specialised labour courts in adjudicating many employment rights. This is one of many lessons that the European experience offers to Americans.

There may be some interesting lessons in the contrast between the vibrancy and variability of the one area of employment rights that is almost entirely left to the states and the virtual stagnation of the law of collective labour rights that is exclusively federal and largely insulated from majoritarian control. In any federal system, one of the endemic challenges is finding the right balance between federation-wide uniformity and local control and experimentation. The existing balance has been struck in the United States by a series of uncoordinated accommodations to historical change constrained by a constitutional commitment to federalism that we have been taught to regard as wise. On the whole, it is no model. But it does offer a varied set of experiences – natural experiments, perhaps – that may offer some incidental lessons.

One rather elementary lesson may be that there are pitfalls to both complete federation-wide uniformity and unfettered regional experimentation. Uniform federal law, particularly where the law is relatively immune to revision as in the case of the NLRA, may stagnate without the stimulation of either local experimentation or democratic reexamination. (Whether that is any kind of a lesson for a more simply majoritarian parliamentary system is unclear.) On the other hand, the opposite picture of dynamic and highly variable state laws governing individual employee rights looks a lot better when we focus on the most innovative states than when we focus on those that have adhered to a nearly unreconstructed rule of employment at will. Whether because of institutional traditions of judicial reticence or a sympathy for employer prerogatives, the states that have largely resisted the erosion of employment at will, including New York, leave a lot of employees without the benefit of what other states deem to be 'fundamental' rights of privacy, liberty and security.

In principle, the solution may seem rather obvious: create federation-wide minimum standards – the most fundamental rights, together with adequate but not extravagant enforcement procedures and remedies – while allowing local variations above that minimum. That may not work for all areas of the law; sometimes uniformity is necessary. But it seems like the right starting point. And it seems to be roughly the starting point within the European Union with respect to social and labour rights. That solution has prevailed in the United States with respect to most minimum standards legislation: the Fair Labor Standards Act, as well as the Family and Medical Leave Act, for example, set a floor in terms of minimum wages, maximum hours and leave time; but states and even localities (depending on state law) remain free to establish a higher minimum wage, a lower maximum work-week or more generous parental leave policies. The difficulty, again, is in constructing a floor at the right level. That is not something on which the American experience is likely to be instructive.

Finally, it would be unseemly – perhaps un-American – to conclude these reflections without a further word or two on the role of contract and the market. The presumptive validity of the terms of individual employment contracts, and the comparatively small role played by regulation – fundamental or otherwise – is the heart of the American model of employment law in the private sector (outside the 10 per cent that is unionised). The regime of individual contract was elevated to constitutional status during the *Lochner* era. But even since the deconstitutionalisation of liberty of contract, most terms and conditions of employment of American workers are a product of individual (or, in the shrinking union sector, collective) contracts. As compared with much of western Europe, our minimum standards are, in many respects, minimum indeed. With respect to retirement and health benefits, the law mandates nothing at all (though it regulates whatever employers do offer), and many workers have neither. Most striking of all is the fact that basic job security is left to the realm of contract: unless employers promise not to do so, they are free to fire their employees without any justification.

By leaving more to the domain of contract, the American labour market has gained flexibility, and perhaps job growth, while American workers experience greater economic insecurity and inequality than their employed European counterparts. The balance of advantage in this contract-based regime favours the most skilled workers as compared with the less skilled, and it tilts against workers in general, at least in the short term, when slack market conditions weaken their bargaining position. Putting aside painful and all-too-recurrent questions about the viability of generous labour protections in an increasingly porous and global economy, decisions about how much to leave to the market is perhaps the most fundamental labour question of all. The American experience provides not a model but a useful body of knowledge about the consequences of one sort of answer to that question.

9

The impact of fundamental social rights on Japanese law

TAKASHI ARAKI

I. Introduction

One of the significant features of Japanese labour law is that it has its basis in the Constitution. The Japanese Constitution, which was promulgated in 1946 and took effect the next year, contains provisions on minimum standards of living (art. 25), on the right to, and obligation to provide education (art. 26), on the right to work and on working conditions (art. 27) and on workers' rights to organise, bargain and act collectively (art. 28).

Apart from these fundamental social rights provisions, the Japanese Constitution contains a long list of human rights. Furthermore, international law concerning human rights also affects fundamental social rights in Japan.

To examine the impact of the fundamental social rights on the political and judicial arena in Japan, this chapter first overviews the fundamental human and social rights guaranteed in the Constitution. Second, it looks at how constitutional provisions on social rights affect the legislative process. Third, the following three dimensions will be overviewed to analyse the impact of the fundamental rights on the judiciary: judicial review of the state's acts; indirect application of fundamental rights to private citizens through the concept of public policy; and case law development concerning dismissal regulation as an example of furthering social rights. Fourth, the impact of international human rights law on Japanese social policy is analysed. In conclusion, a brief summary of

The author expresses his gratitude to Christopher Nyland and Walter Hutchinson for their valuable comments on the draft.

the impact of social rights on Japanese law and features of the Japanese
approach to the social rights will be provided.

II. Fundamental human rights and social rights
in the Japanese Constitution

The current Japanese Constitution provides a long list of fundamental
human rights, including the guarantee of fundamental human rights
(art. 11), rights to be respected as individuals and to pursue happiness
(art. 13), equality under the law and prohibition of discrimination by
reason of race, creed, sex, social status or family origin (art. 14), freedom from slavery, bondage or involuntary servitude (art. 18), freedom
of thought and conscience (art. 19), freedom of religion (art. 20), freedom of assembly, association, speech and all other forms of expression
(art. 21), freedom to choose and change residence and occupation and
to move to foreign countries (art. 22) and academic freedom (art. 23).

Among these fundamental human rights some provisions relate to
employment relations and can fall under the wide category of fundamental social rights in the European context. For instance, Article 13
concerning the right to pursue happiness is now interpreted as a general clause protecting new human rights such as the right to privacy.
Article 14 concerning equality under the law directly relates to equal
treatment at workplaces. Article 18 requires social policy prohibiting
forced labour. Article 19 on freedom of thought gives rise to question-
ing the legality of asking applicants' political preference or activities in
the past at hiring.[1] Freedom to choose one's own occupation, prescribed
in Article 22, guarantees the worker's right to choose an employer, and
also the employer's right to do business. However, unlike in the European
debate, Article 21 concerning freedom of assembly and association is not
deemed as covering workers' rights to organise labour unions, because
the Japanese Constitution explicitly guarantees these rights by a separate
article (art. 28) as explained below.

Besides the above-mentioned fundamental human rights or traditional rights to freedom, the Japanese Constitution prescribes fundamental social rights in the following four provisions. Article 25, commonly
called the provision of the 'right to live', proclaimed the principle of the

---

[1] The *Mitsubishi Jushi* case, Supreme Court, 12 Dec. 1973 (27-11 *Minshu* 1536).

welfare state.[2] Article 26 proclaimed the right to and the obligation to provide education.[3] Articles 27 and 28 deal squarely with labour and employment relations, as seen below. These provisions on fundamental social rights are influenced significantly by the German Weimar Constitution.

III. The impact of constitutional fundamental social rights on the legislature

In the developments of Japanese labour law after the Second World War, constitutional provisions on fundamental social rights had an immense impact.

The right to work

Article 27 Paragraph 1 of the Constitution ('All people shall have the right and the obligation to work') was interpreted as requiring two political obligations on the part of the state:[4] first, the state shall intervene in the labour market so as to enable workers to be offered suitable job opportunities; second, the state bears a political obligation to guarantee the livelihood of those workers who cannot obtain such opportunities. In accordance with the former legislative mandate, various statutes were enacted such as the Employment Security Law of 1947, which regulates employment placement services, recruitment and labour supply businesses, the Employment Measures Law of 1966, which proclaims general principles of labour market policies, the Law Promoting the Development of Occupational Ability of 1969, the Disabled Employment Promotion Law of 1960, and the Older Persons' Employment Stabilisation Law of 1971. In accordance with the latter mandate, the Unemployment Insurance Law of 1947 and its successor, the Employment Insurance Law of 1974, were enacted.

---

[2] Art. 25: 'All people shall have the right to maintain the minimum standards of wholesome and cultured living. In all spheres of life, the State shall use its endeavours for the promotion and extension of social welfare and security, and of public health.'

[3] Art. 26: 'All people shall have the right to receive an equal education correspondent to their ability, as provided by law. All people shall be obliged to have all boys and girls under their protection receive ordinary education as provided for by law. Such compulsory education shall be free.'

[4] Kazuo Sugeno, *Japanese Labour Law*, trans. Leo Kanowitz (Tokyo and Seattle, 1992), 15.

Article 27, Paragraph 1 also mentions the obligation to work. The literal meaning of the phrase implies industrial conscription. However, since such an interpretation is not appropriate, the 'obligation to work' is interpreted to mean that the state has no obligation to countenance those who do not have the intention to work. Thus the availability of unemployment benefits is confined to those who intend to work.

Labour standards

Article 27 Paragraph 2 of the Constitution ('Standards for wages, hours, rest and other working conditions shall be fixed by law') requires the state to enact laws regulating terms and conditions of employment. Accordingly, the Labour Standards Law (LSL) and the Workers' Accident Compensation Insurance Law were enacted in 1947. The LSL is a comprehensive piece of protective labour legislation establishing minimum standards of working conditions. The international labour standards established by the ILO conventions were fully acknowledged in the LSL's enactment. For example, setting a forty-eight hour working week was thought to put a heavy economic burden on Japanese employers. However, in order to be seen to be acknowledging international standards and to be playing its part in the international community, the Japanese legislature adopted these standards.

Subsequently, two chapters contained in the LSL were singled out and became two independent statutes: the Minimum Wages Law of 1959 and the Industrial Safety and Health Law of 1972. Faced with the increased insolvency after the first oil crisis in 1973, the legislature enacted the Security of Wage Payment Law of 1976.

Article 27 Paragraph 3 of the Constitution, concerning the prohibition of child labour ('Children shall not be exploited') is incorporated into the child labour protective provisions of the LSL of 1947.

The collective rights of workers

Article 28 of the Constitution ('The right of workers to organise and to bargain and act collectively is guaranteed') proclaims general principles governing collective labour relations. Any legislative or administrative act that infringes these rights without reasonable justification is therefore unconstitutional and void. Workers are immune from any criminal or civil liability for proper union activities. Article 28 is understood to stem from the provision in the Weimar Constitution of 1919 which guaranteed freedom of association and stated the third-party effect (*Drittwirkung*) among private individuals. Thus, in the opinion of most, Article 28 is construed as regulating not only relations between the state and private citizens but also relations between private citizens (that is, employers and workers). Consequently, workers have a cause of action against an employer who has infringed their union rights. For instance, dismissal of a worker by reason of legal union activities is deemed as null and void, violating the constitutional norm.[5]

Article 28 is further interpreted as entrust the Diet with enacting statutes to effectuate basic union rights. Accordingly, the Trade Union Law (TUL) of 1949 set the requirements for qualifying as a union, established the unfair labour practice system which prohibits employers' anti-union actions including refusal of collective bargaining, gave a normative effect to collective bargaining agreements, and established the Labour Relations Commissions. The commissions are administrative tripartite bodies that adjudicate unfair labour practice cases and resolve collective labour disputes.

The Labour Relations Adjustment Law was also enacted in 1946, to facilitate the resolution of collective labour disputes. Under this law, the Labour Relations Commissions are entrusted with the conciliation, mediation and arbitration of labour disputes.

From a comparative perspective, it is noteworthy that the Japanese law not only gives civil and criminal immunity to proper acts of trade unions but also encourages collective bargaining by administrative intervention through the unfair labour practice system.

---

[5] See Satoshi Nishitani, *Rodo Kumiai Ho (Trade Union Law)* (1998), 36; Nobuyoshi Ashibe, *Kenpo shinpan (Constitutional Law)*, new edn (Tokyo, 1997), 248. Other human rights provisions in the Constitution are generally understood as regulating exclusively the relations between the state and individuals, and thus they have no 'third-party effect' between private individuals. Accordingly, fundamental rights provisions have legal effect between private individuals, if any, only through the 'public policy' concept found in Art. 90 of the Civil Code, which invalidates legal acts violating public order and good morals. Some influential labour law scholars apply the same theory to Art. 28 too. According to them, dismissals for union activities can be nullified because such dismissals are in violation of the public policy reflecting the norms expressed in Art. 28 of the Constitution. See Sugeno, *Japanese Labour Law*, 20.

The unfair labour practice system incorporated into the TUL of 1949[6] was modelled on the US Wagner Act (National Labour Relations Act of 1935).[7] Article 7 of the TUL of 1949 prohibits three types of anti-union actions by employers: the disadvantageous treatment of union members, refusal to bargain, and domination of and interference in union administration. Violation of these prohibitions is addressed by administrative orders of the Labour Relations Commission.[8]

For instance, when an employer refuses to bargain with a labour union on terms and conditions of employment or other employment-related subjects, the labour union can file the case with the Labour Relations Commission. When the Commission finds that there is a refusal of collective bargaining without good reason, it orders the employer to bargain with the union in good faith. Violation of the order can be punished by administrative fines, criminal fines and imprisonment.

Such state intervention to encourage and promote collective bargaining is the outcome of the constitutional guarantee of fundamental

---

[6] The original TUL enacted in 1945 prohibited disadvantageous treatment of union members because of their membership, and also prohibited yellow-dog contracts, which oblige workers not to join a union, by the imposition of criminal provisions. The gravity of such criminal penalties, however, led to the 1945 TUL being applied only in a few instances. In fact, only 3.6 per cent of the cases brought to the Labour Relations Commissions were prosecuted, and 1.6 per cent resulted in convictions. In response to the ineffectiveness of the former system, the TUL of 1949 changed the criminal penalty system into a system of administrative remedies by which the Labour Relations Commission orders remedial measures to rectify the consequences of unfair labour practices. The Wagner Act in the United States was a model for this modification. The 1949 revision also added several prohibited acts, such as the refusal to bargain, and domination of and interference in union administration.

[7] However, there are significant differences between the American unfair labour practice system and that of Japan. First, since the TUL does not adopt an American-style exclusive representation system, Japanese minority unions are entitled to the same rights and protections as majority unions. Second, unlike the US National Labour Relations Act, as amended by the Taft–Hartley Act of 1947, the TUL of 1949 has not incorporated the notion of unfair labour practices on the part of unions. Third, the Labour Relations Commissions in Japan are tripartite bodies. Although only the neutral members retain the adjudicatory function for unfair labour practice cases, members appointed by labour and management play an important role in promoting settlement of cases. Fourth, neutral members of the Labour Relations Commission in Japan are appointed on a part-time basis, and attorney certification is not required. Although the merit of this practice is to utilise the wisdom of those well acquainted with labour relations rather than with legal expertise, there is a criticism that fact-finding and drafting of orders by non-lawyers are sometimes inaccurate or inadequate to withstand judicial review in the courts. Fifth, unfair labour practice cases can also be brought to ordinary courts for damages or annulment of juristic acts under Japanese law.

[8] There are Local Labour Relations Commissions instituted in each prefecture as the first instance, and the Central Labour Relations Commission in Tokyo, a reviewing agency.

social rights. Although the unfair labour practice system significantly restrains employers' freedom of business and may well contravene their fundamental rights, such social policy is deemed as constitutional by the existence of the social rights provisions in the Constitution.

IV. The impact of the constitutional fundamental social rights on the judiciary

As mentioned above, the fundamental social rights in the Constitution have provided important political and legislative grounds for developing social policy in Japan. How, then, have the fundamental rights guaranteed in the Constitution affected the Japanese courts' interpretation? Discussion should be divided into three areas: judicial review of the state's acts; judicial intervention in the acts of the private citizen through the public policy concept incorporating norms of constitutional fundamental rights; and case law developments realising fundamental rights.

The courts' attitude towards judicial review: respect for the legislature's discretion

The judicial review system

Fundamental human and social rights in the Constitution make acts by the state that violate them unconstitutional. The Constitution endows the judiciary with the power to examine the constitutionality of legislative and administrative acts.

Unlike some European countries, however, Japan has no constitutional court. Judicial review of the constitutionality of legislative acts or other state acts is entrusted to ordinary courts and ultimately to the Supreme Court. Article 81 of the Constitution states: 'The Supreme Court is the court of last resort with power to determine the constitutionality of any law, order, regulation or official act.' Since this power of judicial review has been modelled on the US judicial review system, it is established that the court cannot review the 'abstract' allegation of unconstitutionality of state acts unrelated to resolving concrete cases.[9]

---

[9] The *Keisatsu Yobitai* case, Supreme Court (Grand Bench), 8 October 1952 (6-9 *Minshu* 783). (The allegation that establishing the police reserve army was against art. 9 of the Constitution, which proclaims renunciation of military force, was dismissed because the allegation is abstract and is not related to concrete legal issues.)

Therefore, Japanese courts can review the constitutionality of state acts only when it is necessary to adjudicate concrete, not abstract, legal issues contested in the case.

The reluctance of the court to find unconstitutionality

Japanese courts are said as a general rule to be reluctant to find the legislative and administrative acts unconstitutional and so allow legislatures wide discretion.[10] With regard to social rights, since the constitutional provisions are interpreted as being 'programmatic', or at least not sufficiently concrete to give specific rights to private citizens, the courts' deferral to the legislature becomes further evident.

For instance, in the famous *Asahi* case, a person living on social benefits sued the government for not providing a minimum standard of living guaranteed by Article 25 of the Constitution. Although the district court upheld the plaintiff's claim, the Supreme Court in an *obiter dictum*[11] stated that whether a specific measure met the standard of 'wholesome and cultured living' as provided by the Constitution was primarily determined by the Ministry of Health and Welfare. Unless it exceeds the scope of discretion, the court may not interfere.[12]

The most heated debate concerning fundamental social rights occurred with regard to the restriction on the fundamental right of government employees to engage in collective action. In the 1960s and 1970s, the Supreme Court decisions showed unstable fluctuation between constitutionality without conditions and constitutionality with strict conditions.

Immediately after the Second World War, employees in the public sector enjoyed the same rights to organise, to bargain collectively and

[10] Yuji Iwasawa states: 'The Japanese courts will find a statute unconstitutional only when it is obvious that the restriction contained in the statute is excessively unreasonable. A minimum level of reasonableness is usually sufficient to justify restrictions of human rights.' Yuji Iwasawa, *International Law, Human Rights, and Japanese Law: the impact of international law on Japanese law* (Oxford, 1998), 304. Hiroshi Oda, however, evaluates the system of constitutional review as having worked fairly well in postwar Japan: Hiroshi Oda, *Japanese Law*, 2nd edn (Oxford, 1999), 40, 124. Regarding the general overview of the human rights protection by the Judiciary, see Oda, ibid., 102ff.

[11] The appeal itself was dismissed because the plaintiff died, and the alleged right was held not heritable by successors. However, considering the importance of issues raised in this case, the Supreme Court, in an exceptional manner, expressed its interpretation of the nature of art. 25 of the Constitution.

[12] The *Asahi* case, Supreme Court, 24 May 1967 (21 *Minshu* 1043).

to engage in collective acts as did workers in the private sector. However, in 1948, faced with the militant union movement led by leftists, General Douglas MacArthur, Supreme Commander of the occupying Allied Powers, ordered the Japanese government to deprive public sector employees of their right to bargain collectively and to strike. As a result, all public employees in both the national and local civil services are prohibited from striking and a violation is punishable by criminal sanctions.

The prohibition covers not only civil servants whose services are directly related to the government authority but also those working in public enterprises, such as mail services, printing services, local transport, and so forth. Personnel in the Self-Defence Forces, the police service, the Maritime Safety Service, the prison service, and the fire defence service are prohibited not only from striking but also from organising labour unions.

The Supreme Court initially adopted the position that the workers' fundamental rights enshrined in Article 28 of the Constitution can be restricted for reasons of public welfare (Art. 12, Constitution),[13] or on the basis that civil servants are 'servants of the whole community' (Art. 15 Para. 2, Constitution), and thus it held statutory prohibition of strikes to be constitutional.[14] However, in judgements in the 1960s, the Supreme Court abandoned this attitude and adopted the so-called 'reasonable narrow interpretation'. In the light of the constitutional guarantee of workers' right to strike and the established interpretation that the term 'workers' includes civil servants, the prohibition of public employees' strike can only be constitutional by interpreting the prohibition and sanctions against violations narrowly.[15] This approach was followed by two other Supreme Court Grand Bench decisions.[16] However, in 1973 the Grand Bench of the Supreme Court explicitly reversed its previous

---

[13] Art. 12 reads: 'The freedom and rights guaranteed to the people by this Constitution shall be maintained by the constant endeavour of the people, who . . . shall always be responsible for utilising them for the public welfare.'

[14] The *Kokutetus Hirosaki Kikan-ku* case, Supreme Court, 8 April 1953 (7-4 *Keishu* 775). The *Wakayama-ken Kyoso* case, Supreme Court, 14 July 1965 (19-5 *Minshu* 1198) also admitted wide legislative discretion and held the restriction of local civil servants' right to strike constitutional.

[15] The *Zentei-Chuyu* case, Supreme Court, 26 October 1966 (20-8 *Keishu* 901).

[16] The *Tokyo-to Kyoso* case, Supreme Court, 2 April 1969 (23-5 *Keishu* 305); the *Zenshiho Sendai Anpo* case, Supreme Court, 2 April 1969 (23-5 *Keishu* 685).

judgement and confirmed the constitutionality of the prohibition of strikes by national civil servants.[17] This interpretation has to date been repeatedly confirmed in subsequent cases of local civil servants and employees in public enterprises heard by the Supreme Court.[18] Apart from grounds previously mentioned for restricting government workers' basic rights, such as public welfare, the Supreme Court newly referred to the principle that terms and conditions of the employment of government employees must be determined by statutes or by parliamentary democracy, and thus they should not be entrusted to collective bargaining.

In any event, the Japanese Supreme Court does not actively seek to find legislation unconstitutional. In the arena of social policy where state intervention is envisaged, it is not surprising that the legislature's discretion is highly respected.

The application of fundamental social rights to private individuals through public policy

Unlike relations between the state and individuals, the human rights and social rights provisions in the Constitution are understood as not being directly applicable to the relationship between private citizens. However, norms declared in the fundamental rights clauses in the Constitution can indirectly apply to private parties through the 'public policy' concept found in Article 90 of the Civil Code, which invalidates legal acts violating public order and good morals.[19]

Here the courts' approach seems to be of a flexible and balancing nature, because whether a private person's act is deemed to violate public order or not depends on the consciousness of social norms or on prevailing practices at particular times. At the very least, such an approach is different from the approach determining whether human rights that are deemed to be of inviolable and inalienable value are infringed at all.

Such a flexible approach by the Japanese courts is best illustrated by the cases concerning discrimination.

[17] The *Zen-norin Keishoku-ho* case, Supreme Court Grand Bench, 25 April 1973 (27 *Keishu* 547l).
[18] The *Iwate-ken Kyoso* case, Supreme Court Grand Bench, 21 May 1976 (30-5 *Keishu* 1178); the *Zentei Nagoya Chuyu* case, Supreme Court Grand Bench, 4 May 1977 (31-3 *Keishu* 182); the *Kitakyushu-shi Kotsu-kyoku* case, 8 Dec. 1988 (42-10 *Minshu* 739).
[19] The *Mitsubishi Jushi* case, Supreme Court, Grand Bench, 12 Dec. 1973 (27 *Minshu* 1536).

Discrimination by reason of thought and creed

The *Mitsubishi Jushi* case[20] raised the question of worker selection on the basis of thought and creed. In this case, the employer refused to hire a university graduate as a regular employee upon completion of the probationary period,[21] on the grounds that he had made a false declaration with regard to his political activities. This was made in his personal statement, submitted to the company at the time of the recruiting examination, and the employer held that making a false statement in itself disqualified him as a managerial candidate. The court faced the question as to whether the company's refusal ran counter to the constitutional provisions of equality under the law (Art. 14, Constitution[22]) and freedom of thought and creed (Art. 19, Constitution), as well as the prohibition of discrimination in employment on account of creed under the Labour Standards Law (art. 3, LSL[23]).

The Supreme Court held that the human rights provisions of the Constitution do not apply directly to relations between private individuals and that Article 3 of the Labour Standards Law refers to the post-hiring working conditions but does not regulate hiring itself. Emphasising that the Consitution guarantees companies' freedom to do business and to execute contracts, the Supreme Court ruled that even if a company refused to employ a person with a certain creed or certain beliefs on account of such characteristics, the failure to hire cannot be automatically held to be illegal.

In connection with the freedom of hiring, this case raised the question of whether a company was permitted to investigate an applicant's beliefs or creed in the hiring process. The Supreme Court held the view that it was not illegal to do so because the refusal itself to hire on account of beliefs or creed was not unlawful.

In the light of the Supreme Court's emphasising that 'employment relations in a company... call for mutual trust in the context of a

---

[20] Ibid.

[21] It is common practice for Japanese employers to set a probationary period, lasting anywhere from three to six months, for regular workers at the initial stage of employment.

[22] Art. 14 of the Constitution reads: 'All of the people are equal under the law and there shall be no discrimination in political, economic or social relations because of race, creed, sex, social status or family origin.'

[23] Art. 3 LSL reads: 'An employer shall not engage in discriminatory treatment with respect to wages, working hours or other working conditions by reason of the nationality, creed or social status of any worker.'

continuous human relationship, all the more so in a society like Japan where lifetime employment is an established fact of life . . .',[24] we can see that long-term employment practices seem to influence the Court's interpretation of the employer's freedom to hire. Under the long-term employment practices, a regular worker, once employed, cannot be dismissed without compelling reason. Therefore the Court perhaps considered that employers should be free to investigate a candidate's personality *before* concluding a regular employment contract in order to ascertain whether they could start such a long-term relationship.

Since the situation regarding long-term employment has changed and consciousness of discrimination has increased, it is not clear when decisions not to hire an applicant by reason of beliefs or creed are contested, whether the Supreme Court will maintain the position described above. In any event, it is noteworthy that the Supreme Court at the time treated the issue of freedom of thought and creed in the context of the employers' needs in the context of the practice of long-term employment.

Age discrimination and fundamental rights

Japanese courts are cautious in accepting the notion of age discrimination. Even in very recent cases where the mandatory retirement system was contested as age discrimination, courts approved the reasonableness of the system under the long-term employment practice.[25]

Sex discrimination and public policy

In sex discrimination cases, by contrast, the courts have actively intervened in and modified practices by utilising the public policy concept.

While the Labour Standards Law prohibits wage discrimination by reason of sex (art. 4, LSL), it does not prohibit discriminatory treatment. Therefore, various discriminatory practices regarding women in Japanese companies, such as mandatory retirement upon marriage or earlier mandatory retirement age applying to women only, were contested in court as being against public policy. Though these practices are currently prohibited by the Equal Employment Opportunity Law (EEOL), prior to the enactment of the EEOL discriminatory treatment

[24] The *Mitsubishi Jushi* case, Supreme Court, 12 Dec. 1973, (27 *Minshu* 1536).
[25] The *Aru Efu radio Nihon* case, Tokyo High Court, 26 Aug. 1996 (47-4 *Rominshu* 378); the *Tokyo Daigaku* case, Tokyo District Court, 14 April 1997 (1617 *Hanji* 140).

was only addressed by individual cases alleging such treatment to be contrary to public policy.

The interpretation that differential treatment violates public policy accumulated in the lower courts. For instance, mandatory retirement upon marriage applied simply to women,[26] and work rules stipulating a younger retirement age (30) for women, as against 50 for men, were held to be against public policy.[27] The Supreme Court endorsed these lower court attitudes by holding that setting a separate mandatory retirement age for women (55 for women, 60 for men) is based on no reasonable grounds and amounts to discrimination against women by reason of sex. Therefore, such a differentiated mandatory retirement violated public policy and was thus null and void.[28]

This established public policy theory concerning discriminatory retirement systems extends to other forms of discriminatory treatment in employment. For instance, the court held that differential treatment of men and women regarding promotion constituted a tort, and ordered damages in recognition of the wage difference caused by the failure to promote.[29] Furthermore, in recent years the court found unfavourable treatment over promotion to be illegal sex discrimination and confirmed the plaintiff's promoted status.[30]

Gradation of fundamental rights?

The aforementioned cases show that the Japanese courts have not treated categorically the issues involving the indirect application of fundamental rights. In the framework of public policy or public order, fundamental rights issues are viewed in the context of the employment system. As a result, even in the cases where some fundamental rights in the European sense can be seen as having been infringed, courts are reluctant to hold such action illegal when it is deemed to be reasonable in the light of prevailing practices under the current employment system.

Courts tend to treat sex discrimination cases as a matter of inviolable fundamental rights, while age discrimination seems to be treated as more

---

[26] The *Sumitomo Semento* case, Tokyo District Court, 20 Dec. 1966 (17 *Rominshu* 1407).

[27] The *Tokyu Kikan Kogyo* case, Tokyo District Court, 1 July 1969 (20-4 *Rominshu* 715).

[28] The *Nissan Jidosha* case, Supreme Court, 24 Mar. 1981 (35 *Minshu* 300).

[29] The *Shakai Hoken Shinryo Hoshu Shiharai Kikin* case, Tokyo District Court, 4 Jul. 1990 (565 *Rodo Hanrei* 7).

[30] The *Shiba Shinyo Kinko* case, Tokyo District Court, 27 Nov. 1996 (704 *Rodo Hanrei* 21); –, Tokyo High Court, 22 Dec. 2000 (796 *Rodo Hanrei* 5).

an issue of employment policy than as a fundamental rights issue. This might reflect the difference in maturity of respective fundamental rights. Emerging new norms, such as the prohibition of age discrimination, seem to be treated as a matter of social policy rather than as a matter of inviolable fundamental rights in Japan.

Case law developments furthering fundamental social rights

Another important scene of interplay between judiciary and fundamental social rights is case law developments that realised the idea of fundamental social rights.

Unlike European countries, Japan has no statute that requires just cause for dismissals. Though thirty days' advance notice for dismissals is required by the provision of the Labour Standards Law and discriminatory dismissals are prohibited by the relevant regulations, in principle, Japanese written laws maintain the employer's freedom to dismiss.

Since Article 27 of the Constitution sets out the right to work and Article 25 requires minimum standards of wholesome and cultured living, labour law scholars have contended that a law restricting employers' freedom to dismiss should be enacted. However, such a law, generally requiring just cause for dismissal, has not yet been enacted.

However, as is well known for lifetime or long-term employment, dismissal is severely restricted in Japan. It is not statutory law but *case law* that places such restriction on arbitrary dismissals and also on economic dismissals.

Immediately following Japan's defeat in the Second World War, when there was a shortage of food, lack of employment opportunities and superfluous workforce, a dismissal meant the loss of livelihood for many workers. Even after Japan put such difficult times behind it and the long-term employment practice was firmly in place, a dismissal was detrimental to a worker's seniority, a decisive factor in the seniority-based personnel management and wage systems, for the seniority he had gained through his previous employment would not necessarily carry over to his new employment. Dismissal also placed such a worker at a serious disadvantage as finding comparable employment was extremely difficult in Japan's inactive external labour market.

Under such circumstances, Japanese courts felt that workers should be provided with a degree of protection by restricting the employer's right to dismiss at will. Relying on the general clause of the Civil Code that prohibits abuse of rights (Civil Code art. 1, para. 3), Japanese courts handed down decision after decision holding that an objectively unreasonable or socially unacceptable dismissal was an abuse of the right to dismiss. Such dismissals were declared null and void. The theory of 'abuse of the right to dismiss' was thus created by judicial precedent in lower courts and finally endorsed by the Supreme Court in 1975.[31]

Under this case law, an employer is required to demonstrate the existence of just cause. Courts interpret just cause very strictly, and tend to deny the validity of the dismissal unless there has been serious misconduct by the worker. A court will consider all of the facts favourable to the worker's case and subject the reasonableness of the dismissal to strict scrutiny.[32]

Furthermore, when the recession triggered by the oil crises in the 1970s caused large-scale corporate restructuring, Japanese courts established protection against dismissals for economic reasons. Since the long-term employment practice had taken root in Japanese corporate society by that time, major companies refrained from resorting to employment adjustment through dismissals. After careful consultation with their enterprise-based unions, corporate management chose to take various cost-cutting measures to avoid layoffs as much as possible. The unions also cooperated with management in implementing relocation and transfer programmes designed to avoid employment adjustment dismissals.

Taking these larger companies' practices as a model, Japanese courts established general rules concerning economic dismissals. The courts set out the following four requirements allowing dismissals for business reasons: (i) there must be an economic necessity to reduce the number of

---

[31] The *Nihon Shokuen Co.* case, Supreme Court, 25 April 1975 (29 *Minshu* 456).

[32] A typical decision illustrating this high standard of just cause is the Supreme Court's decision in the Kochi Broadcasting Co. case (The *Kochi Hoso Co.* case, Supreme Court, 31 Jan. 1977, 268 *Rodo Hanrei* 17). In this case, a company dismissed an announcer who overslept and missed broadcasting the morning news twice within a two-week period. While the Supreme Court admitted that the announcer was not blameless, it nullified the dismissal as excessively cruel and socially inappropriate. In so ruling, the court considered the fact that the worker's failures were not caused by malice but by negligence; that whereas the co-worker who was supposed to wake up the announcer had also overslept, the co-worker was not dismissed but simply reprimanded; that the worker apologised immediately after the first incident, and in the second incident his attempt to hide his mistake was the result of his awkwardness due to his repeated failures.

employees; (ii) dismissals must be the last resort, so that every possible measure to avoid layoffs must be attempted, such as a reduction in overtime, reduction of salaries of executives and managers, attrition and non-replacement, solicitation for voluntary retirements, transfers and so on; (iii) the selection of employees to be dismissed must be made on an objective and reasonable basis; and (iv) the employer must faithfully consult with unions or employees.

The validity of economic dismissals has been determined by whether all these four requirements are met or not. If one of the four requirements is not satisfied, the dismissal has been regarded as an abuse of the right to dismiss.[33]

If the employer's exercise of the right to dismiss is judged to be abusive and, therefore, invalid, the employer is obliged not only to pay the wages covering the period of dismissal but also to reinstate the dismissed worker, as the dismissal is null and void.

V. International fundamental social rights and their impact on Japanese social policies

Unlike European countries where various international or supranational sources of fundamental social rights exist,[34] the main sources of international fundamental social rights for Japan are those established within a framework of the United Nations and the International Labour Organisation.

The status of international law in the Japanese legal system

The current Constitution has not been modified since it was proclaimed in 1946. Although domestic social legislation certainly developed in accordance with socioeconomic developments, the development was

[33] One of the Tokyo district court decisions recently rejected the rigid interpretation of economic dismissals because, it said, there are no solid legal grounds for insisting that all four requirements must be satisfied for economic dismissals. According to the Tokyo district court, what the court should determine is whether or not a dismissal is abusive. The so-called 'four requirements' are nothing but 'four factors' in analysing abusiveness. Therefore, according to the Tokyo district court logic, if one of the four 'factors' is not met, such an economic dismissal can be held legal and valid by taking all other factors surrounding the dismissals into consideration.

[34] E.g. European Convention on Human Rights (ECHR) of 1950; European Social Charter (ESC) of 1969 and revised ESC of 1996; Community Charter of 1989; Charter of Fundamental Rights of the EU of 2000.

rather gradual, and as seen above, the content of social legislation was entrusted to the wide discretion of the legislature. New and more vigorous impetus in Japanese domestic legislation came from outside, namely international human rights law.[35]

In Japan international treaties have the force of law without specific measures to incorporate them into the national legal system, and they override domestic laws (art. 98 para. 2, Constitution).[36] However, the Japanese government takes a cautious and strict approach to the ratification of treaties. When the Japanese government decides to enter into a treaty, it makes scrupulous efforts to eliminate any inconsistency and conflict between Japanese domestic law and the treaty. If there is any conflict between them, the government makes sure that domestic law is amended before it enters into the treaty or convention. As a result, ratification is accompanied by a whole set of revisions of existing laws and by new legislation.[37]

Regarding social policy, Japan has ratified the following treaties:

1965 International Convention on the Elimination of All Forms of Racial Discrimination (ratified 1995);
1966 International Covenant on Economic, Social, and Cultural Rights (ratified 1979);
1966 International Covenant on Civil and Political Rights (ratified 1979);
1979 Convention on the Elimination of All Forms of Discrimination against Women (ratified 1985);
1989 Convention on the Rights of the Child (ratified 1994).

In the social policy arena, the ratification of the Convention on the Elimination of All Forms of Discrimination against Women (CEDAW)[38] illustrates how international law played a critical role in domestic social legislation.

---

[35] The impact was substantial not through direct application of international law in the courts, but through political and legislative processes. Iwasawa states: 'In Japan, international human rights adjudication has tended to be more effective as a political means to give legitimacy to movements to change domestic laws rather than as a legal weapon to win actual cases in the courts' (Yuji Iwasawa, *International Law*, 308).

[36] Art. 98 Para. 2 of the Constitution provides that international treaties to which Japan is party should be observed faithfully, and since the ratification by the Diet is needed, it is generally agreed that international treaties are superior to statute laws. See Iwasawa, *International Law*, 28; Oda, *Japanese Law*, 50.

[37] Iwasawa, *International Law*, 306; Kazuo Sugeno and Yasuo Suwa, *Introduction to Japanese industrial Relations: A Legal Perspective*, 1 JILL Forum Paper 73 (Tokyo, 1994).

[38] For details of Japan's signing and ratifying the CEDAW, see Iwasawa, *International Law*, 205ff.

Ratification of CEDAW and the enactment of the
Equal Employment Opportunity Law in 1985

In 1980, the Japanese government signed CEDAW, adopted by the United
Nations in 1979. Japan took it as an international duty to ratify the Convention by the end of the UN Decade for Women. In order to do so, the
government needed to make necessary adjustments in national legislation. Although the Labour Standards Law had since 1947 prohibited
wage discrimination by reason of sex, there were no statutes prohibiting 'discriminatory treatment' such as discrimination in the process of
recruitment, hiring, promotion, allocation of jobs and so on, and the
issue was entrusted to the case law development process. As mentioned
above, Japanese courts had developed case law making some types of discriminatory treatment, such as mandatory retirement upon marriage or
retirement at an age lower than that of men, against public policy. However, case law protection is only available for those who litigate. The high
cost of litigation in Japan in terms of money and time, and a social reluctance to embark on it, impeded the right of women to enjoy case law
protection. Furthermore, case law protection was insufficient concerning discrimination in recruitment, hiring, promotion and assignment
of jobs. Thus legislation prohibiting sex discrimination in all aspects of
employment was long awaited.

However, such legislation requires a fundamental reform of the firmly
rooted male-centred employment tradition in Japan. After heated debate on the new legislation's impact on the traditional male-centred
work patterns and practices, the role of women in family and society,
and the desirable balance between equality and protection, the Equal
Employment Opportunity Law (EEOL) was finally enacted in 1985. If
there were no international pressure to ratify CEDAW, it is questionable
whether Japan could have enacted the EEOL in 1985.[39]

From 1985 EEOL to 1997 EEOL

Partly due to the fact that the legislation was only possible through
a compromise between labour and management, or liberal and
conservative parties, and partly due to the gradualism in Japanese

[39] Ibid., 246.

legislative policy elaborated later, the 1985 EEOL took a conservative attitude towards intervening in established male-centred employment practices.

Prohibition of discriminatory treatment by the 1985 EEOL was limited to discrimination in vocational training, fringe benefits, mandatory retirement age, mandatory retirement by reason of marriage, pregnancy or childbirth, and dismissals (1985 EEOL arts. 9, 10, 11 (1997 EEOL arts. 6, 7, 8)). These prohibitory provisions are mandatory and nullify contracts which violate them. Damages caused by violating actions can be claimed in tort suits.[40]

By contrast, the 1985 EEOL refrained from direct intervention in the main arena of differential treatment between men and women, that is, in recruitment, hiring, assignment and promotion. Instead, the law merely provided that employers have a *duty to endeavour* to provide women with opportunities equal to those provided to men (1985 EEOL arts. 7 and 8), and the Ministry of Labour could lay down guidelines with respect to the measures which employers should endeavour to implement (1985 EEOL art. 12). The Ministry of Labour issued such guidelines in 1986 and reinforced them in 1994.

The 1985 EEOL faced three severe criticisms,[41] but within some ten years the law was modified (1997 EEOL) and these criticisms were addressed.

First, one-sided support of women was criticised. Although the 1985 EEOL prohibited disadvantageous treatment for women vis-à-vis men, more favourable treatment of women was allowed following the logic that it would promote women's employment. Therefore, whereas restricting recruitment to male candidates would violate the EEOL, restricting it to women (e.g. by recruiting for part-time jobs for women only) would not, because recruiting only for women would provide more employment opportunities for women. Such one-sidedness was severely criticised in that it allowed the continued entrapment of women in low-paying occupations.

---

[40] However, unlike the LSL, the EEOL is not sanctioned by criminal provisions.

[41] Mutsuko Asakura, 'The Equal Employment Opportunity Law in the Second Stage', 1116 Jurisuto 51 (1997). See also Tadashi Hanami, 'Equal Employment Revisited', 39-1 Japan Labour Bulletin 5 (2000). In addition to these three defects, Hanami emphasises the policy-makers' confusion of equality with protection, and their limited view on discrimination focusing solely on gender while disregarding other types of discrimination based on race, age or handicap.

Although the 1997 EEOL still maintains a position prohibiting discrimination by reason of being a woman, and has not reached a genuine discrimination prohibition law for both sexes, it prohibits preferential treatment for women when such treatment fixes job categories for women or maintains women's job segregation by sex.

Second, the 1985 EEOL was castigated as a paper tiger, lacking an effective enforcement mechanism because it contained insufficient sanctions against violation of the law. The 1985 EEOL did not prohibit discrimination in terms of recruitment, hiring, assignment and promotion, but merely set forth a 'duty to endeavour' not to discriminate against women. By contrast, the 1997 EEOL explicitly prohibited discrimination concerning recruitment, hiring, assignment and promotion. As a new form of sanction against violations of the EEOL, the 1997 EEOL has introduced the practice of publicising the violating company's name.

Third, the mediation procedures under the 1985 EEOL did not work. From 1986, when the 1985 EEOL took effect, until 1994 the mediation procedure was not utilised at all because the procedure could not be begun if one party to the dispute (normally the employer) did not agree to it. The 1997 EEOL therefore allows mediation procedures to be initiated at the request of one party.

Gradual and soft-law approach

Faced with the international pressure to ratify the CEDAW, Japan started to engage in sweeping legislative changes,[42] enacting the EEOL in 1985. Japan's equal employment policy concerning the elimination of sex discrimination began with a modest intervention entailing a duty to endeavour rather than outright prohibition, which would entail drastic modifications of current practices. Through administrative guidance and campaigning, a gradual but steady modification of societal and companies' consciousness towards equal employment was sought. After ten years' experience of the 1985 EEOL, the 1997 revision of the EEOL witnessed no overt opposition to prohibiting discriminatory treatment in all stages of employment.

[42] Though this article focuses on employment issues, ratification of the CEDAW required legislative changes to attain equal treatment between the sexes in terms of nationality, education, social security and so forth. See Iwasawa, *International Law*, 205 ff.

It should also be noted as a feature of Japan's equal employment policy that the policy harmonising work and family life has developed simultaneously with the anti-sex discrimination policy. The policies of prohibiting discrimination and of facilitating equality were in reality pursued together.[43]

Such a soft-law approach utilising administrative guidance is one of the most significant characteristics of the social policies in Japan. Certainly such a gradual approach takes time. But the Japanese legislature has considered such an approach to be more effective in the end than direct legal intervention. When indirect intervention has not worked and more stringent regulations are needed, or when a society has accepted new norms and direct legal intervention will no longer cause serious confusion, regulations can take more direct and mandatory forms. This gradual and soft-law approach utilising 'duty to endeavour' coupled with administrative guidance, has quite often been adopted in recent social policies in Japan.

VI. Conclusion: a matter of fundamental rights or of policy?

The fundamental social rights enshrined in the Japanese Constitution played an important leading role in Japanese social legislation, especially in the years immediately following the Second World War. Reflecting the mandate to effectuate the right to work, the government enacted a series of laws to enable the labour market to function and to provide necessary protection against unemployment. Upon a constitutional mandate to establish, by statute, minimum working conditions, various protective labour laws were enacted. The constitutional guarantees of workers' right to organise, bargain and act collectively led to the enactment of the Trade Union Law, which imposes on employers a duty to bargain and encourages collective bargaining by administrative intervention under the unfair labour practice system.

---

[43] It is also noteworthy that harmonisation measures also developed in the same manner as the EEOL. The 1992 Law introduced childcare leave as a mandatory right, but it simply set a duty to endeavour to provide family care leaves. Five years later, the 1997 Law made family care leaves mandatory. To effectuate the policies harmonising work with family life, the government started a campaign to encourage family-friendly measures among firms by giving excellent company awards. See Takashi Araki, 'Equal Employment and Harmonization of Work and Family Life: Japan's Soft-Law Approach', (2001) 21, 3 Comparative Labor Law and Policy Journal 451.

Fundamental human and social rights have also affected the judiciary. Their impact differs according to three phases. First, courts review the constitutionality of legislation and administrative acts, tending to respect the legislature's wide discretion and refrain from finding unconstitutionality. Second, courts adjudicate the legality of the acts of private individuals by transforming the fundamental rights values into public policy. Under the framework of public policy, fundamental rights issues are often examined from the viewpoint of whether the treatment in question is reasonable or not in the context of the Japanese employment system. Under such a framework, current practices or prevailing treatment in society are decisive factors in determining what constitutes a violation of public policy. As a result, even in cases where fundamental rights can be seen as having been infringed, the courts are reluctant to hold such infringements as illegal when similar practices are common. However, with respect to sex discrimination, courts have more actively intervened to put right current practices. This suggests that there is a difference of approach depending on how well established the various fundamental rights are seen to be. Emerging new norms, such as the prohibition of age discrimination, are treated as a matter of social policy rather than as a matter of inviolable fundamental rights. Third, case law on employment security can be deemed an outgrowth of fundamental social rights.

International treaties and conventions have affected social legislation significantly. This chapter analysed the impact of international human rights law on domestic legislation, by taking the ratification of the CEDAW as an example. Here the Japanese legislature adopted a gradual and soft-law approach.

Fundamental rights or policy?

As Bob Hepple has pointed out, the long list which constitutes the EU Charter of Fundamental Rights contains at least three categories of norms: individual rights, recognised and respected rights, and pure objectives.[44] In accordance with the expansion of the fundamental rights list, it will be necessary to distinguish the types of fundamental human

---

[44] Bob Hepple, 'The EU Charter of Fundamental Rights' (2001) 30 Industrial Law Journal 228.

and social rights. Some fundamental rights should be regarded as core rights and thus as truly inalienable and inviolable. Others are rather peripheral and merged into social policy matters. From this point of view, the treatment of fundamental social rights in Japan suggests that the core is smaller and peripheral area is wider than in the European debate. This allows Japan to adopt a gradual and soft-law approach to dealing with fundamental social rights issues.

When a fundamental right is deemed to be inviolable and inalienable, any agreement infringing it will be nullified through state intervention in the freedom of contract, and in the natural mechanisms of the market. The delineation between core and peripheral rights denotes the extent to which the state will intervene in the free functioning of the market. The main feature of Japan's approach to fundamental social rights is that even if Japan admits that the intended policy relates to a core social right, it adopts a gradual approach. As illustrated by the gradual development of the EEOL, even in the sex discrimination issue, which is deemed a core fundamental right in other countries, Japan first adopted less interventionist methods. By utilising administrative guidance and public information campaigns vigorously, the EEOL aimed to create new social norms and let them take root. After such a new social norm has been established, the issue initially seen as a matter of policy will then become a matter of inalienable fundamental rights. At this stage, infringement of this right is no longer condoned, and is legally prohibited. This gradual approach might be deemed as ignoring the inviolable nature of fundamental rights, because in the process of transition, it does not legally prohibit their violations. However, it might be evaluated as a method for correcting practices deemed socially inappropriate, but that are deeply rooted in consensus-oriented societies like Japan's. It might also be seen as a means of implementing fundamental social rights while avoiding the socioeconomic confusion caused by too drastic and excessive state intervention.

10

Enforcement: the law and politics
of cooperation and compliance

BOB HEPPLE

Social rights are like paper tigers, fierce in appearance but missing in tooth and claw. One of the paradoxes of the recent explosion of charters and declarations at international and European levels, national codes of practice and guidelines, and even new individual legal rights is that these lack effective enforcement procedures and sanctions. I propose to discuss three tendencies which make it difficult to realise the promise of social rights. These are the increasing reliance on 'soft law', the privatisation of enforcement, and the restrictions placed on collective solidarity by national laws.

I. The growth of soft law

Social rights are sometimes expressed in binding legal instruments, with enforcement mechanisms, but increasingly they take the form of non-binding recommendations, codes of practice and guidelines. The former are usually referred to as 'hard law' and the latter as 'soft law'.

In public international labour law, ratified ILO conventions are the best-known example of hard law. They create legally binding obligations on member states, subject to international supervision. ILO recommendations cannot create international legal obligations and so are usually described as 'soft law'. But the distinction with conventions is to a large extent more a matter of theory than practice. Recommendations have some significant features in common with conventions: they are drawn up by the same lengthy and careful tripartite procedures, and are subject to the same follow-up procedures as conventions apart from those designed to monitor the application of ratified conventions.[1] On the basis of a study of a selection of recommendations that entail varying degrees of difficulty in implementation, Francis Maupain concludes that ILO recommendations, like unratified conventions, 'can exercise a real influence on national law and practice, with the degree of influence varying widely depending on the subject matter'.[2] What is much more difficult to assess, however, is the extent of 'compliance' in the strict sense. Maupain suggests that some other terminology may be more appropriate 'to describe what the limited evidence suggests, that in many cases there is a selective impact of some of the normative provisions of the instrument, but not necessarily of the instrument as an integrated whole'.[3]

There is a declining rate of ratification of recently adopted ILO conventions. This may be due to a number of reasons, including the unwillingness of governments to take on such commitments in the face of global competition, the reduced resources of states to shoulder the administrative burdens of reporting and compliance, and the growth of federalism which complicates ratification of international instruments. Membership of the EU may also be an obstacle to ratification. The ECJ has said that in areas where the EC has laid down only minimum requirements member states are free to adopt more stringent measures laid down in ILO conventions, but in those areas where the EC has harmonised rules, the EC alone has competence.[4] In 1994[5] and again in 1997, the then ILO Director-General suggested that greater use should be made of recommendations, on the basis of the somewhat circular argument that recommendations have the same impact as non-ratified conventions. In practice, until 1998 recommendations were limited to supplementing conventions on points of detail.[6]

---

[1] One important difference is that while a member state may be required to explain how effect could be given to an unratified convention and the difficulties which prevent or delay ratification, they need not specify the mechanism by which it is proposed to give effect to a recommendation, but must specify modifications which may be found necessary in adopting or applying a recommendation.

[2] Francis Maupain, 'International Labor Organization Recommendations and Similar Instruments', in D. Shelton (ed.), *Commitment and Compliance: The role of non-binding norms in the International Legal System* (Oxford, 2000), 372 at 383.

[3] Ibid., at 393.   [4] Opinion 2/91 [1991] ECR I-1061.

[5] *Defending Values, Promoting Change*, Report of the Director-General, International Labour Conference, 81st session (Geneva, 1994).

[6] An autonomous recommendation on job creation in small and medium-sized enterprises was adopted in 1998.

In an attempt to strengthen compliance with non-ratified core conventions – those on the 'fundamental' rights of freedom of association and effective recognition of collective bargaining, the elimination of all forms of forced or compulsory labour, the effective abolition of child labour and the elimination of discrimination in respect of employment and occupation – the ILO adopted, in June 1998, the Declaration on Fundamental Principles and Rights at Work. This is described in the Annex on 'Follow-up' as 'strictly promotional', and not a substitute for the 'established supervisory mechanisms'. The annual follow-up concerning non-ratified 'fundamental' conventions entails merely some adaptation of the present application of Article 19(5)(e) of the ILO Constitution. There will also be a global report, submitted to the International Labour Conference for tripartite discussion, relating to each category of fundamental principles and rights during the preceding four-year period 'to serve as a basis for assessing the effectiveness of the assistance provided by the Organisation, and for determining priorities for the following period'. There are no new sanctions. In particular, it is expressly stated in Article 5 that nothing in the Declaration and its follow-up may be used for 'protectionist trade purposes'. Arguably, this does not foreclose the use of trade sanctions where the purpose is not 'protectionist'. Labour standards which are incorporated in multilateral agreements, such as the WTO, where no single state can exert unilateral protectionist power, would not seem to fall foul of Article 5. But for the present the WTO firmly resists demands for a link between trade and labour standards.

Another example of soft international law is the ILO's disappointing Tripartite Declaration of Principles Concerning Multinational Enterprises and Social Policy (1977), which bears a close resemblance to the OECD's Guidelines for Multinational Enterprises (1976), and as with those Guidelines compliance is voluntary.[7] Neither is legally enforceable, and they cannot be invoked before national courts or tribunals. The ILO Declaration has been ineffective because of the absence of sanctions to secure compliance with its standards, even by countries which adopt them.[8] Although about two-thirds of countries submit triennial reports on their observance of the Declaration, less than half of these consult the social partners in preparing their replies. The disputes procedure

---

[7] On the origins of the Declaration see O'Higgins, Ch. 2 above.
[8] Jill Murray, 'Corporate Codes of Conduct and Labour Standards', in R. Kyloh (ed.), *Mastering the Challenge of Globalisation* (Geneva, 1998).

is aimed purely at interpretation, has no means of enforcement and is rarely used.[9] The chapter on employment and industrial relations in the OECD Guidelines has proved to be rich in principle, but weak in enforcement. National contact points (NCPs) in each country are supposed to promote the Guidelines, collect information, handle inquiries and assist in solving problems which may arise between business and labour in matters covered by the Guidelines. In individual cases, where NCPs have failed to resolve the matter, 'clarification' may be sought from the Committee for International Investment and Multinational Enterprises (CIME). About 30 cases have been brought to CIME's attention, but the number has declined in recent years, with only seven alleged violations in the period 1991–2000. These procedures have been criticised by trade unions on the grounds that NCPs have almost ceased to exist in some countries, and the CIME has generally been unwilling to interpret the vague text so as to favour trade union positions.[10] There was a full-scale review of the Guidelines in 1998–2000 with subsequent reviews of the text and follow-up procedures. Despite the changes, there is little reason to expect that they will have a significant influence so long as they remain soft law.[11]

A final example of soft law at international level is the rapid proliferation of corporate codes of conduct issued by transnational corporations (TNCs). I have discussed these elsewhere,[12] showing that what they share in common is that they are *voluntary* written commitments to observe certain standards in the conduct of business, usually including labour and employment rights. The choice of particular labour issues is highly selective and they are usually made unilaterally without the involvement of trade unions. They are ineffectively implemented, with inadequate (if any) monitoring, a lack of training and incentives for local managers to comply, and an absence of sanctions. Most codes make no reference to the consequences of non-compliance; a few mention

---

[9] B. Hepple, 'Labour Regulation in International Markets', in S. Picciotto and R. Mayne (eds.), *Regulating International Business* (London, 1999), 194.

[10] Ibid., 194–6.

[11] For a more optimistic forecast see P. Tergeist et al., 'The Organisation for Economic Co-operation and Development', in R. Blanpain (ed.), *International Encyclopedia for Labour Law and Industrial Relations* (The Hague, 2000), para. 165; see too R. Blanpain, in idem (ed.), *Multinational Enterprises and the Challenges of the 21st Century* (The Hague, 2000), ch. 4.

[12] B. Hepple, 'A Race to the Top? International Investment Guidelines and Corporate Codes of Conduct', (1999) 20 Comparative Labor Law and Policy Journal 347, at 357–60.

'working with suppliers or business partners to make improvements', but termination of a contract or business relationship for non-compliance is a rarity. However, an important distinction needs to be made between codes of this kind adopted by TNCs and those which are externally imposed to create political pressure for a change in national laws and practices. Examples of the latter are the Sullivan Principles, intended to put pressure on American corporations in apartheid-era South Africa, and the MacBride Principles, intended to put pressure on American companies to adopt anti-discrimination and affirmative action policies in Northern Ireland. Christopher McCrudden[13] concludes that both of these sets of principles had some important effects. In South Africa they were a useful focus for local political activities, they brought about some changes in working conditions, they led to increased company funding of social causes, and they put pressure on government to recognise black trade unions. But at the same time many opponents of apartheid saw them as legitimating investment rather than withdrawal. In Northern Ireland, the MacBride Principles, supported by Irish-American interests and opposed by the British government and business, were largely successful in securing new fair employment legislation in 1989. However, it is more difficult to estimate the extent to which the Principles, as distinct from other causes, brought about change in companies.

There has also been increasing use of soft law measures in respect of EC social policy. Catherine Barnard[14] points out that most EC measures adopted under the 1974 and 1989 action programmes were legally binding hard law. By contrast the Medium-Term Action programme 1995–7, its successor in 1998–2000 and the Strategic Objectives 2000–5 rely heavily on soft-law measures which are purely persuasive. Soft law is also the main means of implementing the new EC Employment Title. A number of reasons may be suggested for this shift from directives to weaker instruments. One is the principle of subsidiarity in Article 5 (ex art. 3b) of the EC Treaty which has been interpreted as meaning that recourse should be had to binding measures only as the last resort.

---

[13] 'Human Rights Codes for Transnational Corporations: What Can the Sullivan and MacBride Principles Tell Us?' (1999) 19 Oxford Journal of.Legal Studies 167.

[14] EC Employment Law, 2nd edn (Oxford, 2000), 82–3; and generally, S. Sciarra, 'Social Values and the Multiple Sources of European Social Law' [1995] 1 ELJ 60 at 78–79; Beveridge and Nott, 'A Hard Look at Soft Law', in P. Craig and C. Harlow (eds.), Lawmaking in the European Union (Deventer, 1998).

Preference is now given to voluntary codes of conduct.[15] Another is the absence of political agreement on many issues. The Commission not infrequently attempts to secure the agreement of reluctant member states by making recommendations or preparing codes as a preliminary to tougher measures to be brought forward when political circumstances change. A third reason is the belief that soft measures are more flexible, allowing the Commission to use persuasion and best practice models as a means of achieving social objectives. But flexibility can be achieved in other ways, for example by giving member states optional methods of implementing a directive (e.g. the European Works Councils Directive), or by allowing derogations from certain standards (e.g. the Working Time Directive), or by giving lengthy time periods for implementation (e.g. the Framework Employment Equality Directive, and the National Information and Consultation Directive). The difference between flexible directives, which leave a measure of discretion to member states, and codes of practice or guidelines, is that the objectives of directives are legally binding on member states, while codes and guidelines are not.

The EU Charter of Fundamental Rights (December 2000) was supported by the United Kingdom purely as an exercise in transparency. It has no independent legal status, may not be interpreted in conflict with existing international and European human rights structures, is not supposed to affect the existing legal relations between citizens and domestic authorities, and creates no 'new' rights. Nor does it enlarge EU competence. The 'unresolved political question is whether the UK will be able for long to resist the incorporation of the new Charter – which effectively supersedes the 1989 [Charter of Fundamental Rights of Workers] – into the [EU] treaties'. [16]

Within the United Kingdom codes of practice represent an increasingly popular form of soft law, some being softer than others, but all representing a preference for a 'voluntary' approach. There are four main types. The first two types amplify standards laid down in legislation, and may have legal effects, while the last two are voluntary and without legal consequences. First, there are those made by the Secretary of State under statutory powers. The main codes are those on picketing,

---

[15] See the Edinburgh Council conclusions II, Guidelines, 3rd para., point 3, EC Bull 12/1992, 25–6.

[16] B. Hepple, 'The EU Charter of Fundamental Rights' (2001) 30 ILJ 225, at 230; see further Weiss, ch. 3 above.

industrial action ballots and notice to employers, discrimination in the field of employment against disabled persons, and on part-time work. More recently, the DTI has issued a code of practice on access to workers during recognition and derecognition ballots. Failure to observe any provision of one of these codes does not of itself render a person liable in any proceedings, but they are admissible in evidence in proceedings before courts, tribunals and the CAC, and, where relevant, must be taken into account in determining any question. The second type of code is that issued by a regulatory agency under statutory powers. Those issued include the ACAS codes on disciplinary and grievance procedures, disclosure of information to trade unions for collective bargaining purposes and time off for trade union duties and activities; the Health and Safety Commission codes on safety representatives and safety committees; the CRE code on racial discrimination in employment; and the EOC codes on equal opportunities and equal pay. While these are not expressed to be admissible in courts, they are admissible in employment tribunals and must be taken into account where relevant. The third category consists of codes for which there is no express statutory basis and whose legal status is ambiguous. This includes the DfEE Code of Practice on Age Diversity in Employment, and DfEE Guidance on matters to be taken into account in determining questions relating to the definition of disability. Finally, there is the type of code issued by voluntary organisations such as the TUC dispute principles and procedures, and the CIPD code of practice on employee data, which are not legally enforceable.

There are many reasons for the popularity of soft law. One, which may actually help effective enforcement, is to amplify broad legally binding standards and sometimes to recommend voluntary action which goes beyond strict requirements. ILO recommendations are an example, as are the first two UK types of code of practice, issued under statutory powers and capable of being used as an aid to interpretation and enforcement. A second reason is far less acceptable. This treats codes as exclusive alternatives to binding instruments. Examples have been noted at international and EC level. In the UK, an example is the code on age diversity in employment which was put forward as an alternative to age discrimination legislation but is widely regarded as being entirely ineffective.[17]

---

[17] See B. Hepple, M. Coussey and T. C. Choudhury, *Equality: a new framework: report of the independent review of UK anti-discrimination legislation* (Oxford, 2000), App.1, para. 5.4; Cabinet Office, *Winning the Generation Game* (London, 2000).

A leading advocate of the voluntary or 'best practice' approach has been the Better Regulation Task Force[18] in relation to company equality policies, an approach with which the government has regrettably agreed. The Task Force held out the promise that if voluntary methods did not work, then legislation could be used 'at a later date'. In July 2001, the new 'pro-business' Secretary of State for Trade and Industry was reported to have contrasted legislation or 'hard law', which she described as a 'pretty blunt instrument', with 'soft law' such as voluntary standards, best practice models and codes of conduct which she said 'are good ways to secure changes in workplace culture'.[19]

This evolutionary approach is profoundly mistaken. First, it has always failed in the past. An example is the Race Relations Act 1968, which left enforcement in respect of racial discrimination in employment to voluntary bodies in forty industries.[20] This had to be abandoned in the 1976 Act because it exerted no pressure on management to change entrenched practices. There is no reason to believe that purely voluntary codes (like that on age discrimination) will succeed any better in the future in a technologically more complex society under the pressures of global competition. Secondly, the antithesis between soft law and hard law is a false one. One form of regulation (voluntarism) is not an alternative to another (legal enforcement). 'The point is that a voluntary approach may work in influencing the behaviour of some organisations (e.g. a leading edge company whose markets are among ethnic minorities will readily want to project an equality policy), but not others who for economic or social reasons are resistant to change.'[21] The theory of 'responsive regulation'[22] persuasively suggests that regulation needs to be responsive to the different behaviour of various organisations. Although regulators start with attempts to persuade those subject to them to cooperate, they need to be able to rely on progressively more deterrent sanctions until there is compliance. In order to work, there must be a gradual escalation of sanctions and, at the top, sufficiently strong sanctions to deter even the most persistent offender. When a low sanction

---

[18] Better Regulation Task Force, *Review of Anti-Discrimination Legislation* (1999), 4.
[19] *Financial Times*, 10 July 2001.
[20] See B. Hepple, *Race, Jobs and the Law in Britain*, 2nd edn (Harmondsworth, 1970), 175–202.
[21] Hepple, Coussey and Choudhury, *Equality: a new framework*, para. 3.4.
[22] See esp. I. Ayres and J. Braithwaite, *Responsive Regulation:Transcending the Deregulation Debate* (Oxford, 1992).

fails, more severe ones need to be available. The theory is supported by much empirical evidence.[23]

II. The privatisation of enforcement

Labour law developed in part as a response to the distinction between the 'private' sphere of economic life – what Adam Smith called 'civil society' – and the 'public' sphere of all that was controlled and administered by the state.[24] This distinction was conceptualised in the continental countries as that between private and public law, and was challenged by those who were subjected to the domination of private power in the economic sphere but were gradually securing the rights of political and social citizenship. Protective labour legislation changed its character from the gift of the liberal state into the 'rights' of workers. Independent state inspectorates (starting with the British factory inspectors) played an important role. As the idea spread of integrating workers into liberal society, so safety delegates, workers' delegates and 'mixed' labour courts (starting with the French *conseils des prud'hommes*), emerged in Europe as participants in a system of publicly accountable enforcement of workers' rights.

Britain stood apart from these developments. Except for health and safety, private rather than public means of negotiation and enforcement were seen as the most effective way of resolving disputes. Trade union activity, collective bargaining sanctioned by industrial action, with relatively few legal supports and protected from common law courts by the trade dispute immunities, were the principal means of enforcement. Non-legally binding procedural agreements, usually at industry or regional level, were at the heart of the British system until the 1970s.[25] From 1896 until the 1970s government-supported conciliation, mediation and arbitration were intended to foster and promote voluntary collective bargaining arrangements, and not to replace them. Between 1979 and 1998 the situation changed dramatically. In 1980, two-thirds of all establishments recognised trade unions; by 1998, the figure was

---

[23] See Hepple, Coussey, and Choudhury, *Equality: a new framework*, paras. 3.1–3.4.
[24] B. Hepple, 'Introduction', in B. Hepple (ed.), *The Making of Labour Law in Europe* (London, 1986), 19.
[25] See W. R. Hawes, *Employment Relations in Britain: 25 years of the Advisory, Conciliation and Arnitration Service* (Oxford, 2000), ch. 1, 2–3.

two-fifths. In 1984, the pay of workers was determined by collective bargaining in three-fifths of establishments; by 1998 that figure had halved to 29 per cent. The way in which bargaining was organised changed: industry-wide arrangements all but disappeared, and the scope of bargaining narrowed considerably. Industrial action declined sharply, falling in the early 1990s to the lowest level since 1897, when official records began. These changes were in part due to severe restrictions placed on unions and the withdrawal of state support for collective bargaining under the Conservative administrations. They also reflect the effects of technological change and global competition. The growing body of new individual rights introduced since 1971 has been enforced not primarily by collective bargaining but largely by individual complaints to tripartite employment (formerly industrial) tribunals. About four out of ten of these cases are settled through ACAS conciliation, three out of ten are withdrawn, and the rest go to hearings before tribunals, where success rates are relatively low. In the discrimination field, the EOC, CRE and DRC provide some support for individuals and also have strategic enforcement roles.

At the very moment when employment tribunals have come to the centre-stage of enforcement of individual rights, with over 130,000 registered claims a year, a serious attempt is being made by the government to deter workers from using them. The poorest applicants, with no right to representation, may be denied a hearing by recent reforms which enable tribunals to order increased deposits of £500 (previously £150) to be paid as a condition of proceeding to a full hearing if the case appears to have no reasonable prospects of success. Cases may be now struck out on the grounds of having no reasonable prospect of success. Since the reasons for the employer's action, in a dismissal or discrimination case, are often peculiarly within the employer's knowledge there is a risk that cases will be decided in this way on the basis of a partial or incomplete grasp of the facts. Employees may also be scared to proceed in the knowledge that the amount which a tribunal may award as costs without assessment against a party whose case is found to be unreasonable or misconceived has been raised from £500 to £10,000.[26] Further proposals which would have the effect of limiting access to tribunals were announced at the end

---

[26] Employment Tribunals (Constitution and Rules of Procedure) Regulations 2001, SI 2001, No. 1171, with similar regulations in Scotland.

of July 2001,[27] and are being implemented in the Employment Bill 2002. These include barring applications to a tribunal unless the employee has set out his or her grievance in writing and sent a copy to the employer within a specified time; compelling tribunals to reduce compensatory awards to employees by up to 50 per cent if statutory procedures are not completed; and requiring tribunals to disregard procedural flaws where the tribunal thinks that it would have made no difference had the proper procedure been followed – a speculative exercise which the House of Lords condemned and stopped in 1987.[28] These and other reforms to be introduced by regulations under the Bill may deny access to justice to many employees whose rights have been infringed.

The government is rightly trying to encourage conciliated settlements, not content with the fact that 75 per cent of applications are currently withdrawn, settled privately or settled through ACAS.[29] However, the government is also seeking to encourage other private organisations to act as conciliators alongside ACAS, apparently with none of the guarantees of impartiality and quality which distinguish ACAS's work as a public agency.[30]

An even more significant shift from the public law system into the private sphere is to be found in the new 'arbitration alternative' to employment tribunals,[31] available in England and Wales since May 2001. This has to be characterised as 'private' because it requires a waiver of statutory rights in return for the dubious privilege of what is in effect private arbitration. Unlike the United States, where the Supreme Court[32] has recently confirmed the legality of pre-dispute waivers (dubbed the modern 'yellow dog' contract),[33] the British arbitration scheme for unfair dismissal is permitted only where there is an existing dispute.

---

[27] Department for Trade and Industry, *Alternative Dispute Resolution: Consultation Paper* (London, 2001).

[28] *Polkey* v. *A.E.Dayton Services Ltd* [1987] IRLR 503, HL.

[29] DTI, *Alternative Dispute Resolution*, para. 2.7, and ch. 4.   [30] Ibid., para. 4.13.

[31] The scheme was introduced initially in England and Wales, after considerable delay, under the Employment Rights (Dispute Resolution) Act 1998, which inserted a new s. 212A into the Trade Union and Labour Relations (Consolidation) Act 1992. Details will be found in *The ACAS arbitration scheme for the resolution of unfair dismissal disputes: a guide to the Scheme* (London, 2001).

[32] *Circuit City Stores Inc* v. *Adams* No. 99-1379, (21 March 2001); discussed by Estlund, ch. 8 above.

[33] Katherine Stone, 'Mandatory arbitration of individual employment rights: the yellow dog contract of the 1990s' (1996) 73 Denver University Law Review 1017–50.

However, this does not alter the private nature of the arbitration. The waived rights which the employee would have had, had the matter been heard by an employment tribunal, are extensive: the right to a public hearing, the cross-examination of witnesses, compelling the attendance of witnesses, the production of documents to be ordered, and the right to a published and full reasoned decision. Most important of all, the parties have to waive their rights to have the dispute resolved in accordance with the law. To this there are only two exceptions imposed for constitutional reasons, namely matters of EC law and issues under the Human Rights Act 1998.

The terms of reference of the arbitrator, in deciding whether the dismissal was fair or unfair, expressly require him or her not to apply 'legal tests or rules (e.g. court decisions or legislation)'. Instead the arbitrator must 'have regard to general principles of good conduct in industrial relations (including for example, principles referred to in any ACAS disciplinary and grievance procedures code of discipline at work handbook)'.[34] How far this will differ from the approach taken by employment tribunals to the issue of whether the dismissal was fair or unfair under section 98(4) of the Employment Rights Act 1996 (ERA) is uncertain. Since the terms of reference expressly state that 'the arbitrator shall not decide the case by substituting what he or she would have done for the actions taken by the employer',[35] the arbitrator seems to be free to apply the 'band of reasonableness' test mandated for tribunals in *Post Office v. Foley/HSBC v. Madden*.[36] Nor is there any novelty in applying the ACAS guidance; indeed, tribunals are required to have regard to this so far as relevant. However, the arbitrator is freed from the constraints of sections 98(1) and 98(2), which limit the potentially fair reasons. Does this mean that the employer does not have to demonstrate any reason at all other than the needs of the business?[37] Even when it comes to automatically unfair reasons, 'the arbitrator will take account of, *but not necessarily follow*, the provisions for automatic unfairness in Part X [of the ERA]'.[38] It has been suggested that arbitrators are more likely to award reinstatement than tribunals do. But the wording of the scheme

---

[34] Arbitration Scheme, para. 26.   [35] Ibid.   [36] [2000] IRLR 827, CA.

[37] As suggested by John K. MacMillan, 'Employment Tribunals: Philosophies and Practicalities' (1999) 28 ILJ 33 29.

[38] Arbitration Scheme, para.90 (Emphasis added).

in relation to remedies is almost identical to the statutory provisions. In particular, the arbitrator must take into account exactly the same matters which have proved to be obstacles to the use of this remedy in tribunals: the employee's wishes (most do not ask for this), the practicability of complying with an order, and contributory fault by the employee. The same limits on compensation apply as under the statutory provisions. Unlike tribunals, there is no appeal on a question of law, save in respect of EC law and the Human Rights Act. The only challenges are on jurisdictional grounds or for 'serious irregularity'.[39]

The advantages claimed for the new arbitration scheme in comparison with the tribunals are speed, informality, cheapness and an 'investigative' approach.[40] All of these – as the 1987 Justice report suggested[41] – could be achieved within the public law system of tribunals. Some of the drawbacks of tribunals have been overcome since the original proposals were made for the ACAS scheme. In particular, by 1997 the performance indicator for bringing cases to first hearing within twenty-six weeks was 85 per cent outside London.[42] The real problem is lack of resources. It is clear that the government's main reason for implementing the arbitration scheme is that it will be cheaper for the state to provide than tribunals.[43] For the parties it may also mean lower costs, but even this advantage may be less important now that new tribunal costs rules (above) increase the likelihood of costs awards being made in the case of unmeritorious claims and defences.[44] Moreover, Scotland has led the way in providing legal aid for tribunal representation, and the new community legal service in England and Wales provides a framework for improved assistance for claimants.

---

[39] Ibid., para.162.
[40] See R.Lewis and J.Clark, *Employment Rights, Industrial Tribunals and Arbitration: The Case for Alternative Dispute Resolution* (London, IER,1993); Employment Department, *Resolving Employment Rights Disputes: Options for Reform* (London Cm27023,1994); Department of Trade and Industry, *Resolving Employment Rights Disputes: Draft Legislation for Consultation* (London, Cm3135,1996).
[41] Justice, *Industrial Tribunals* (Chair Bob Hepple) (London,1987), esp. pp.40–42.
[42] Macmillan (1999) 28 ILJ at 45–46.
[43] Linda Dickens,'Doing more with less: ACAS and individual conciliation', in B. Towers and W. Brown (eds.), *Employment Relations in Britain* (London, 2000), 89.
[44] Employment Tribunals (Constitution and Rules of Procedure) Regulations 2001, SI 2001 No. 1171, r. 14.; and see too, *Benyon* v. *Scadden* [1999] IRLR 700, where the EAT encouraged tribunals to exercise their discretion to award costs more freely.

The argument that an investigative approach is more likely in arbitration than in tribunals[45] is not consistent with the existence of arbitration systems (e.g. in the United States and South Africa) which adopt much the same adversarial approach as tribunals do. The new tribunal rules now include case management powers, for the first time imposing an express duty on the parties to assist the tribunal in this respect. An arbitration approach was not necessary to improve this aspect of tribunals.

Whatever views one takes about these matters of procedure, these do not touch on two fundamental objections to the new system The first is that it does not seriously address the inequality of resources of the parties in a system of individual rights, and may actually exacerbate this. This was the main concern of the Justice report, which proposed two strategies to overcome this inequality: (i) an investigative approach which reduced the need for representation in the majority of cases; and (ii) improvements in the adversarial system, including legal aid for representation, and an upper-tier court to deal with cases involving complex issues of fact or law. Both these strategies lay firmly within the bounds of a public system of labour law, not the private realm. Running through the arbitration scheme is the expectation of outside help to the employee in deciding whether to waive statutory rights (the requirements for a compromise agreement have been relaxed), preparing a written statement of case, and presenting evidence. But most employees are unlikely to have that access to advice and assistance, and there will be little scope for later redress if things go wrong. The arbitrator has even less scope for helping an unrepresented party than does a tribunal chair. The arbitrator has no powers to help by subpoenaing witnesses, ordering the production of documents or imposing sanctions on an un-cooperative employer. The 'investigative' approach is no substitute for those powers in the background, particularly if the arbitrator is to maintain the appearance of impartiality.

The second objection is the substitution of the unfettered discretionary power of the arbitrator for the rule of law in the workplace. It must be emphasised that this is not an arbitration of statutory rights. There is a waiver of those rights. The proceedings will be confidential,

---

[45] Jon Clark, 'Adversarial and Investigative Approaches to the Arbitral Resolution of Dismissal Disputes: a Comparison of South Africa and the UK' (1999) 28 ILJ 319.

and the reasons for the award will be brief. This will deprive unions of the weapon of publicity, which is an aid to organisation and helps to shame an employer into adopting fair practices. Instead of applying objective legal standards, the arbitrator will apply 'good industrial relations practice'. The property rights of the employer generally means that what is 'good' practice is determined by the employer. Even ACAS guidelines, freed from the constraints of the law, can be manipulated when the arbitrator has an unfettered discretion. It is the 'common law' of the shop laid down by the employer, not employment law developed by tripartite tribunals, which is apparently to be applied. The arbitrator may come to be expected to act as 'labour relations physician' or 'labour relations psychiatrist', rather than as neutral adjudicator.[46] Instead of a judicial process of applying laws enacted through the democratic process, private arbitration may simply be used by management to further corporate objectives and to increase control, rather than to promote the public policy objectives of legislation. This is a worrying domestic counterpart in Britain to the privatisation that has already occurred internationally through the widespread use of corporate codes of conduct, depending on private enforcement, at the expense of improved mechanisms of public international law.[47]

III. Restrictions on collective solidarity

'The dilemma which globalisation poses for labour law is that the more comprehensive and effective legislation or collective bargaining is, the more likely it is that [multinational corporations] will wish to relocate.'[48] The threat of 'strikes' by capital are greatly facilitated by the new mobility of international capital, and by the legal guarantees of free movement of capital, goods and services. The freedom of movement of individual workers is no counterpart to these freedoms. One of the paradoxes of the new European social model is that it relies on the social dialogue, which depends on strong representation of management and labour at European, national and sectoral level, but at the same time provides no

---

[46] See Katherine Stone, 'The Post-war Paradigm of American Labor Law' (1981) 90 Yale LJ 1509, 1559–64.

[47] See Hepple (1999) 20 Comparative Labor Law and Policy Journal 347.

[48] Hepple, 'New Approaches to International Labour Regulation' (1997) 26 ILJ 353, at 355; and see Wedderburn, Ch. 1 above.

mechanisms for strengthening and protecting collective organisations. Indeed, the procedures under Article 137 (ex art. 118) EC do not apply to the right of association, the right to strike or the right to lock-out.[49] The main emphasis of EC collective labour law has been on the subjects of information and consultation, but the sanctions for non-compliance are essentially a matter for national law and practice subject to the overriding requirements of 'adequacy' and 'proportionality'. Article 28 of the EU Charter of Fundamental Rights, based on the revised European Social Charter (art. 21), recognises the 'right to negotiate and conclude collective agreements at the appropriate level and, in cases of conflicts of interest, to take collective action to defend their interests, including strike action'. However, there is no EC law which protects strike action or international solidarity.[50]

Morgan and Blanpain argued as long ago as 1977 that 'if the decision-making power of the enterprise crosses national boundaries, as can be the case with multinational enterprises ... employees should equally be able to express solidarity beyond national boundaries'.[51] Yet transnational industrial action is subject to severe legal restrictions, sometimes outright prohibition, in almost every country, and these restrictions have increased over the past two decades. A recent survey[52] indicates that among OECD member states only Belgium appears to leave national and international solidarity action unregulated. Outright prohibition is, of course, a feature of UK law, a legacy of market individualism which has been left undisturbed by New Labour. In most other OECD countries solidarity action is permissible only if certain strict conditions are satisfied.

The ILO's response to this has been equivocal and contested.[53] Although the new Director-General has spoken strongly about the need for the ILO to contribute to the empowerment of workers, the ILO's Governing Body has not moved beyond inconclusive discussions. The 1998 ILO Declaration, with its reassertion of freedom of association and collective bargaining as fundamental rights, does provide a framework

---

[49] Art. 137(6) EC Treaty.   [50] See further Weiss, Ch. 3 above.

[51] A. Morgan and R. Blanpain, *The Industrial Relations and Employment Impacts of Multinational Enterprises: an Inquiry into the Issues* (Paris, 1977), 32–3.

[52] Paul Germanotta, *Protecting Worker Solidarity Action: A Critique of International Labour Law* (IER, 2002). I am grateful to the author for allowing me to see this important paper in draft form.

[53] See O'Higgins, Ch. 2 above.

for new ILO initiatives. The crucial issue is the extent to which the ILO's supervisory bodies, in particular the Committee of Experts of the Application of Conventions and Recommendations (CE) and the Committee on Freedom of Association (CFA), are willing to recognise that solidarity action, particularly across national boundaries, is encompassed by the freedom of association. The right to strike, including the right to solidarity action, is not expressly recognised in ILO Convention No. 87 on Freedom of Association, but the CE has derived the right to strike from Articles 3 and 10 of the Convention. In relation to solidarity action, the CE and CFA have generally taken the position that 'a general prohibition on sympathy strikes could lead to abuse, and workers should be able to take such action, providing the initial strike they are supporting is itself lawful'.[54] The applications of those standards have been ambiguous. In relation to the United Kingdom the CE has recently repeated that 'workers should be able to participate in sympathy strikes provided the initial strike they are supporting is itself lawful'.[55] In 1989, the CE said that 'where a boycott relates directly to the social and economic interests of the workers involved in either or both the original dispute and the secondary action, and where the original dispute and the secondary action are not unlawful in themselves, then that boycott should be regarded as a legitimate exercise of the right to strike'.[56]

The main problem with the CE's approach is that it makes lawful sympathy or secondary action dependent upon the lawfulness of the primary dispute. If the law applied is that of the country in which the primary dispute occurs, this limitation may make it impossible to take solidarity action with workers in a country where strikes are prohibited or severely restricted. Testing the legality of the primary dispute by the law of the country in which the sympathy action occurs is also beset with difficulties because of the different institutional arrangements and collective bargaining procedures in each country. Application of the law of the country in which the sympathy action occurs would involve

---

[54] ILO, *Freedom of Association and Collective Bargaining*, General Survey (Geneva, 1994), para. 168; and see Tonia Novitz, 'Freedom of Association and "Fairness at Work"' (1998) 27 ILJ 169.

[55] ILO, *Report of the Committee of Expoerts*, Report III (Part IA), International Labour Conference, 87th session (Geneva, 1999); and ILO, *Report of the Committee of Experts*, Report III (Part IA), International Labour Conference, 77th session (Geneva, 1989).

[56] Committee of Experts, 1989 Report.

artificial modifications of unfamilar systems. It would, therefore, make sense for the ILO's supervisory committees to apply simply a test of 'common interest' between the workers involved in the primary and secondary actions.

At present section 244(3) of the Trade Union and Labour Relations (Consolidation) Act 1992 allows a dispute relating to matters occurring outside the United Kingdom to constitute a 'trade dispute' only if the person(s) whose actions in the United Kingdom are said to be in contemplation or furtherance of a trade dispute relating to matters occurring outside the United Kingdom 'are likely to be affected' by the outcome of the dispute in respect of one or more of the matters specified in section 244(1) of the Act. This prevents solidarity action (even if all the other restrictions on industrial action are surmounted) where there is no immediate connection between the outcome of that dispute and UK workers.[57] This is unduly restrictive, as the ILO supervisory bodies have recognised. The criterion should be whether the sympathy action relates directly or indirectly to the social or economic interests of the workers involved, and the test of this should essentially be a subjective one, that is a genuinely held belief of the workers taking the secondary action. Sympathy action of this kind will rarely be taken if the workers do not feel that they have something to gain, either immediately or through the implicit promise of future support from those with whom they are expressing solidarity.

IV. Conclusion

Social and labour rights may be seen, in Antoine Lyon-Caen's words, as 'principles of action'.[58] But once voluntary cooperation fails, they have to be translated into enforceable rights if they are to be instruments of change.

A preliminary point is that none of these rights will be effective if they can be circumvented by the use of contingent work, outsourcing and the like which fall outside the scope of labour law. The ILO's new vision of 'decent work' – 'opportunities for women and men to obtain decent and productive work, in conditions of freedom, equity, security and

---

[57] G. S. Morris and T. J. Archer, *Collective Labour Law* (London, 2000), para. 6.21.
[58] Above, Ch. 6.

human dignity'[59] – is notable for its universality.[60] Unlike classical labour law, it does not presuppose the existence of a contract of employment or employment relationship. It is not limited to 'dependent' or 'subordinated' labour on which labour legislation has traditionally been focused. Although principles of non-discrimination between part-time and full-time and temporary and permanent workers have now entered EC labour law, some national systems continue to legitimise inequalities between blue-collar and white-collar workers, workers in private and public sectors, the employed and the self-employed, those at work and those seeking work. The objective of decent work acknowledges the basic equality of all these groups in both the formal and informal sectors.[61] The social rights of labour are universal. To become effective labour law must become social law.

Enforcement mechanisms in a new world of universal social rights have to take account not only of changes in the labour market and the organisation of work, but also the complexities of new technology, and the growth of small enterprises (where enforcement is particularly difficult). These changes are taking place at a time when organised labour is in decline and the state has diminishing political will and inadequate resources for enforcement. The state is withdrawing from prime responsibility for the conditions of labour and seeks to promote self-reliance and self-help.

One response to these developments has been increasing reliance on soft law. This can sometimes be effective where it is used – as in the case of ILO Recommendations supplementing conventions, and in some UK codes of practice – to take corporations 'beyond compliance'. Soft law may encourage them to adopt best practices beyond minimum legal requirements. However, when soft law is used as an excuse or justification for not providing binding sanctions in the case of non-compliance, it is at best naïve and at worst abject surrender to those whose only motive is profit. Soft law can play a significant part in systems-based approaches, for example health and safety enforcement, and achieving equality of opportunities. Here the aim is to achieve change by cooperation of management, workers and their representatives, and state regulators. In this

---

[59] *Decent Work*, Report of the Director-General of the ILO to the 87th Conference of the International Labour Conference (Geneva, 1999).

[60] Amartya Sen, 'Work and rights' (2000) 139 Int. Labour. Review 119.

[61] B. Hepple, 'Equality and empowerment for decent work' (2001) 140 Int. Labour Review 5.

tripartite approach, soft law can express flexible standards. However, the success of such approaches requires long-term commitment, adequate resources and ultimate sanctions. While such an approach may work well where there are common interests, for example in occupational health and safety and equal opportunities, it is unlikely to be appropriate in cases of conflict of interests, for example the achievement of equal pay for women where the government remains tied to 'voluntary' pay reviews under industrial 'champions'.

Another reflection of the decline of state activity has been the reduction of resources for enforcement. Agencies are understaffed and insufficiently funded. The new system of private arbitration, although presented simply as a cheap form of alternative dispute resolution, is a worrying threat to the rule of law in the sphere of employment. Different standards may be applied in different industries and even to different workers in similar circumstances in the same enterprise. It may accentuate the inequality between employer and employee.

Industrial action has been a relatively negligible feature of labour relations in recent years. But in the new global economy, where legal alternatives are weak and ineffectual, the restrictions in nearly all countries on expressions of collective solidarity across borders deny workers the opportunity to exercise what countervailing power they may still have. Attempts to broaden the legal framework for such action are likely to be beset with difficulties and much opposition, but the ILO should take a lead and the EC should bring collective bargaining and the right to strike in from the cold into the mainstream of EC social law. There are many other ways in which collective solidarity may be improved as well, for example networking via the Internet, the use of new rights to union recognition[62] and to information and consultation. For the rising generation of human rights and labour lawyers there is an exciting challenge to help devise legal procedures and meaningful sanctions appropriate to the brave new world of social rights.

---

[62] See Lord Wedderburn, 'Collective Bargaining or Legal Enactment: the 1999 Act and Union Recognition' (2000) 29 ILJ 1, at 38–42, for the problems with the sanctions under the recognition legislation.

INDEX

Note: An explanation of abbreviations used in the index is to be found in the table of abbreviations.

To avoid unhelpful repetition or dispersal of entries, entries have been by subject rather than country, the latter being indicated, as appropriate, as part of the heading or as a subheading.